29 LEGIONS OF MIDDLE-EARTH

51 THE TWO TOWERS

ALSO IN THIS ISSUE

LEGIONS OF MIDDLE-EARTH

UNLEASH THE LEGIONS!

Legions of Middle-earth is a new 128-page expansion for The Lord of the Rings strategy battle game. Collect an army and take your battles to a whole new level!

Legions of Middle-earth is a 128-page expansion for The Lord of the Rings

LEGIONS OF MIDDLE-EARTH			£12
Sweden	Kr180	Denmark	Kr150
Norway	Kr180	Euro	€20

Product code: 60041499019

Written by Mat Ward

ON SALE AUGUST 5TH

Released 12/08/06 in Northern Europe.

>>> MORE ON PAGE 29

THE TWO TOWERS

Relive the events of The Two Towers book and film with this 96-page journey supplement. Packed with new scenarios, character profiles, painting guides and scenery projects.

The Two Towers is a 96-page journey supplement for The Lord of the Rings

THE TWO TOWERS			£12
Sweden	Kr180	Denmark	Kr150
Norway	Kr180	Euro	€20

Product code: 60041499018

Written by Graham McNeill & Adam Troke

ON SALE AUGUST 5TH

Released 12/08/06 in Northern Europe.

>>> MORE ON PAGE 51

EASTERN INVADERS

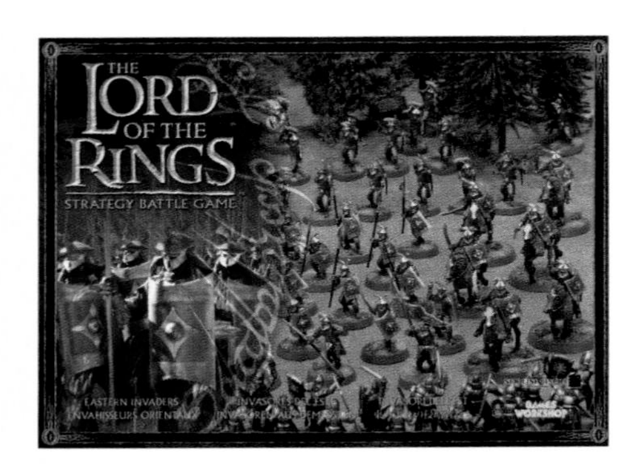

The Easterlings are a hard people, armed and armoured to rival the best warriors found anywhere in Middle-earth. These warriors of the mysterious Rhûnish lands are dedicated to the Dark Lord's cause.

This box set contains 48 metal and plastic Citadel miniatures, creating the basis of an Easterling army of over 400 points.

This box set contains:

- 6 Easterlings Kataphrakts
- 16 Easterlings with bows
- 8 Easterlings with spears
- 16 Easterlings with swords
- 1 Easterling Banner Bearer
- 1 Easterling Captain

EASTERN INVADERS			**£50**
Sweden	Kr750	Denmark	Kr650
Norway	Kr750	Euro	€80

Product code: 99111499070

ON SALE AUGUST 5TH

Released 12/08/06 in Northern Europe.

BOX SET SAVES YOU £16!

A selection of the models included in this box set

MUSTER OF ROHAN

Rohan is a comparatively new kingdom of Men, gifted to Eorl and his folk in recognition of the great service they had done Gondor in times of peril. Famed horsemen and bold warriors, Rohan has ever stood firm against the shadow of Sauron.

This box set contains 55 metal and plastic Citadel miniatures, creating the basis of a Rohan army of over 450 points.

This box set contains:
- 36 Warriors of Rohan
- 12 Riders of Rohan
- 3 Royal Guard on foot
- 3 Royal Guard on horse
- 1 Captain of Rohan

MUSTER OF ROHAN			£50
Sweden	Kr750	Denmark	Kr650
Norway	Kr750	Euro	€80

Product code: 99111499068

ON SALE AUGUST 5TH

Released 12/08/06 in Northern Europe.

BOX SET SAVES YOU £14!

A selection of the models included in this box set

NEW!
Rohan Captain

THE HOST OF CIRITH UNGOL

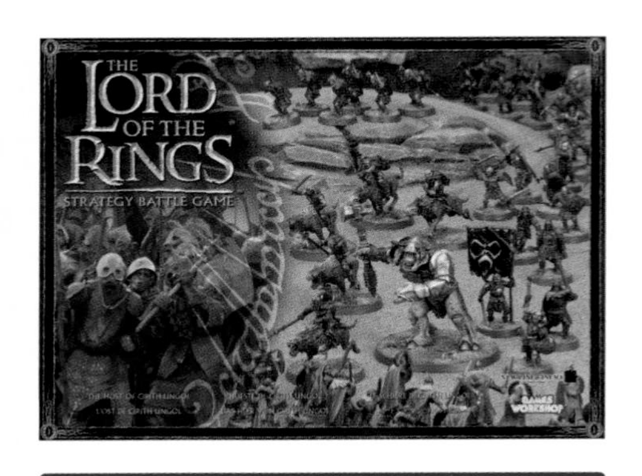

Cirith Ungol is also called Spider Pass, for its tunnels harbor Shelob, the great Spider and spawn of Ungoliant. The tower of Cirith Ungol was built by Gondor, but is now a bulwark of Mordor, infested by a legion of vile Orcs and Uruk-hai.

This box set contains 51 metal and plastic Citadel miniatures, creating the basis of a Cirith Ungol army of over 500 points.

This box set contains:

36	Orc Warriors
6	Warg Riders
1	Mordor Troll
6	Mordor Uruk-hai
1	Mordor Orc Captain
1	Mordor Orc Banner Bearer

HOST OF CIRITH UNGOL			£50
Sweden	Kr750	Denmark	Kr650
Norway	Kr750	Euro	€80

Product code: 99111499067

ON SALE AUGUST 5TH

Released 12/08/06 in Northern Europe.

BOX SET SAVES YOU £17.50!

A selection of the models included in this box set

DEFENDERS OF MINAS TIRITH

Minas Tirith is the chief stronghold of Gondor, and the most frequently tested of all the enemies of Mordor. At its heart is the Tower of Ecthelion, where the Stewards of Gondor have long held court. The proud warriors of Minas Tirith are superbly equipped and well-trained, always ready to heed the call to war!

This box set contains 40 metal and plastic Citadel miniatures, enough to create the basis of a Gondor army of over 400 points.

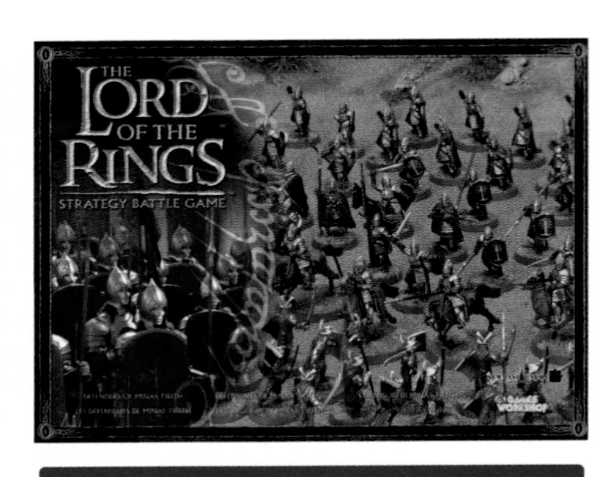

This box set contains:

- 5 Knights of Minas Tirith
- 27 Warriors of Minas Tirith
- 3 Citadel Guard with spear
- 3 Citadel Guard with bow
- 1 Banner Bearer
- 1 Captain of Minas Tirith

DEFENDERS OF MINAS TIRITH			£50
Sweden	Kr750	Denmark	Kr650
Norway	Kr750	Euro	€80

Product code: 99111499066

ON SALE AUGUST 5TH

Released 12/08/06 in Northern Europe.

BOX SET SAVES YOU £10.50!

A selection of the models included in this box set

LEGION OF THE WHITE HAND

Isengard is a mighty fortress, with Orthanc – the tower of Saruman – at its heart. The ferocious legions of Isengard are truly a force to be feared. Disciplined ranks of Uruk-hai warriors, reinforced by the technology of Saruman.

This box set contains 65 metal and plastic Citadel miniatures, creating the basis of an Isengard army of over 600 points.

This box set contains:

- 30 Uruk-hai Warriors
- 24 Uruk-hai Scouts
- 3 Uruk-hai Berserkers
- 6 Uruk-hai with crossbows
- 1 Uruk-hai Captain
- 1 Uruk-hai Banner Bearer

LEGION OF THE WHITE HAND			£50
Sweden	Kr750	Denmark	Kr650
Norway	Kr750	Euro	€80

Product code: 99111499069

ON SALE AUGUST 5TH

Released 12/08/06 in Northern Europe.

BOX SET SAVES YOU £11.50!

A selection of the models included in this box set

Pictures for illustrative purposes only. Product contents may vary. Products sold unpainted and unassembled. Certain Citadel products may be dangerous if used incorrectly. Prices correct at time of going to press, please contact us for current availability and prices. Prices quoted are for products sold by Games Workshop through its own stores, catalogue or website. Independent retailers are responsible for determining their own prices.

URUK-HAI SCOUTS

This box set contains 24 plastic Uruk-hai Scouts

URUK-HAI SCOUTS			£15
Sweden	Kr180	Denmark	Kr150
Norway	Kr180	Euro	€20

Product code: 99121499019

Sculpted by: Alan Perry and Michael Perry

ON SALE AUGUST 5TH

Released 12/08/06 in Northern Europe.

Contents of one sprue illustrated below. Box set contains two sprues.

THÉODRED

This blister pack contains a metal Théodred model, both on foot and mounted

THÉODRED			£12
Sweden	Kr150	Denmark	Kr125
Norway	Kr150	Euro	€17.50

Product code: 99061464104

Sculpted by: Alan Perry & Aly Morrison

ON SALE AUGUST 5TH

Released 14/08/06 in Northern Euro

ERKENBRAND

This blister pack contains a metal Erkenbrand model, both on foot and mounted

ERKENBRAND			£12
Sweden	Kr150	Denmark	Kr125
Norway	Kr150	Euro	€17.50

Product code: 99061464105

Sculpted by: Michael Perry

ON SALE AUGUST 5TH

Released 15/08/06 in Northern Europe.

ROHAN OUTRIDERS

This blister pack contains one Rohan Outrider on foot, and one mounted

ROHAN OUTRIDER			£10
Sweden	Kr140	Denmark	Kr115
Norway	Kr140	Euro	€15

Product code: 99061464106

Sculpted by: Alan Perry & Michael Perry

ON SALE AUGUST 5TH

Released 13/08/06 in Northern Europe.

One random mounted model and one random foot model supplied

URUK-HAI

FERAL URUK-HAI

This blister pack contains three metal Feral Uruk-hai miniatures

FERAL URUK-HAI			£6
Sweden	Kr100	Denmark	Kr85
Norway	Kr100	Euro	€11.50

Product code: 99061462038

Sculpted by: Alan Perry

ON SALE AUGUST 5TH

Released 12/08/06 in Northern Europe.

UGLÚK & VRASKÛ

This blister pack contains a metal Uglúk and a metal Vraskû model

UGLÚK and VRASKÛ			£10
Sweden	Kr140	Denmark	Kr115
Norway	Kr140	Euro	€15

Product code: 99061462037

Sculpted by: Aly Morrison & Alan Perry

ON SALE AUGUST 5TH

Released 12/08/06 in Northern Europe.

DUNLENDINGS

DUNLENDING WARRIORS

This box set contains nine metal Warriors of Dunland and one Dunlending Captain

DUNLENDING WARRIORS			£20
Sweden Kr270		Denmark	Kr225
Norway Kr270		Euro	€30

Product code: 99111464111

Sculpted by: Alan Perry & Michael Perry

ON SALE AUGUST 5TH

Released 12/08/06 in Northern Europe.

DUNLENDING WARRIORS

This blister pack contains three random metal Dunlending Warriors

DUNLENDING WARRIORS			£6
Sweden Kr100		Denmark	Kr85
Norway Kr100		Euro	€11.50

Product code: 99061464108

Sculpted by: Alan Perry & Michael Perry

ON SALE AUGUST 5TH

Released 12/08/06 in Northern Europe.

DUNLENDING COMMAND

This blister pack contains a metal Dunlending Captain and a Dunlending Banner Bearer

DUNLENDING COMMAND			£6
Sweden Kr100		Denmark	Kr85
Norway Kr100		Euro	€11.50

Product code: 99061464107

Sculpted by: Alan Perry & Michael Perry

ON SALE AUGUST 5TH

Released 12/08/06 in Northern Europe.

THE BALROG

This box set contains one plastic Balrog kit

THE BALROG			£35
Sweden	Kr400	Denmark	Kr350
Norway	Kr400	Euro	€50

Product code: 99121499016

Sculpted by: Steve Saleh, Michael Perry, Alex Hedstrôm and James Mason

ON SALE AUGUST 5TH

Released 17/08/06 in Northern Europe.

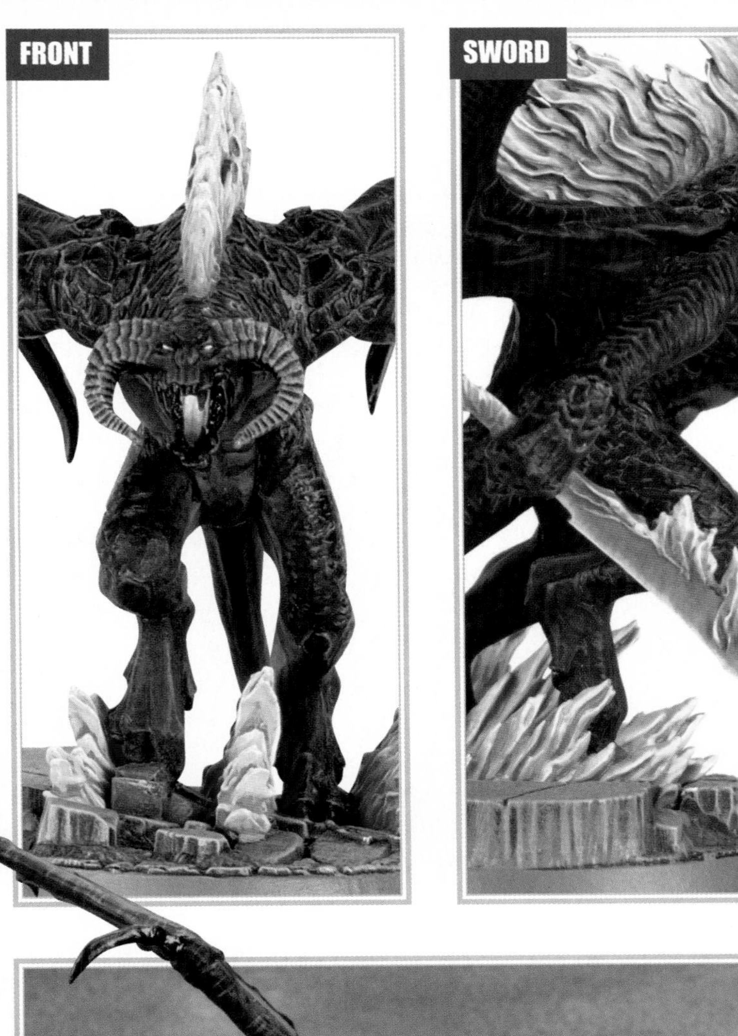

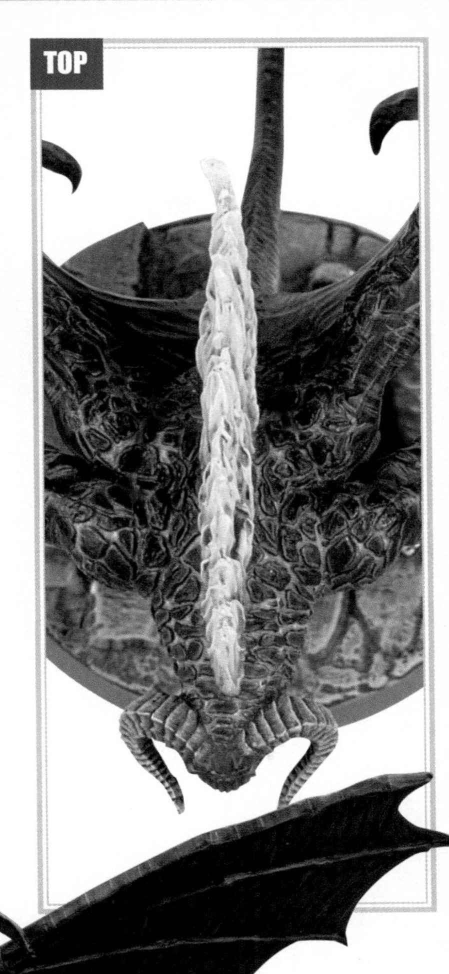

The Balrog is a mighty creature of great age and power – a monster of a rare and horrific kind. Of all the evil powers in the world it is amongst the most potent and formidable.

BLACK LIBRARY

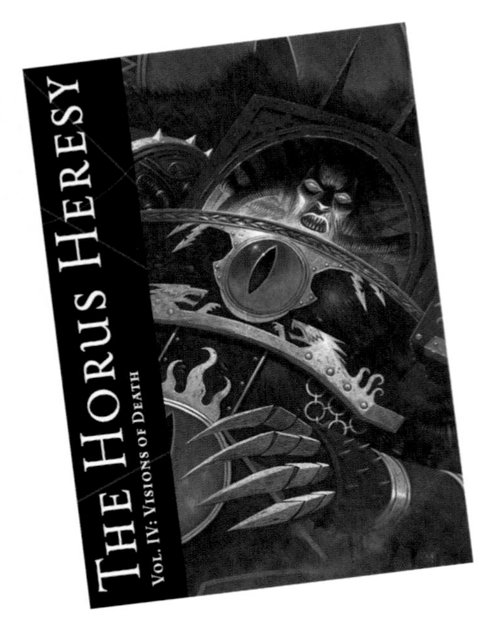

HORUS HERESY VOL IV: VISIONS OF DEATH

Set 10,000 years before the current Warhammer 40,000 timeline, this book details the massive and catastrophic civil war that engulfed humanity. Packed with high quality artwork from Sabertooth Games' collectible card game and lavish background information from Games Workshop guru Alan Merrett, the Horus Heresy series builds up into an invaluable and definitive guide to the darkest period in the history of mankind.

HORUS HERESY VOL IV — **£15.00**
by Alan Merrett, edited by Nick Kyme

Sweden	Kr250	Denmark	Kr200
Norway	Kr250	Euro	€25

ISBN: 1-84416-340-7

ON SALE JULY 29th

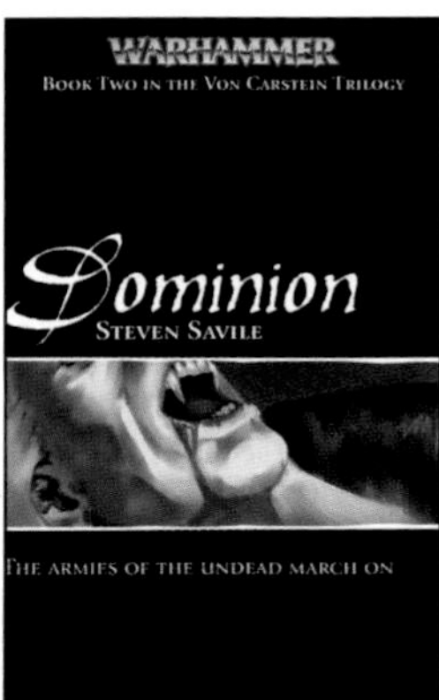

DOMINION

The Vampire Counts have ravaged the Old World for many generations and those of the von Carstein bloodline are the most feared. Dominion tells of the epic rise and fall of the infamous vampire Konrad von Carstein. As mighty armies are raised and swept away, the legions of the undead continue to grow, the von Carsteins at their head.

DOMINION — **£6.99**
by Steven Savile

Sweden	Kr120	Denmark	Kr100
Norway	Kr120	Euro	€13

ISBN: 1-84416-292-3

ON SALE JULY 29th

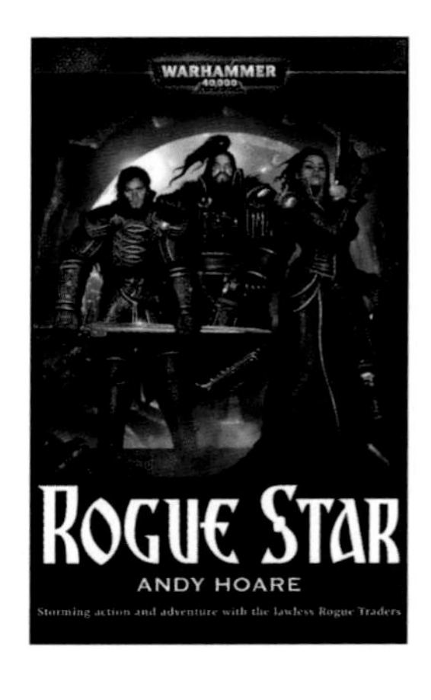

ROGUE STAR

Lucian Gerrit is a rogue trader – a starship captain granted ancient trading rights along the Eastern Fringe. But his family's fortunes have been steadily declining. In a final gamble to restore his ancestral glory, Gerrit commits his family's assets to aid a planetary governor in a long-standing war – in the escalating conflict, he may lose more than his livelihood!

ROGUE STAR — **£6.99**
by Andy Hoare

Sweden	Kr120	Denmark	Kr100
Norway	Kr120	Euro	€13

ISBN: 1-84416-375-X

ON SALE JULY 29th

Black Library publishes a range of novels and sourcebooks that delve deep into the worlds of Warhammer and Warhammer 40,000. These are available in many of our stores world-wide, as well as in bookshops in certain countries. However, if you are finding it difficult to get hold of any of their publications, then go to their website, where their books may be purchased directly.

www.blacklibrary.com

BACK FROM THE DEAD

Once the Proctor-General of Necromunda Hive City, Erik Bane's life has fallen apart at the seams. When a desperate girl enters the settlement, fleeing from a deadly gang, Bane steps up to regain his former glory. As a deadly plague sweeps through the underhive transforming citizens into zombies, Bane realises that he may have to give up more than he ever bargained for.

BACK FROM THE DEAD — **£6.99**
by Nick Kyme

Sweden	Kr120	Denmark	Kr100
Norway	Kr120	Euro	€13

ISBN: 1-84416-376-8

ON SALE JULY 29th

FORGE WORLD

TAU TX-24 PIRANHA UPGRADE KIT

This new conversion kit contains resin components to upgrade the standard plastic Piranha model into the TX-24. With new weaponry and features, this version of the Piranha is a valuable addition to any Tau army.

Model designed by Darren Parrwood.

1 Rear detail, illustrating new jet engines and side fairings.

2 New enclosed crew compartment offers greater protection for your warriors.

BLACK TEMPLARS VENERABLE DREADNOUGHT

This new Venerable Dreadnought kit for the Black Templars Space Marines is a multi-part resin model. A selection of resin Dreadnought arms are available separately.

Model designed by Simon Egan.

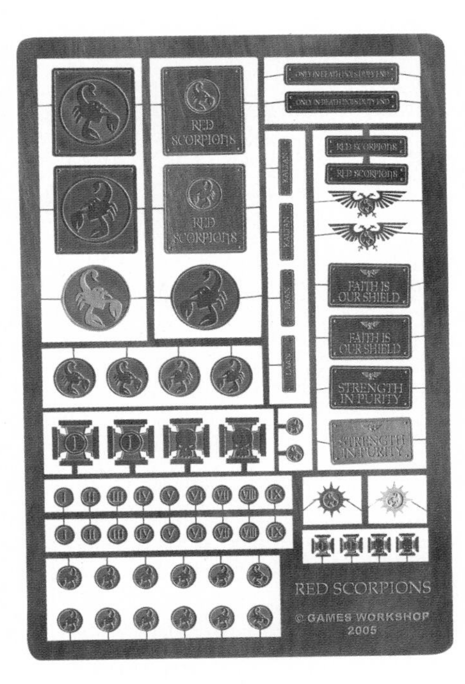

RED SCORPIONS BRASS ETCH

The new brass etch sprue for the Red Scorpions Space Marines features more than 60 symbols of various sizes to customize your Red Scorpions army.

IMPERIAL INQUISITION Collector's Guide

We will be watching you

The Inquisition, is a secretive body founded in the earliest days of the Imperium.The Inquisition stands ready to defend Humanity against the myriad of dangers posed by the witch, deamons and aliens. Such is the power wielded by an Inquisitor that they can call upon every branch of the armed forces of the Imperium and none can refuse his call. Even the Space Marines may be called upon to aid an Inquisitor should the threat be geater than he and any locally requisitional forces are able to counter. The Forces of the Imperial Inqisition Collectors' Guide is the most comprehensive resource ever compiled for anyone who has an interest in Forces of the Imperial Inqisition models.
This full colour, 72-page book is packed full of:

- Complete components lists, including pictures and codes.
- Forces of the Imperial Inqisition; Colour schemes of known Inquisitors and their forces.
- Imperial Inqisition themed Golden Demon winning entries from around the world.
- The best Imperial Inqisition dioramas and conversions.
- Awesome Imperial Inqisition armies.

FORCES OF THE IMPERIAL INQUISITION Collectors Guide

Collectors Guide			£6
Sweden	Kr100	Denmark	Kr85
Norway	Kr100	Euro	€11.50

Product code: 99040107001

ON SALE AUGUST 12TH

* see page 125 for a list of all the Collectors guides available.

NECROMUNDA REDEMPTIONISTS

REDEMPTIONIST GANG

This boxed set contains eight metal Redemptionist models on foot.

REDEMPTIONIST GANG	£20
Product code: 99110599159	
Sculpted by: Adam Clarke	

ON SALE AUGUST 12TH

DIRECT ONLY

Priest

Deacon

Brethren

Brethren

Deacon

Brethren

Brethren

Zealot

You can find all these products online by logging on to: www.games-workshop.co.uk/store

WAAAGH! THE ORCS!

The Orcs are back, and they're meaner than ever! In White Dwarf 322, we will unveil the latest edition of the Orcs and Goblins army book, along with a whole raft of new models to support it.

Orcs and Goblins players will find all of their favourite parts of the army represented with shiny new rules, as well as some new additions, such as the Forest Goblin Spider Riders. Some notable heroes also make a welcome return, such as the infamous Warlord Skarsnik and his faithful Squig Gobbla.

The army has a whole host of new special rules, magic items and spells, which really characterise the savage nature of the greenskin horde, and make them more of a force to be reckoned with than ever before.

White Dwarf 322 will bring you notes from the author of the book, Mat Ward, along with a massive inaugural battle report, so you can see the new army in action for yourselves, with all their shiny new rules and tricks on display.

New Miniatures

Accompanying the new rules is a veritable host of new models, from new versions of old favourites to brand new troop types.

▶ *Two of the fantastic new Night Goblin Bosses to lead your army.*

▲▶ *This new plastic box set provides more options for your Spider riders.*

Orcs & Goblins Army Book

The new Orcs and Goblins army book is the place to start for all greenskins players, featuring background, rules, the army list and hobby information. Tool up your Bosses with deadly new weapons, and choose an army worthy of the Waaagh!

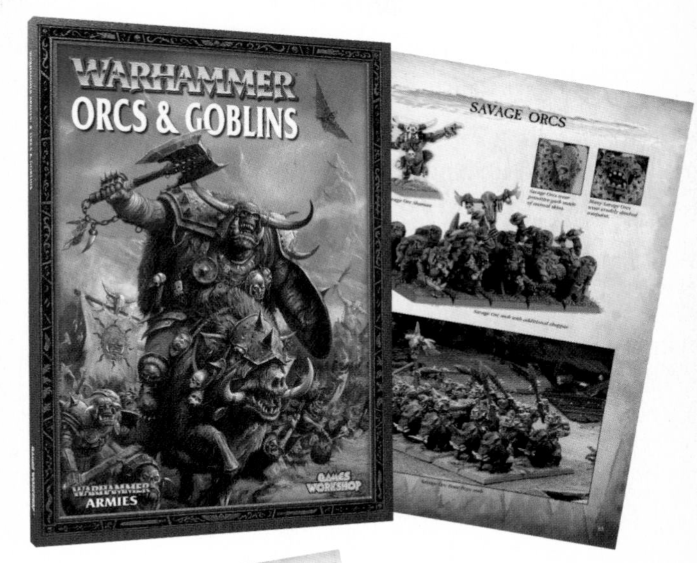

WAAAGH! SKARSNIK

WAAAGH! MAGIC

THE POWER OF THE WAAAGH!

WAAAGH! Miscast Table

AZHAG THE SLAUGHTERER

THE CROWN OF SORCERY

THE BATTLE OF BUTCHER'S HILL

SPECIAL RULES

MAGIC ITEMS

► This Orc standard bearer is part of a multi-part Orc Boss plastic sprue, designed by Alex Hedström. this kit will allow you to create foot and mounted Heroes and Lords for your army!

GAMESDAY & GOLDEN DEMON 2006

DESIGN STUDIO TO INVADE EN MASSE!

This year's Games Day will feature the Design Studio like never before. An increased contingent will be present on Games Workshop's biggest and best day of the year – Games Day!

Rumours abound that the Studio will be bringing special treats (showing off what's coming out in the future) and showing hobbyists how we go about making our models and games from start to finish.

There are even tales of a giant game of Warhammer involving the 'three-ups' from the brand new Warhammer boxed game – Battle for Skull Pass!

For more on this year's Games Day, a glimpse at the new limited edition model, and a full report on last year's event turn to **page 108.**

WARHAMMER

Grand Tournament & exclusive new offer!

Here's a treat for all you Warhammer Grand Tournament players! Buy your ticket and get exclusive access to the new Warhammer Rulebook and Warhammer boxed set, Battle for Skull Pass. Better still, you can also buy the strictly limited edition Ultimate Warhammer Rulebook (with a leather case and tapestry style cover), and the Warhammer Special Gamers' Edition specially designed for those attending events! Turn to **page 64 and 80** to find out more about these great products.

All three of this year's Warhammer Grand Tournament Heats will use the new edition, so get a copy of the rules on September 9th (launch day) and make sure you have enough time to read them and formulate devastating new strategies!

Tickets for all three heats are now available from Direct. If you already have your ticket, you can still give the guys a ring about this promotion.

Call now to order:
0115 91 40000

Boxed Game Redemption

Don't forget, buy the boxed set now and get the new rulebook FREE when it's released. Offer lasts from 1/6/06 to 8/9/06

IMPORTANT

ADVANCE NEWS – PRICE CHANGES

As of the 2nd October Games Workshop UK will be changing the prices on a selection of our products. To give you as much notice as possible, so you can get your products at the current price, we've listed the major changes below:

- **All blisters priced £3 to £7 will increase by £1**
- **Paint brushes will increase by 50p.**

You still have several weeks to get these products at the old prices, so you can take full advantage of this notification! Visit our website for a full list of the changes at *www.games-workhop.co.uk/news.*

COVENT GARDEN, LONDON

Official Opening Party! Saturday 5th August 2006

Our Covent Garden Hobby Centre is holding an Official Opening Party on the 5th August to celebrate the new store opening in the heart of London's pedestrianised piazza! (There might even be tea and cake – Grombrindal)

SPECIAL GUESTS!

Alan Perry

Michael Perry

The Design Studio special guests will be at the Opening Party from 10:00am to 1:00pm.

Alan & Michael Perry

Two of Games Workshop's most prolific, talented and longest serving (25 years) Citadel Miniatures sculptors are going to be at Covent Garden. Alan and Michael sculpted all of the new models (check out the examples below) for The Two Towers Journey.

SPECIAL EVENTS!

The Lord of The Rings painting competition

Win signed copies of WD320, Legions of Middle-earth Expansion and The Two Towers Journey for The Lord of The Rings Strategy Battle Game! Simply bring along a single miniature for The Lord of The Rings. There will be two categories, under 16 and over, and they'll be judged by our special guests.

Question and Answer

Quiz our guests on the new The Lord of The Rings Expansion, Journey and miniatures.

Signings

Get your new Expansion and Journey signed on the day it's released, and feel free to bring along any other Games Workshop books our guests have been involved in.

www.games-workshop.co.uk/coventgarden

OPENING TIMES:
Monday – Saturday:
10.00am to 7.30pm
Sunday:
11:00am to 5.00pm

ADDRESS:
Unit 33, The Market,
Covent Garden
London,
WC2E 8RF
Tel: ***0207 240 5106***

The store is already open if you cannot make it on the Official Opening Party and want to go before.

WIN signed copies!

THE LORD OF THE RINGS

Legions of Middle-earth	05/08/06	£12.00
Legion of the White Hand	05/08/06	£50.00
The Host of Cirith Ungol	05/08/06	£50.00
Defenders of Minas Tirith	05/08/06	£50.00
Eastern Invaders	05/08/06	£50.00
The Muster of Rohan	05/08/06	£50.00
The Two Towers	05/08/06	£12.00
Theodred (foot & mounted)	05/08/06	£12.00
Erkenbrand (foot & mounted)	05/08/06	£12.00
Uruk-hai Scouts	05/08/06	£15.00
Balrog (Plastic)	05/08/06	£35.00
Dunlending Warriors box set	05/08/06	£20.00
Dunlending Warrior command	05/08/06	£6.00
Dunlending Warriors blister pack	05/08/06	£6.00
Uglúk & Vraskû	05/08/06	£10.00
Feral Uruk-hai	05/08/06	£6.00
Rohan Outrider	05/08/06	£10.00

NEXT MONTH

Ent	26/08/06	£20.00
Haldir's Elves Command	26/08/06	£6.00
Morgul Stalkers	26/08/06	£6.00
Dead Marsh Spectres	26/08/06	£6.00
Isenguard Troll	26/08/06	£15.00
Osgiliath Veterans	26/08/06	£6.00
Defenders of Rohan	26/08/06	£25.00
Rohan Captain (foot & mounted)	26/08/06	£10.00
Rohan Banner Bearer (foot & mounted)	26/08/06	£9.00

WARHAMMER 40,000 NEXT MONTH

Space Marine Megaforce	02/09/06	£100.00
Tau Empire Megaforce	23/09/06	£100.00

WARHAMMER NEXT MONTH

Battle for Skull Pass	09/09/06	£40.00
Battle for Skull Pass paint set	09/09/06	£12.00
Warhammer rulebook	09/09/06	£30.00
Warhammer Collectors Edition (Direct Only)	09/09/06	£60.00
Warhammer Gamers Edition (Direct Only)	09/09/06	£60.00
Warhammer Dice Tin	09/09/06	£6.00
Warhammer Special Edition Fanatics	09/09/06	£7.00
Orcs & Goblins Army	23/09/06	£145.00

OTHER RELEASES

Necromunda Redemptionists	12/07/06	£20.00
Forces of the Imperial Inquisition Collectors' Guide	12/07/06	£6.00
Horus Heresy vol. IV: Visions of Death	29/07/06	£15.00
Dominion	29/07/06	£6.99
Rogue Star	29/07/06	£6.99
Back from the Dead	29/07/06	£6.99

DON'T FORGET

You can buy our products from the following sources

- Games Workshop stores Page 116
- Independent trade stockists Page 116
- GW Online store Page 092
  www.games-workshop.co.uk/store
- Games Workshop Direct Page 122

COMING NEXT MONTH

WARHAMMER

Warhammer rulebook

THE LORD OF THE RINGS STRATEGY BATTLE GAME

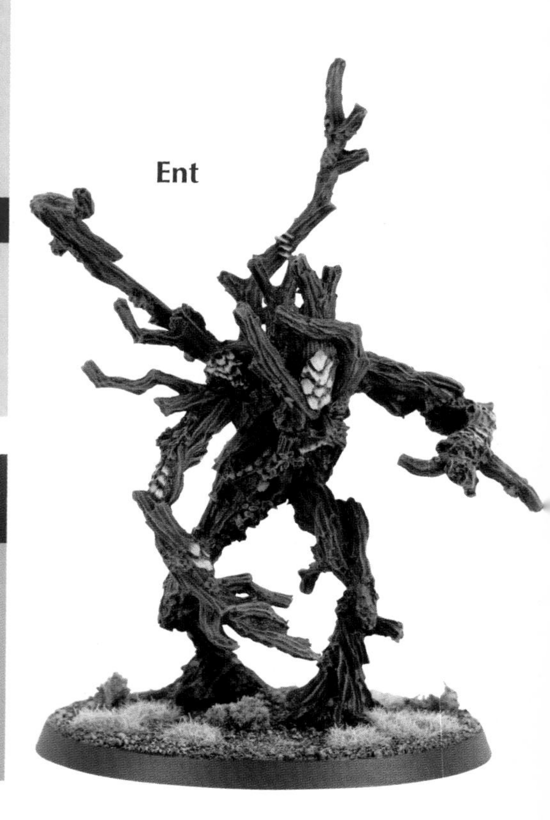

Ent

Legions of Middle-earth™

THE LORD OF THE RINGS
STRATEGY BATTLE GAME

EXPANSION

Designer's Notes
Jervis Johnson reveals what the publication of Legions of Middle-earth means for the game.

Sample Armies
We take a look at a few sample armies, based on the new lists from the expansion.

Battle Report
Alessio Cavatore and Graham McNeill commit to battle over the ruins of Osgiliath.

The Great Battle

Let slip the Wargs of war! With 49 army lists, the new Legions of Middle-earth expansion gives you all the information you need to fight battles with themed armies.

Legions of Middle-earth is big news here at Games Workshop HQ. Drums roll out everywhere, from the pits of Isengard to the halls of the Dwarves, as armies of freshly painted miniatures march forth to do battle. Yet no doubt some of you are thinking "Battles? I thought the game allowed you to re-enact scenes from The Lord of the Rings?" Well, you'd be right. The fact is, it's both! We got Jervis Johnson, veteran Games Designer and the brains behind the project, to explain just what in Middle-earth is going on.

"We'd just finished the latest version of the rules manual," he says, "and I began thinking about how people were actually playing The Lord of The Rings strategy battle game. We've always had a good idea of how people play our other games, but I can't say we were as confident with how gamers played The Lord of the Rings. It's skirmishy, yet there is a strong narrative element to it. I wanted to know how this worked out there."

See, Jervis' job is to cogitate on such matters. So he set out on a road trip, visiting numerous clubs and stores in search of the answers, sort of like a friendly Nazgûl seeking The One Ring.

# of Our Time...

"I went out to loads of clubs and stores. One thing that was immediately apparent was that gamers loved the game. They loved the miniatures range and they loved the background. As I expected, a lot of people were playing the scenarios that you get in the supplements and the rules manual, but there was this other group of people who were collecting themed armies and fighting pitched battles. And these gamers said that although the rules manual tells you how to play battles, they felt it was a little unstructured. The battle scenario in the rules manual lets you have all sorts of models on either side, just as long as they are either all Good or all Evil; there wasn't much direction in it to help players with theming armies. So this expansion was designed to address the needs of those people who like to play battles between two matched forces, those who enjoy the satisfaction of going 'Ha ha! I won! I am the best general!'" And who doesn't enjoy that?

Jervis is keen to point out that this is not the only way to play the game, and nor is it all about tournament style games.

"We are not being dictatorial. This is just one way of exploring the hobby; I actually discovered that a lot of gamers switch between the different kinds of The Lord of the Rings game, playing a battle one week and then saying 'Okay, next week we'll do the Weathertop scenario'. All these forms of gaming are equally valid, and we are going to continue releasing supplements like The Fellowship of The Ring and Shadow in the East. But while the other supplements focus on a specific journey through parts of the The Lord of the Rings story, here we try to give you a game that gives you even more options.

IN THE BOOK

49 Army lists
12 Points match battle scenarios
13 Answers to FAQs
7 Region-specific terrain generators

ALSO!

Sneaky peek – as we don't want to make our nice new army expansion obsolete as soon as it is released, some of the army lists include the names of miniatures we haven't made yet…

49 Army lists!

GOOD
- The Fellowship of The Ring
- Arnor
- The Grey Company
- The Shire
- Rivendell
- The Grey Havens
- Eregion
- Lothlórien
- Thranduil's Halls
- Fangorn
- The Riders of Eorl
- The Host of the Hammerhand
- Théoden's Host
- The Tower of Ecthelion
- Minas Tirith
- The Fiefdoms
- The Army of the High King
- The Rangers of Ithilien
- The Dead of Dunharrow
- Durin's Folk
- Khazad-Dûm
- Erebor

CHAMPIONS OF GOOD
- The Wild Men of Druadan Forest
- The Wanderers in the Wild
- The Wizards
- The Eagles of the Misty Mountains
- Guardians of the Carrock

EVIL
- Moria
- Angmar
- The Dwellers Below
- Isengard Raiders
- The Legions of the White Hand
- Dunland
- Sharkey's Rogues
- Cirith Ungol
- The Black Gate
- Dol Guldur
- Minas Morgul
- Barad-dûr
- The Easterlings
- Variags of Khand
- Khandish Mercenaries
- The Serpent Horde
- Harad
- Far Harad
- The Corsair Fleets
- Umbar

CHAMPIONS OF EVIL
- Monsters of Middle-earth
- The Nazgûl

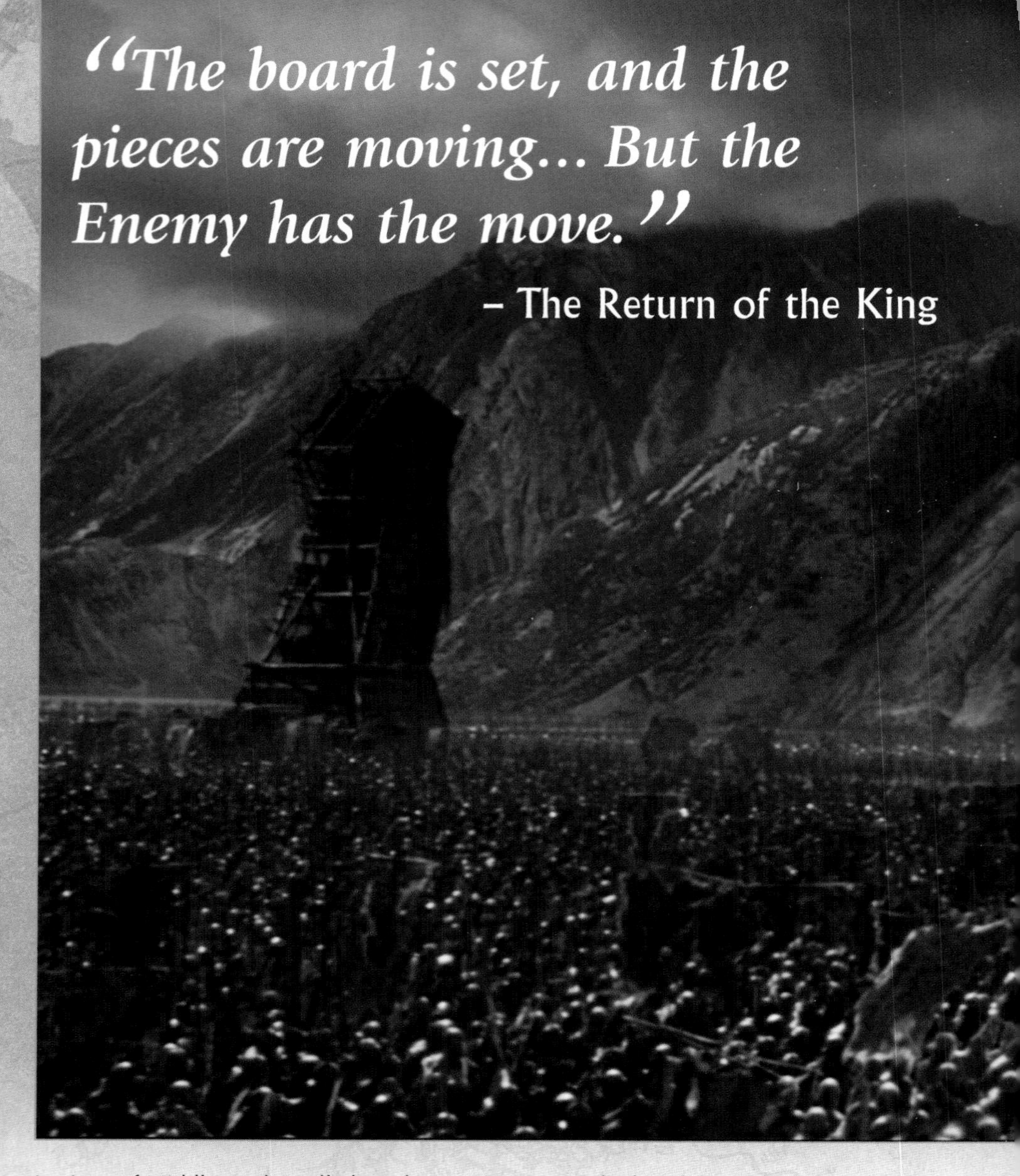

Legions of Middle-earth is all about letting gamers choose how they want to play. You can decide who fights who."

Some of these new options are embodied in the scenarios, of which there are 12. These are all balanced game set-ups which make it easy for you to create a battle where you can pit your tactical abilities against an opponent and get a clear winner.

"They are all based on what I call mirroring, which means that the same victory conditions and set-up rules apply to both sides," Jervis explains. "They're also designed to work with whatever terrain people have. Players pointed out that if they wanted to play the journey-style scenarios that they'd often have to make a specific piece of scenery. Some people love that – I met one guy whose whole hobby was pretty much making beautiful terrain for his club mates, but then not everyone has the time to do that, and then there is also the issue of what models you have painted up. It is a lot of fun getting scenery and models ready for a specific game, but sometimes you just want to turn up with an army and play."

Although players have themed their armies for a while anyway, this expansion gives clear guidelines on who and what can fight together. It is a pure gaming supplement. The characteristic profiles for all the models can be found elsewhere, and this has given us the chance to cram Legions of Middle-earth with loads of interesting army variants.

"The book is divided into Good and Evil forces, which are further broken down into several different sections based on specific regions or races," says Jervis, "for example, the Woodland Realms. For each

of these areas you have a variety of army lists. You might want a Wood Elf army, but do you want a Thranduil's Halls host or a Lothlórien army?"

Furthermore, certain Heroes are also restricted – Denethor can't be in an army with Aragorn, King Elessar, for example. This lets you pick up on themes within themes, and give your army a strong sense of time and place.

"Mat Ward, who wrote the book, can be thanked for that," says Jervis. "It needed someone like Mat, who has such a depth of knowledge about Middle-earth's background, to bring it all to life, and create variant armies that were interesting yet true to JRR Tolkien's work."

Another important aspect of the expansion is the allies system, as Middle-earth's wars are often waged by coalitions of creatures.

"We wanted to give you the opportunity to recreate that, so half your points can be spent on allies from different army lists. The cool thing is that you can concentrate your theme on one army list, then expand that collection by adding extra bits to it if you fancy something different. Of course, most gamers will find themselves adding units here and there until they actually have enough Citadel miniatures for two armies."

The big thing about all this is that it's not a new direction for the game, nor is it a replacement for the established ways of playing. On the contrary, Legions of Middle-earth offers a deepening of The Lord of the Rings Strategy Battle Game hobby. If you want proof of that, check out our Two Towers feature elsewhere in this issue. Surely this is a good month to raise your flag over Middle-earth.

These powerful heroes make fantastic leaders for your legions.

Théoden's Host

Westfold Guards

Erkenbrand with Horse
75 points

1 Captain of Rohan with shield and heavy armour
55 points

8 Riders of Rohan
104 points

4 Riders of Rohan with throwing spears
60 points

3 Rohan Royal Guard with horses and throwing spears
54 points

8 Warriors of Rohan with shields
56 points

8 Warriors of Rohan with shields and throwing spears
72 points

2 Rohan Royal Guard with throwing spears
24 points

www.games-workshop.co.uk /store/westfoldguard

I don't know about you, but for me, the best scene in the entire The Lord of the Rings trilogy was the Ride of the Rohirrim. The sight of thousands of charging horsemen smashing into the Orcs outside Minas Tirith has to be one of the most spectacular pieces of cinema ever committed to celluloid. I defy anyone not to feel their heartbeat quicken as the music swells and King Théoden of Rohan rides along the line of warriors with his sword clattering against their spears. From that moment on, I knew that if I were to collect a force for The Lord of the Rings, it would have to be Rohan.

A good portion of my army was always going to be based around Riders of Rohan, so I started out with 12 of these guys. Cavalry are the best value for points in the game as far as I'm concerned; they're fast moving, can quickly react to enemy threats and anyone on foot has to walk warily when there's cavalry around that can knock them to the ground before trampling all over them! I chose Erkenbrand to lead the Riders of Rohan, since he's one tough customer and is loaded up with Might, Will and Fate. Since Heroes can often get ganged up on by lots of cheaper troops, I chose three Rohan Royal Guard on horseback to fight alongside him.

I also wanted a solid core of infantry, so chose 16 Warriors of Rohan with a Captain of Rohan to lead them. I then picked three Rohan Royal Guard on foot, since their Fight Value of 4 could make all the difference between winning and losing a fight if the dice results in a tie. Working together, there's not much this army can't handle and it has the speed and durability to succeed in almost any mission. Forth Éorlingas!
Graham McNeill

Legion of the White Hand

Hrashtâk's Raiding Party

1 Uruk-hai Captain with heavy armour and crossbow *60 points*

1 Uruk-hai Warrior with banner *39 points*

13 Uruk-hai Warriors with shields *130 points*

8 Uruk Hai Scouts with bows *72 points*

11 Uruk Hai Scouts with shields *99 points*

3 Uruk-hai Berserkers *45 points*

5 Uruk-hai Warriors with crossbows *55 points*

www.games-workshop.co.uk /store/hrashtaksraidingparty

With Uruk-hai, the trick is one of quantity, rather than quality – Saruman's finest are so expensive that the cost of elite troops quickly mounts up. Numbers really do count in The Lord of the Rings, and it's worth packing as many models into your army as you can. Therefore Uruk-hai Scouts are my main troops, mainly because they're cheaper than their comrades. Fortunately there is no such thing a weak Uruk-hai. With Fight and Strength 4, these chaps can happily clobber their way through anything other than Elves and, as the Firstborn are even more expensive than Uruk-hai, you can use superior numbers to deliver a beating.

I'll be aiming to win the fights – to increase my chances of this, I'll have the Uruk-hai Banner Bearer stay close to this group. The bow-armed Scouts will advance more slowly and give supporting fire to my main attack wave. However, they're just as effective in close combat as my other warriors – if possible they'll pitch in!

The crossbow troops need to find a hill and start picking off dangerous-looking foes. The Warriors with shield stand at the front of my attack wave, using their Defence of 6 to shelter the more lightly armoured troops behind.

The Berserkers will be kept in the heart of my formation, safe from archery, until I've closed with the enemy. When the battle lines meet, they'll be unleashed on the biggest target I can find.

The Captain (I used the new Vraskû model to represent him) is best employed where the attack is stalling, but I'll choose my combats carefully. His Fight and Strength of 5 allow him to carve his way through Warriors and Captains, but Aragorn could ruin my day... **Mat Ward**

The Easterlings

The Army of Lhanzaghad

2 Easterling Captains with Easterling halberds
110 points

2 Easterling Warriors with banners
64 points

6 Easterling Warriors with shields and spears
60 points

12 Easterling Warriors with shields
96 points

12 Easterling Warriors with bows
96 points

5 Easterling Kataphrakts
70 points

www.games-workshop.co.uk/store/thearmyoflhanzaghad

Easterlings are a durable army. With good Courage and Defence values, they can take a beating that would break an Orc army to fragments. The weapon and troop options available to the Easterlings make their overall tactics simple yet effective: hold the foe with your infantry, pepper them with arrows and then unleash your gleaming Kataphrakts into the fray.

Easterling Warriors with shield and Easterling Warriors with shield and spear are reliable and solid troops, Defence 6 with a shield and a match for almost any Good troops. Divided into two groups of 12 (6 with shield and 6 with spear and shield) they create two small formations that can join together if necessary.

To prevent the enemy from flanking or disrupting your main infantry formations, direct the fire of your Easterling Warriors with bow carefully, targeting enemy cavalry or Heroes. They are competent, rather than exceptional, archers, so they must concentrate their fire.

The Kataphrakts are shock troops, designed to break apart an enemy formation once it has been stopped by Warrior phalanxes. Whilst it is possible to perform a pre-emptive cavalry charge with these Kataphrakts, they are too few in number in this army to make a stand without support from infantry, instead they should crush the foe against a wall of unyielding shields and spears.

Lastly, one each of the Easterling Captains and Warriors with banner join each of the groups of Warriors. The fighting power of the group, augmented by the presence of a banner, whilst the Captain increases not only the hitting power of the unit but also the tactical flexibility, thanks to Heroic actions.

Mat Ward

Tower of Ecthelion

The noble Men of Gondor have had a tough time of it, with their constant battles against the Dark Lord. However, their might of arms makes them a great choice for Good players.

Taking most of the box set contents as the core of my force, I flicked through the pages of Legions of Middle-earth and decided on a Tower of Ecthelion army. There was really only one reason for this, and that reason is Boromir. In full armour and packing an astonishing 6 points of Might, Gondor's favourite son was the obvious choice for my general. Looking down the list for another Hero to swell my army, I made sure I could accommodate Beregond too. The inclusion of this Citadel Guard Hero makes the force historically viable as well as hard-hitting – Beregond was assigned to Boromir's personal guard, after all.

The basic Warriors of Minas Tirith are no pushovers, with their heavy armour providing protection against bowfire. A healthy smattering of spears and a banner bearer will ensure that the soldiery have some staying power in a prolonged fight. The Knights are among my favourite models, and with five of them in the box it seemed churlish not to take the lot.

In battle I use large blocks of infantry to hold vital areas of the board. In this case, the swordsmen and spearmen, led by Beregond. I keep Boromir nearby, but I like to keep powerful Heroes like this on their own, ready to nip in and help out where they're needed most. The archers move up slowly in support of the infantry block, loosing off some speculative volley fire shots early on. That leaves the Knights, who I'll use as a flanking force, threatening enemy infantry.

Mark Latham

The Tower Guard

Boromir, Captain of the White Tower
175 points

Beregond of Gondor
25 points

1 Warrior of Minas Tirith Banner Bearer
32 points

5 Knights of Minas Tirith
65 points

8 Warriors of Minas Tirith with spears and shields
72 points

8 Warriors of Minas Tirith with swords and shields
64 points

8 Warriors of Minas Tirith with bows
64 points

www.games-workshop.co.uk/store/thetowerguard

Cirith Ungol

Gorbag's Ravagers

Gorbag ***45 points***

Orc Captain with shield ***45 points***

1 Orc Banner Bearer ***30 points***

8 Orcs with spears ***48 points***

8 Orcs with shields ***48 points***

4 Orcs with bows ***24 points***

3 Orcs with two-handed weapons ***18 points***

4 Warg Riders with spears and shields ***60 points***

2 Warg Riders with bows ***26 points***

2 Mordor Uruk-hai ***16 points***

4 Mordor Uruk-hai with two-handed weapons ***36 points***

1 Mordor Troll ***100 points***

www.games-workshop.co.uk /store/gorbagsravagers

The new Host of Cirith Ungol box set contains so much stuff that it makes picking a 500 point list very easy indeed.

I really wanted Gorbag to lead the army, because having a named character from the book or the film at the head of your force makes it immediately more atmospheric. Once I added Gorbag to the box contents, my force was already 'over-pointed', so I was left to strip it down to accommodate this deadly Hero.

The army has a good solid core of infantry, being nearly 40 models strong altogether. Although these are mostly Orcs, who are, let's admit it, hardly the best fighters in Middle-earth, the sheer weight of bodies on the field should mean that they will nearly always outnumber the opposition; very handy for trapping lone Heroes in fights. Six Warg Riders are nothing to be sniffed at either – these fast troops are great for getting round behind the enemy or isolating small pockets of the opposing force.

Although Orcs are a cowardly rabble, this army does have a hard centre to it – six Mordor Uruk-hai and a Mordor Troll. The Uruk-hai are easily the match of most other races' troops, while the Troll is just awesome. These monsters are so powerful that they can easily deal with the warriors of an opposing army, and will even give many of the less mighty Heroes pause for thought before engaging them.

A force of Cirith Ungol is a fantastic shock force for the budding Evil player. I think that, to expand this army in the future, I'd look to the allied lists – perhaps the Black Gate or Barad-dûr. However, I'd confidently state that this force would give any 500 points worth of Good guys a run for their money. **Alessio Cavatore**

Domination of Osgiliath

Legions of Middle-earth Battle Report

Amidst the ruins of Osgiliath, something wicked stirs... the forces of Cirith Ungol have arrived across the Anduin, eager to feast on Man-flesh!

Scenario

The battlefield is dominated by four objectives – in this case a militia barracks, ruined manor house, granary and blacksmith's forge. Each of these buildings contains either vital supplies for the ongoing struggle for Osgiliath, or are strategically important positions.

Winning the Game

The game may end as soon as one force has been broken. At the end of each turn after this condition has been met, roll a dice. On the score of a 1 or 2, the game ends. At this point, the player who has the most models within each objective building has claimed it.

Major Victory
You have captured all four buildings.

Minor Victory
You have captured three buildings.

Draw
You have captured two buildings or less.

Game Statistics

Scenario
Domination

Forces
Cirith Ungol and The Black Gate

The Tower of Ecthelion and Rangers of Ithilien

Players
Graham McNeill
Alessio Cavatore

Points
750

Location
Osgiliath

Timeline
The War of The Ring

Faramir's Guard

Alessio Cavatore

Alessio Cavatore has written several books for Warhammer and The Lord of the Rings strategy battle game. He is responsible for the rules content of Games Workshop's three main game systems.

Alessio: I wanted my force to represent the defenders of Osgiliath. In particular I was thinking of the tragic scene when Faramir rides out at the head of the knights of Minas Tirith to try and re-capture the lost city. Using the contents of the Host box, I formed the core of my army from a solid group of Warriors of Minas Tirith and Citadel Guard, always very difficult to kill on account of their heavy armour. The box also contains a Captain and Banner Bearer – perfect to lead my infantry.

Since I already had some knights in my basic force, I expanded their numbers considerably (and gave them a banner as well!) and then bought Faramir in his knightly garb to lead them. Together they form a mighty strike force, though I hoped they'd do better than getting themselves shot to pieces like in the film!

I completed my force by buying a group of Rangers of Gondor to offer me some nice extra firepower. As Faramir was riding out with his knights, I put Madril in charge of these brave bowmen.

My force was picked from two different army lists. The first was chosen from the Tower of Ecthelion list, and included Faramir, the knights and the bow-armed Warriors of Minas Tirith, plus the Citadel Guard and a couple of warriors to make sure I kept to the army's bow-limit.

The second (allied) contingent was picked from the Defenders of Osgiliath list and was led by Madril. It included the Rangers and enough Warriors of Minas Tirith without bows to make this allied contingent legal as well.

We were ready to do battle with the forces of Mordor.

Faramir with heavy armour and horse	***85 points***
Beren, Captain of Minas Tirith with shield	***55 points***
Madril	***55 points***
6 Rangers of Gondor	***48 points***
13 Knights of Minas Tirith	***169 points***
1 Knight of Minas Tirith with banner	***38 points***
3 Citadel Guard with longbows	***30 points***
3 Citadel Guard with spears	***27 points***
8 Warriors of Minas Tirith with shields and spears	***72 points***
8 Warriors of Minas Tirith with shields	***64 points***
8 Warriors of Minas Tirith with bows	***64 points***
1 Warrior of Minas Tirith with banner	***32 points***

Take the City!

Graham: I've got 750 points of Evil to storm the ruins of Osgiliath and capture it for the Dark Lord. No problem, right? I decided to use the Host of Cirith Ungol largely because I wanted to use Shelob to psyche out Alessio. My opponent has an amusing (well, to me at least) phobia of spiders and, since the model of Shelob is so gruesomely icky, I hoped it might keep him a little off balance. Well, it could work. I started by choosing a solid cadre of Heroes, since I didn't want to be 'out-Mighted' in this scenario. I've always liked the Mouth of Sauron and hoped to use his Transfix power in conjunction with Shelob to give her a better chance of killing any heroes that went up against her. An Orc Captain and Shagrat gave me more Might to play with and the Orc Shaman's Fury power would keep me in the game when casualties became heavy (and you never know, I thought I might roll a few sixes to save the odd Orc here and there).

My Warriors were a much simpler choice; I took the Mordor Troll because there's not much that stands a chance of killing one of these monsters. I surrounded him with a collection of Orcs armed with a variety of weapons. I planned to throw the Uruk-hai and the Orcs with two-handed weapons in first, with the Orcs armed with spears behind them to give them an extra attack. The Warg Riders would provide a mobile force that could strike at any enemy Warriors on foot that strayed too far from the protection of the Knights of Minas Tirith. Though my force wasn't as numerous as I'd like, it had more than enough hard-hitting nasties to crush all before me. The time of Men is over!

Graham McNeill

By day, Graham McNeill works as a mild mannered Games Developer. By night, he doesn't fight crime, nor does he stalk the streets as an avenging superhero. Honest. He doesn't.

	The Mouth of Sauron with armoured horse	***75 points***
	Shelob	***90 points***
	Shagrat	***55 points***
	Gharukh, Orc Captain with shield	***45 points***
	Uldhaur, Orc Shaman	***50 points***
8	**Orcs with spears**	***48 points***
11	**Orcs with shields**	***66 points***
4	**Orcs with two-handed weapons**	***24 points***
4	**Orcs with bows**	***24 points***
1	**Orc with banner**	***30 points***
4	**Warg Riders with shields and throwing spears**	***60 points***
2	**Warg Riders with bows**	***26 points***
1	**Mordor Troll**	***100 points***
6	**Mordor Uruk-hai with two-handed weapons**	***54 points***

Let Battle Commence (Turns 1-5)

As dawn breaks over the desolate ruins of Osgiliath, Faramir's loyal warriors are filled with dread – Orcs of Cirith Ungol infest this once-proud city.

In the opening phases of the game, Graham's forces scurried forwards towards the objectives. A lone Orc archer clambered into the granary that lay nearest the Evil deployment zone, taking up a firing position by a window and claiming the building in the name of the Dark Lord. Meanwhile the bulk of the army, including the Mouth of Sauron, Shagrat and the Mordor Troll, headed south to claim the blacksmith's forge. Shelob scuttled westwards with the Warg Riders in tow, hoping to reach the militia barracks.

In contrast, there was little movement from the forces of Good. Faramir and his knights cantered north, intent on instigating a cavalry battle with the loathsome Wolves of Cirith Ungol. As Graham stood puzzled at Alessio's lack of movement, it wasn't long before all became clear. Having bunched up all of his bow-armed warriors behind the ruined manor house, Alessio had no fewer than 18 shots per turn in volley fire barrages! One arrow found its mark on Shelob, forcing the monstrous Spider to spend a Will point in order to pass her Courage test.

Volley Fire!

Alessio's force contains the absolute maximum number of bow-armed troops available to an army in The Lord of the Rings. By bunching them together as he did in the early turns of the game, he was able to make great use of volley fire. While it's not the most accurate way to take down the enemy, Alessio rolled an inordinate amount of sixes to hit, making Graham think twice about breaking cover with many of his more valuable models.

"I will not yield the river and Pelennor unfought. Osgiliath must be retaken."

– Denethor, The Return of the King

 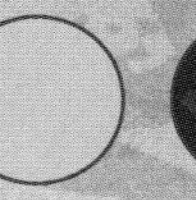  

Objective Tracker

Concerned by the amount of missile fire that his forces were already attracting, Graham began Turn 3 by casting Fury with his Orc Shaman. The large force he was accompanying moved up to the ruins of the forge, consolidating their position. The Wargs began to take pot-shots at the Knights of Minas Tirith – neither set of mounted warriors seemed keen to get into a charging position, as Graham was wary of Alessio's numbers, while Alessio in turn feared Shelob's monstrous charge!

Alessio split up his mass of archers, moving the Rangers and bow-armed Warriors of Minas Tirith into the ruins of the manor house, with the remainder skirting around the edge to get into a more direct shooting position. This group contained 3 Citadel Guard, whose pinpoint accuracy accounted for another wound on Shelob. This time the Spider passed her Courage test without the aid of a Will point. In the fifth turn, the volley fire continued, with the Rangers claiming a Warg. The Warriors of Minas Tirith began to lend supporting fire to Beren and his warriors, who were bearing down on the forge, but could not yet find their range.

Seeing the threat of a mass of Warriors of Minas Tirith advancing towards his forces, Graham sent a detachment to intercept them. With Shagrat, an Orc Shaman and a Banner Bearer amongst them, Graham felt confident they could hold their own. Finally, he sent his Troll storming off to the north of the board to join the Warg Riders in the hope of breaking the deadlock between the two cavalry forces.

Keeping in Formation

When Alessio's spearmen and sword-armed warriors reached the tower near the forge, he arranged his models in a defensively sound formation. Using the tower to shield his flank, Alessio placed the Citadel Guard and the Warriors of Minas Tirith with swords to the front of his lines, with a row of spearmen in support. With a Banner Bearer and a Captain nearby, this phalanx was to prove near impregnable...

Faramir	*Citadel Guard with bow*	*Mouth of Sauron*	*Orc Banner Bearer*
Madril	*Citadel Guard with spear*	*Shelob*	*Mordor Troll*
Captain of Minas Tirith	*Ranger*	*Shagrat*	*Mordor Uruk-hai*
Warrior Banner Bearer	*Warrior with shield*	*Orc Captain*	*Orc with shield*
Knight Banner Bearer	*Warrior with spear*	*Orc Shaman*	*Orc with spear*
Knight	*Warrior with bow*	*Warg Rider with spear*	*Orc with bow*
		Warg Rider with bow	*Orc with two-handed weapon*

Deployment

Orcish Fury

Turns 6 – 9

The bold Men of Gondor advance warily towards the Orc horde, as Shagrat's brutish forces prepare to smash them asunder!

In turn 6, the tense stand-off between the cavalry continued, while Graham's Orcs clattered into the carefully arranged phalanx of Gondorian warriors next to the tower. The rest of the turn proved largely uneventful, with Alessio's shooting proving highly inaccurate. However, this was merely the calm before the storm.

In the seventh turn, Shagrat called a Heroic Move to ensure that the Orc horde could bring their numbers to bear against the Gondorian phalanx. To the north, Alessio decided that the cavalry stalemate had gone on long enough and sped his knights away, hoping they could prove more decisive elsewhere. The bow-armed Gondorians in the manor house sought out better shooting positions, which was just as well, as Graham decided that he was tired of Alessio trying to turn his warriors into pin-cushions, and so redeployed his Troll to take care of the Rangers.

In the Shoot phase the Warg Riders, buoyed by the perceived cowardice of the Knights of Gondor, sent a volley towards their cavalry foes and felled one of them. Madril and the rest of Alessio's missile troops turned their attentions to the hulking Troll, wounding the beast twice. Graham hadn't expected that...

As the vicious melee by the bell tower got underway, the Gondorians gained the upper hand. However, the Fury spell that was earlier cast by the Shaman proved pivotal, saving the Orc Captain from certain death.

While the cavalry battle was turning into a waiting game, the Warg Riders had some success with their bows, taking down a Knight of Minas Tirith.

Militia Barracks

Granary

Manor House

Blacksmiths

Rangers of Gondor

Throughout the game the Rangers of Gondor and their Captain, Madril, had continued to impress. Their impressive shooting values started to come into their own in turn 7, with the Troll falling victim to their deadly arrows. Graham had left them to their own devices for much of the game, and was already starting to regret that decision.

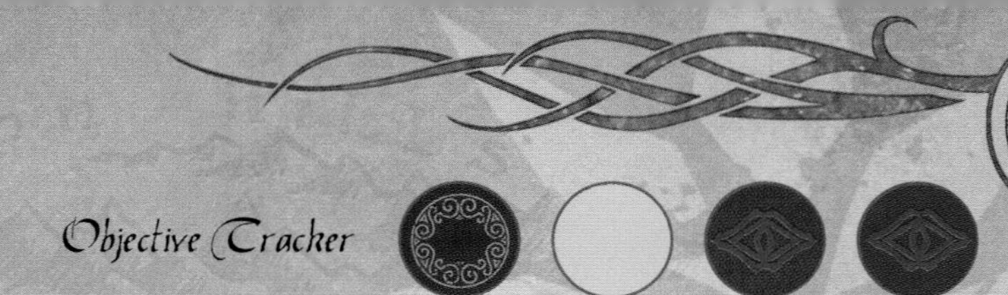

Fury!

The Orc Shaman had so far performed quite poorly, both in the fighting and spell-casting stakes. However, Graham's early success in casting the Fury spell turned out to be priceless – Graham seemed to have an uncanny ability to make crucial Fury saves, keeping his Orcs in the fight when by rights they should have fallen.

Graham gained priority in turn 8, and charged all of his models back into combat to the south. The Troll sped towards the Rangers, while the Warg Riders separated into two groups – the main bulk of them staying put, ready to shoot at the knights again, while four broke away to join up with the Mouth of Sauron. Alessio, meanwhile, had other ideas for Faramir's Knights, moving further away from the Wargs and Shelob, leaving Graham's cavalry out on a limb.

In the Shoot phase the Warriors of Minas Tirith with bows opened fire at the advancing Troll, and Graham could only look on in horror as the brute was shot down! In the Fight phase, the Evil side cut into the wall of spears that lay before them and began to gain the upper hand.

By the start of turn 9 both players realised that they had been far too cautious so far, and made a serious play to get into close combat. The Mouth of Sauron called a Heroic Move and cast Terrifying Aura on himself. Graham's Warg Riders made their move, hurtling into the Knights of Minas Tirith, throwing spears into the mass of horsemen as they charged. One Knight fell before the battle lines met in a frenzy of tooth against steel! Shooting became a risky business, with few archers being able to pick out a distinct target.

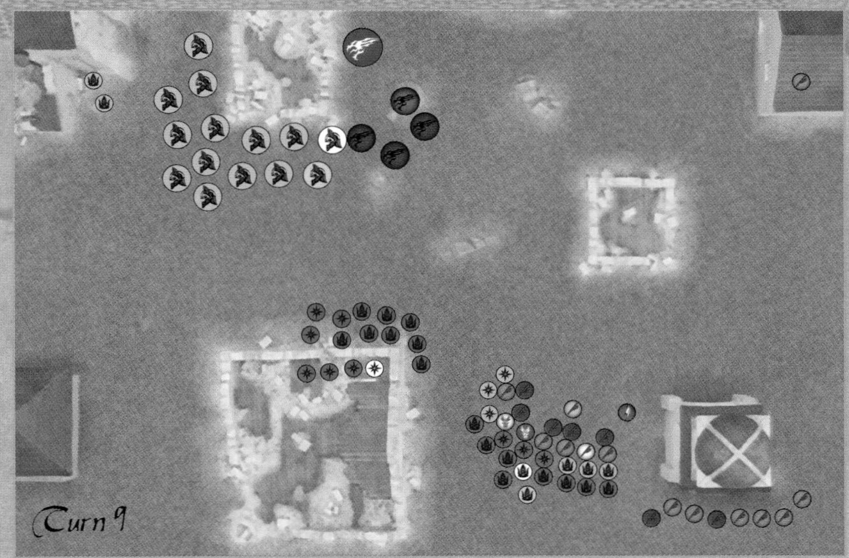

The Fight phase heralded a real turn of luck for Graham, as Shagrat cut down Beren, while his own Captain, Garukh, survived the combat only due to the Shaman's Fury power. Meanwhile Faramir fought two Warg Riders to a standstill, but Shelob was bearing down on him…

“Graham looked on in horror as the Troll was shot down.”

Victory or Death (Turns 10 – 14)

Saddened at the death of Beren, yet buoyed by the felling of the Troll, the Gondorians steeled themselves to reclaim Osgiliath, building by building...

Three of Faramir's Knights charged into the main combat by the bell tower, while the rest battled on relentlessly against the Warg Riders. Faramir took a Courage test, passed it, and crashed into Shelob. The young Captain of Gondor was determined to defeat the beast that dared defile his city! Alessio realised that he was neglecting the objectives, and sent a lone Minas Tirith swordsman north to the barracks to claim it.

Things began to get messy, especially when Graham tried some risky shots into the midst of the combat. Four Orcs unleashed a volley, only to kill the Mouth of Sauron's horse, forcing him to face a charging Knight at a major disadvantage. Alessio's archers stayed in a tight formation, waiting for their chance.

In the large combat carnage ensued – the Knights of Minas Tirith cleaved three Orcs, while the Evil Heroes claimed the Minas Tirith Banner Bearer, a spearman and a Knight in reply. Yet again, Graham passed a Fury save, this time sparing an Uruk-hai its fate. As the turn drew to a close, both generals surveyed the battlefield. With two buildings apiece under their control, and both forces looking rather depleted, there was still all to play for.

Turn 11 began with Heroic Moves being called by both Faramir and the Mouth of Sauron. Crucially, Faramir won the roll-off and charged into Shelob yet again, although he had to expend 2 points of Will to do so. Faramir's Knights intercepted the Mouth of Sauron and the remaining Warg Riders, not only nullifying the Evil Heroic Move, but also ensuring that Faramir and Shelob would fight on equal terms. Finally, Alessio sent the last two knights galloping off towards the tower, where they could either help out in the main fight, or try to take the forge themselves.

The Shoot phase saw Madril and one of his Rangers kill the Orc in the granary, bringing the Good side closer to victory. In some brutal close-quarter fighting, the Good side escaped without taking any wounds. Graham had so far had it mostly his own way, but Alessio seemed to be staging a dramatic comeback.

Faramir and the Mouth of Sauron are two very different kinds of Hero, yet both used their Heroic actions to keep their men in the game when the going got tough.

"Graham had so far had it mostly his own way, but Alessio seemed to be staging a dramatic comeback."

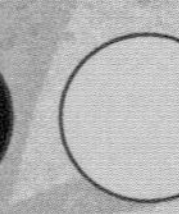

End Game

Alessio managed to sneak two Knights of Minas Tirith straight past the whirling melee that had gone on for so long near the bell tower. Graham simply did not pay these models heed, and as a result they walked into an undefended objective. The moral of the tale is to never underestimate the Knights of Minas Tirith – when the glory of Gondor is at stake, they won't let you down!

At the start of turn 12, Evil took priority, although Faramir called a Heroic Move to usurp the order. Both players had one thing on their minds at this point – throw bodies into the fight. Faramir again charged Shelob, but this time the Spider was aided by two Orcs with two-handed weapons. Graham's bow-armed Orcs also joined the fray, charging into the nearby Knights. Realising the large combat that had raged for most of the game in the centre would probably decide the battle's outcome, Alessio charged Madril and two Rangers into the mass of Orcs, while the two Knights who had previously headed south decided to make for the forge.

In the fighting in the north of the board, it was the Good side that suffered. Faramir took a wound and was forced to expend 2 Fate points to resist it. By the tower the Warriors of Minas Tirith were falling beneath the Orc onslaught, with Madril failing to tip the balance.

Turn 13 saw nearly every model getting into the fight, with the Orc Shaman being forced to call a Heroic Move to keep the advantage with the Evil side, while keeping himself out of harm's way. However, the tenacity of the Men of Gondor finally shone through, with enough Uruk-hai falling to the lances of Faramir's Knights to signal the breaking of the Evil force. Over at the forge, the two Knights of Minas Tirith dismounted and burst into the building, ready to face the two Orcs within. Graham was ready to concede the draw, but Alessio prayed for another turn. The dice was rolled and came up a 4 – play would continue on.

With the Evil force broken, several Orcs fled the field, including the two who were holding the forge. The Shaman spent his remaining Will points to stay in the game, while Shagrat called a Heroic Move to try to keep hold of the objective, but there was no Evil model quite within range of the forge to contest it. With their way unopposed, the two Knights of Minas Tirith consolidated within the building, securing the fate of Osgiliath.

Conclusions

For the glory of Gondor!

Alessio: At the start of this game, I was really worried that Graham was going to overrun me. He had a whole lot of Orcs and two big, scary monsters on his side. However, my plan seemed to work, and I think I proved that there is indeed strength left in Men. The game was very close – much closer than the final score would suggest. However, in retrospect I think I could have broken the deadlock much earlier by being bolder with the Knights. I was far too wary of that Spider...

Luckily I managed to break the Orc army before Shelob could make too much of a mess of Faramir and his Knights. As usual, when an Orc army breaks they tend to dissolve rather quickly, especially if you manage to get rid of those vital Shamans and their Fury. The only real mistake I can find in Graham's tactics was that he needlessly exposed the Orcs guarding one of his buildings to my bowfire, allowing me to clear this particular objective relatively easily. Other than that I think he did rather well and he was unlucky, because if the game lasted one more turn his Orcs, led by the unstoppable Shagrat, would have probably made it inside one of my buildings, and then the result would have been very different.

Men of the Match

I don't think I can pinpoint a single model as the best of the game, as none of them shone particularly during the battle. I will therefore assign this title collectively to my bowmen and rangers, because I'm quite convinced that taking out the Troll before it could make it into combat was an absolutely decisive moment. And they made it just in the nick of time, with their very last arrow!

"I could have broken the deadlock much earlier by being bolder with the Knights."

Orcs of the Match

My Orc Heroes and Shaman get my nomination for best fighters. They did sterling work in holding the combat around the bell tower together with their combination of Heroic moves and the Fury power.

"The mean old Spider didn't have much luck against Faramir."

Think of the Trolls

Graham: Well that didn't work out too well, did it? Though the critters of Cirith Ungol were booted back to the mountains from whence they came, they gave a good account of themselves before they went. Or at least until the last few turns they did. I think my biggest mistake was wavering on what I wanted the Troll to do. With hindsight I should have stuck to my plan of having him trudge forward with the Orcs in support, but I ended up reacting to Alessio and moved him off on his own. And even then I didn't stay on target and ended up moving the Troll in a different direction again! This meant that he got shot to pieces before he had a chance to have an effect on the game.

Alessio played cagily with his force until the right time to strike arrived, unleashing the Knights of Minas Tirith upon my depleted Orcs and Shelob. The mean old spider didn't have much luck against Faramir, though when the Orcs finally managed to help her, she almost accounted for the Hero. I'd also hoped I could break through Alessio's army to reach his objective buildings, so only left a token force behind to guard mine. What a mistake that turned out to be...

CITADEL TOOLBOX Water Effects

Recently we've been experimenting with Water Effects fluid. Here we take a look at mixing this useful liquid with Citadel paints and inks, to achieve some unusual and realistic aquatic effects.

Base painting

The simplest way to add colour to your Water Effects is to paint the surface you are going to apply it to. If you graduate the colour from dark shades in the middle to lighter shades on the outer edges, you get the impression of varying depths of water.

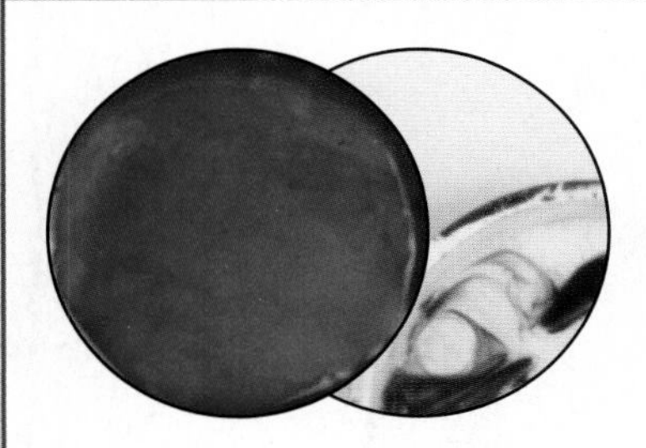

Coloured Water

When you want a strong pigmentation to your Water Effects, you can add ink into the fluid before you pour it. The mix dries translucent and glossy. When adding ink to your Water Effects you need to remember that, when wet, the fluid has a milky appearance but dries clear. Mix the colour paler than you anticipate, as the colour will become richer when it dries.

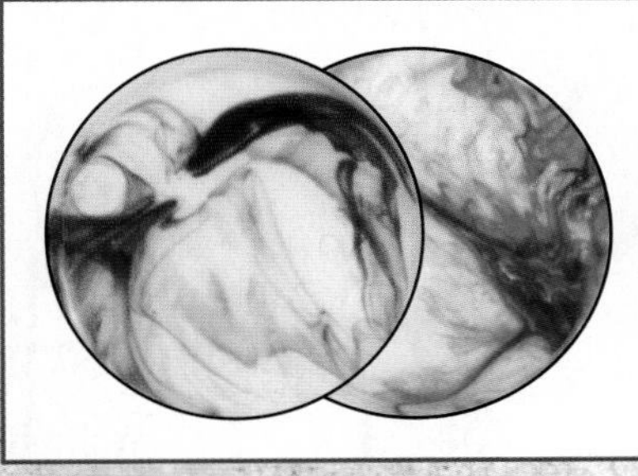

Swirl effects

Instead of mixing the ink with the Water Effects before application, apply the fluid and then add some ink, stirring it with a brush or cocktail stick but without mixing it completely. When dry, the swirls of ink give an interesting effect, like some foreign substance has leaked into the water.

Waste pipes

A set of waste pipes is a quick and easy terrain feature for your games of Warhammer 40,000. To make the waste-pipes scenery piece shown here, we first poured Water Effects onto the base. Next, we mixed some Sunburst Yellow with more Water Effects fluid, before using a brush to apply it to the pipe and pool – the mix dispersed naturally into the pool as it dried.

TESTING METHOD

When mixing Water Effects with paints and inks for the first time, it's well worth testing the effects to ensure you get the right ratio of fluid to pigment. Try painting the underside of some slotta bases with Skull White and use these as test palettes. One other benefit of testing is that it makes you aware of potential problems. In this case, we discovered that adding paint and ink to Water Effects increases the drying time – useful to know when embarking on a large modelling project.

TAU BATTLESUITS

TAU CRISIS BATTLESUIT COMMANDER

1 figure box set

Product Code: 99140113016

Price: £15.00 (NE Band J*)

OUT NOW

TAU XV8 CRISIS BATTLESUIT

1 figure box set

Product Code: 99120113005

Price: £10.00 (NE Band H*)

OUT NOW

TAU XV88 BROADSIDE BATTLESUIT

1 figure box set

Product Code: 99140113005

Price: £15.00 (NE Band J*)

OUT NOW

For more on the Tau Empire and its supporting miniatures range visit:

www.games-workshop.co.uk/tau

NORTHERN EUROPEAN PRICE BANDS*

BAND H		BAND J	
Denmark	kr 125.00	Denmark	kr 200.00
Sweden	kr 150.00	Sweden	kr 250.00
Norway	kr 150.00	Norway	kr 250.00
Euro	€ 17.50	Euro	€ 27.50

THE TWO TOWERS™

THE LORD OF THE RINGS STRATEGY BATTLE GAME

JOURNEY

New Miniatures

Take a look at a dazzling array of new models, from heroes of Rohan to the evil minions of Saruman.

Designer's Notes

Adam Troke takes us on a brand new journey for The Lord of the Rings strategy battle game.

SO IT BEGINS...

THE JOURNEY

The story of The Two Towers is recreated through this new journey by way of the scenarios. The key tales are:

- **Aragorn Legolas and Gimli's journey, including their adventures in Rohan and the battle of Helm's Deep.**
- **Frodo and Sam's journey to Mordor, including their meetings with Gollum and Faramir's Rangers.**
- **Merry and Pippin's escape from the Uruk-hai, their encounter with Treebeard in Fangorn, and the destruction of Isengard.**

N

Fangorn

Rohan

Helm's Deep

Edoras

Amon Hen

Morannon

Mordor

ARAGORN, LEGOLAS & GIMLI - - - -

MERRY & PIPPIN - - - - - - - - - - - - - -

FRODO & SAM - - - - - - - - - - - - - -

What's inside...

The Two Towers is the second journey in this range. Within its 96 pages, you'll find everything you need to recreate the events of the second book and film in The Lord of the Rings trilogy. Inside this tome you will find:

- **17 scenarios, allowing you to play through all the key events from The Two Towers story.**
- **Painting guides for the main characters.**
- **Nine scenery guides, detailing a variety of projects, from modelling dense undergrowth to creating Helm's Deep!**
- **Profiles for the new Heroes and Warriors.**

The latest Journey for The Lord of the Rings Strategy Battle Game is here, allowing you to recreate the events of the books and film through a series of new story-driven scenarios.

The Two Towers journey continues where The Fellowship of The Ring left off. Through seventeen scenarios, it allows players to re-enact the middle part of The Lord of the Rings trilogy, tracing the story as told in the books with a few nods to some of the spectacular film moments. We caught up with Games Developer Adam Troke, co-author of the new supplement, to tell us all about it.

"In The Two Towers you see three stories unravelling together," Adam says. "Frodo and Sam are bound for Mordor with Gollum in tow, and all the dangers that presents. Aragorn, Legolas and Gimli start off trying to rescue Merry and Pippin, as you know – and end up battling for the fate of Rohan! Then, of course, there's Merry and Pippin. They get caught up with Treebeard and the other Ents and get involved in the destruction of Isengard."

Each of the 'journey supplements was planned not only to chart the story of The Lord of the Rings, but also to expand the breadth of involvement of new gamers in the hobby. Adam explains.

"In The Fellowship of The Ring journey supplement, Mat Ward and the team that helped him work on it started a three-part journey – collecting, modelling and gaming. We continue that in this supplement by improving on the standard

Háma, Doorward of Théoden, is just one of the great releases to coincide with The Two Towers journey.

Let's Hunt Some Orc

The Two Towers begins with Aragorn, Legolas and Gimli tracking the Uruk-hai that have imprisoned Merry and Pippin.

Uruk-hai Scouts

The remnants of The Fellowship track their captured friends.

"We must follow the Orcs if there is hope that any of our Company are living prisoners."

– Gimli, The Two Towers

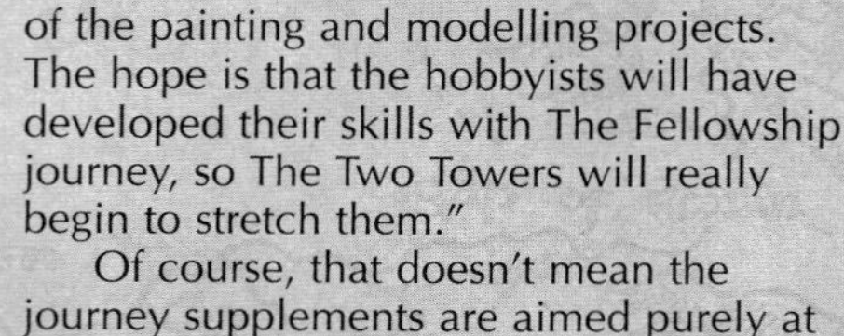

No release of The Two Towers would be complete without the intrepid defenders of Rohan, such as Éomer.

of the painting and modelling projects. The hope is that the hobbyists will have developed their skills with The Fellowship journey, so The Two Towers will really begin to stretch them."

Of course, that doesn't mean the journey supplements are aimed purely at beginners. There's plenty for veteran gamers to get from the scenarios and rules within, and the hobby projects let you have a go at some ambitious pieces, most notably Helm's Deep itself!

It's when talking about the new characters presented in The Two Towers that Adam's enthusiasm boils over.

"This project provided the chance to make more great models. Some of them are obvious, and we've wanted to make them for a while now, like Erkenbrand, Théodred and Háma. Others are just cool ideas, that present great opportunities to add to a force's theme – like the Isengard Troll or the Morgul Stalkers – things that allow us to explore some of the possibilities in Tolkien's wonderful world in a little more depth."

The forces of the White Hand are also reinforced by new releases for The Two Towers. Every army needs leaders, and there are some new Hero choices for Saruman's horde in this supplement. "**Uglúk** is one of those characters that we never covered the first time we visited The Two Towers," says Adam. "Yet for me, one of the most entertaining bits of the whole film is the scene where the miscreant Orcs, led by Grishnákh, attempt to snack on the Hobbits, and Uglúk faces them down. He's a tough, powerful Uruk-hai, comparable to Lurtz, I suppose. What's exciting about Uglúk is his special rule, which reflects a little of the character he displays in the

The Fords of Isen

There have been two battles at the Fords of Isen, and now the forces of Saruman are swelled for these scenarios

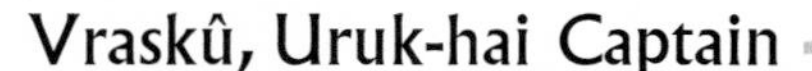

Vraskû, Uruk-hai Captain

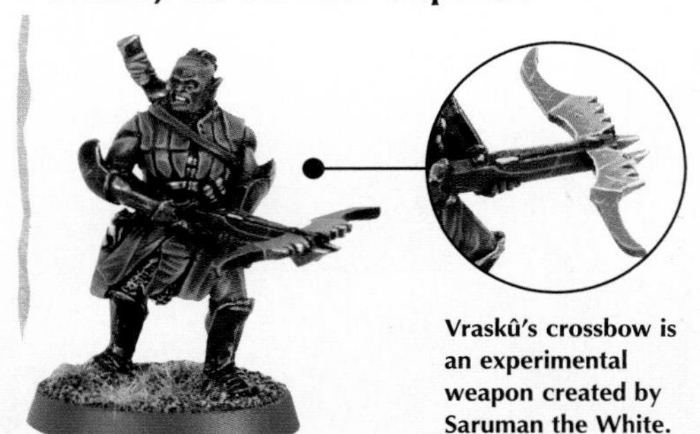

Vraskû's crossbow is an experimental weapon created by Saruman the White.

Uglúk, Uruk-hai Captain

Uglúk thinks nothing of brutally enforcing his command!

Feral Uruk-hai

Old wounds are stitched together with crude metal rings and piercings.

Each Feral Uruk carries a pair of brutal blades.

"We were driven back... over the Isen with great loss; many perished..."

– The Two Towers

film and books. He's not a nice character, and he's quite willing to break heads to get his job done!

"**Vraskû** is another Uruk-hai character, who leads a contingent of scouting Uruk-hai at the Battle of the Fords of Isen. He's a powerful, dependable Uruk-hai Captain, and carries a remarkable crossbow that bears all the hallmarks of Saruman's mechanical tamperings.

With this project we see the release of the new plastic **Uruk-hai Scouts**. "It's about time we made these," says Adam. "They're not just useful for The Two Towers games, but also for gamers who want to collect an Uruk-hai army, or recreate The Fellowship of The Ring scenarios."

"The **Feral Uruk-hai** are another new addition to Isengard, and they nicely complement the existing Isengard range. Embodying the cannibalistic and savage nature of all Orcs, the Feral Uruk-hai are lethal on the battlefield. They don't fight with organised precision, ranked up with pikes and shields like Saruman's siege specialists – these brutes hurl themselves with untamed fury at the enemy."

The new Isengard models aren't the only troops to bolster the armies of Evil in this journey book.

"Perhaps the thing that most excited me about this project were the new Dunlendings," Adam says. "These warriors have poorer wargear than the Rohirrim, but they're still fierce and proud, desperate to reclaim their ancestral lands. The models really capture the barbarity and savagery which Tolkien implies."

The sculptors have produced a set of models that really convey this vision of Dunland, where powerful warriors and desperate Wild Men live side-by-side.

The Dunlending Captain wears armour and carries weapons that are typical of Dunland's elite warriors.

Forth, Éorlingas!

The Horse-lords are bolstered by the arrival of some truly legendary heroes for The Two Towers.

Théodred

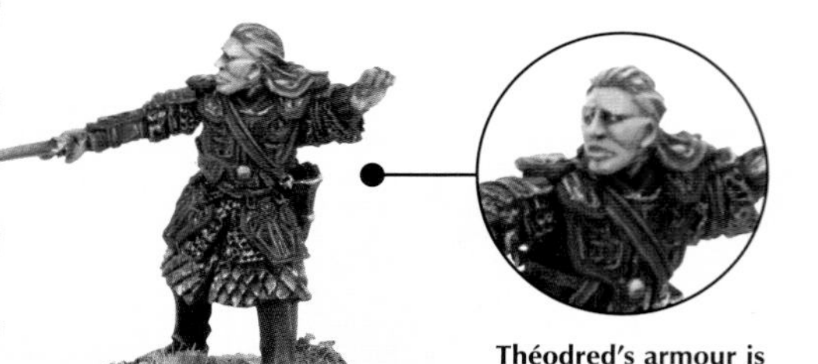

Théodred's armour is particularly elaborate, as befits the son of the King of Rohan.

Erkenbrand

Rohan Outriders

The Outriders are veteran champions of Rohan, each a hero in his own right.

Rohan is one of the big winners from this supplement, as you'd expect, since so much of the action from The Two Towers takes place in the lands of the Horse-lords.

"Take **Erkenbrand** for example," says Adam, "he's a stalwart and bold hero of Rohan. Now, he's there in all his fearsome glory. We see him at the battles of Isen, desperately fighting to hold back a tide of Orcs. Later, he rides to Helm's Deep (though Éomer did this in the movie) and breaks the back of Saruman's army.

"Then you've got **Théodred** – the ill-fated son of Théoden – who is now represented in miniature form, both on foot and mounted. He's cut from the same cloth as his father and cousin, so he's a good, solid Hero. Of course, as we know from the books, he gets slain by Saruman's armies. Don't worry, though, he won't go down without a fight!"

The Ring Goes South

Frodo and Sam now run into even more peril on the road to Mordor, but thankfully find new allies.

Each veteran is a war-weary, scarred and experienced soldier of Gondor.

Morgul Stalkers are fearsome, gaunt-looking Orcs with a vampiric nature.

Tendrils of marsh-weed still cling to the corporeal forms of these long-dead warriors.

Another forthcoming release are the mysterious **Morgul Stalkers**. Adam spills the beans on these frightening monsters.

"We thought that some of the Orcs of Minas Morgul, who serve the Witch-king, would be more sinister than other Orcs, as if the dark power of the Witch-king had corrupted them further. We envisaged them as almost vampiric in nature."

The figure designers then created models of these baleful guardians of the Witch King's city. Orcs like no other, they are deadly agents of Evil.

As if that weren't enough for Frodo and Sam to contend with, the new **Spectres** make the Dead Marshes a very dangerous place too.

With so much new stuff accompanying The Two Towers, you'd be forgiven for thinking that there was no more to come. You'd be wrong! Gondor gets a small nod, thanks to Faramir's part in capturing Frodo and Sam in Ithilien.

"The new addition for Gondor is the **Osgiliath Veterans**," says Adam. "They feature in the first fateful defence of Osgiliath, pushing out the Orcs and retaking the city, if only for a short time. They're hardy, tough, and have absolute faith in their Captains. The models really look like soldiers that have been in the front line for a long time, resonating with the feel of hardened veterans, weary and worn, but unbowed and undaunted."

> **"Morgul Stalkers are baleful guardians of Minas Morgul and deadly agents of Evil."**

March of the Ents

With the release of the new Ents box set, Saruman has even more reason to hide behind the walls of Orthanc...

The Ents of Fangorn

"If we are not hewn down... we could split Isengard into splinters..."

– Treebeard

From the two variations and their components, you can try lots of combinations to make an army of different Ents.

"The **Ents** are one of the key players in The Two Towers, despite their relatively short camera time and page space," says Adam. "Without their help, Isengard would have proven a far harder nut to crack, if Rohan had even possessed the power to do so. Fortunately Treebeard and his happy gang decided to level the White Wizard's fortress, reinforcing why deforestation is a bad thing."

In the game, the Ents are lethal. "Only stuff like Trolls or Sauron have a really good chance of beating them in a fight," Adam explains. "Then there's the fact that they are Woodland Creatures – that's a real advantage, since they can swiftly move through areas of woodland terrain, while other creatures, like Orcs and Uruk-hai, have to halve their movement rate. They can throw stones, smash fortress walls and, frankly, do it all."

A New Power is Rising!

Saruman has one more surprise up his sleeve – one that will be particularly nasty for the defenders of Helm's Deep...

Isengard Troll

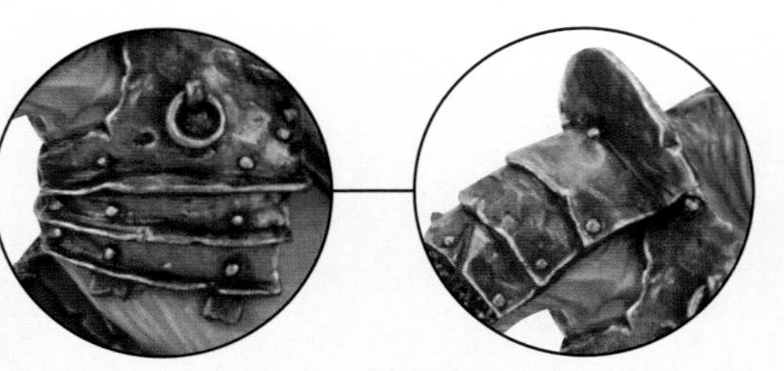

Not content with having Trolls in his service, Saruman has constructed heavy armour and deadly weapons for them, too!

"How shall any tower withstand such numbers and such reckless hate?"

– Théoden

An Isengard Troll bolsters the attack on the Deeping Wall.

Adam is clearly excited by one model in particular...

"Troll!" He cries, when asked what he likes best about Isengard. "At almost every tournament or organised event I've ever attended I've seen at least one enterprising Isengard army with a nicely converted Troll in it. Sometimes it's simply a regular Cave Troll painted with white hand prints on it, while others have been lovingly converted, with scratch-built Isengard wargear.

"The new **Isengard Troll** really scratches that itch. It's somewhere between a Mordor Troll and a Cave Troll in power, but clad in the awesome armour of Isengard. In an army that already specialises in heavy shock attacks, the Isengard Troll is the perfect model to launch that spearhead. One or two of these, backed up by lots of Uruk-hai, should be able to break their way through almost any defence."

Next Month...

MASSIVE HELM'S DEEP BATTLE REPORT!

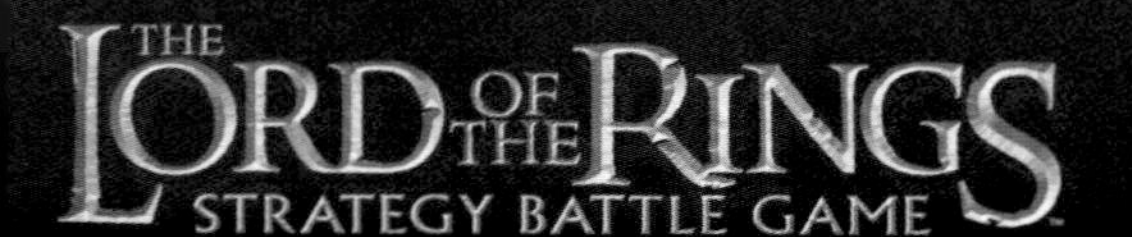

MINES OF

AN INTRODUCTION TO STRATEGY

Recreate The Fellowship of The Ring's journey through Moria with this fantastic boxed set. Bursting with hobby materials, it includes all you need to get playing The Lord of the Rings strategy battle game immediately.

STANDARD BEARER

Veteran games designer Jervis Johnson gets to the core of Warhammer.

2006

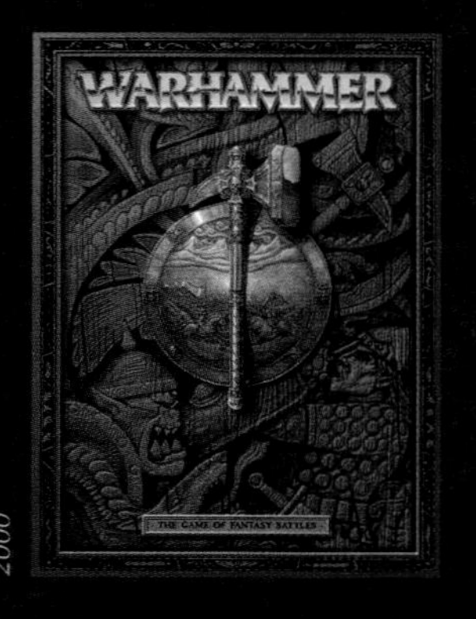

2000

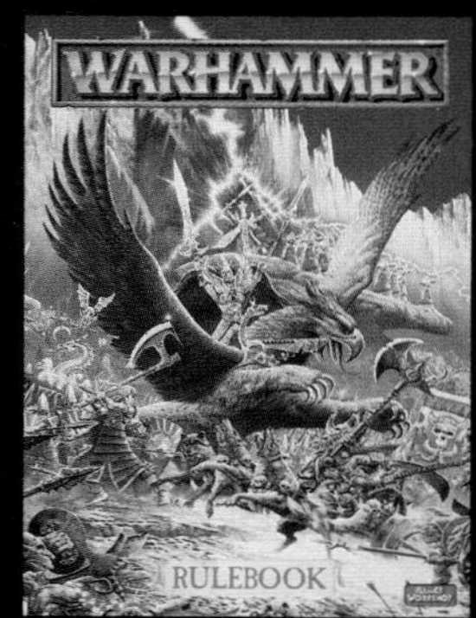

1996

There is fevered activity in the Design Studio at the moment, mainly because next month sees the release of the new edition of Warhammer. Lead developer Alessio Cavatore has worked himself into a frazzle trying to make sure it's the best edition yet, and is now reduced to a quivering wreck staring blankly at his computer screen, occasionally muttering things like "Four in a rank or five?", or "How many models can fit in a building?", and similarly arcane things. Meanwhile, the miniatures designers have been slaving away in an attempt to get as many Citadel Miniatures in the new boxed edition of the game as possible. Every now and then one will come bounding through the Studio yelling "Look, we can fit a Troll on the plastic frame – and a captured Dwarf too!" It really is all very exciting indeed.

I would love to be able to tell you all about the new edition of Warhammer right now, but unfortunately the fearsome techno-magi that run our marketing department have said they will do all kinds of nasty and unpleasant things to me if I blab too much too soon. So, sadly, most of the stuff I know about the new edition of Warhammer will have to remain secret for a few more weeks yet. However, I have been given special dispensation to talk a little bit about why the new edition focuses pretty much exclusively on what we consider to be the 'core' version of the Warhammer game. Trust me, you'll find out more – much more – about the new edition of Warhammer in next month's White Dwarf.

The core Warhammer game

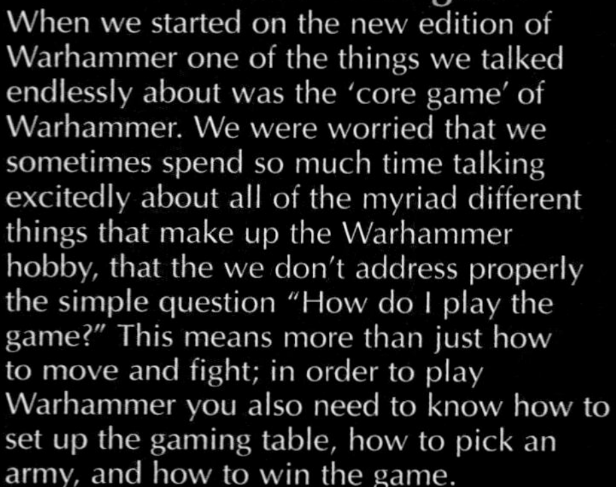

When we started on the new edition of Warhammer one of the things we talked endlessly about was the 'core game' of Warhammer. We were worried that we sometimes spend so much time talking excitedly about all of the myriad different things that make up the Warhammer hobby, that the we don't address properly the simple question "How do I play the game?" This means more than just how to move and fight; in order to play Warhammer you also need to know how to set up the gaming table, how to pick an army, and how to win the game.

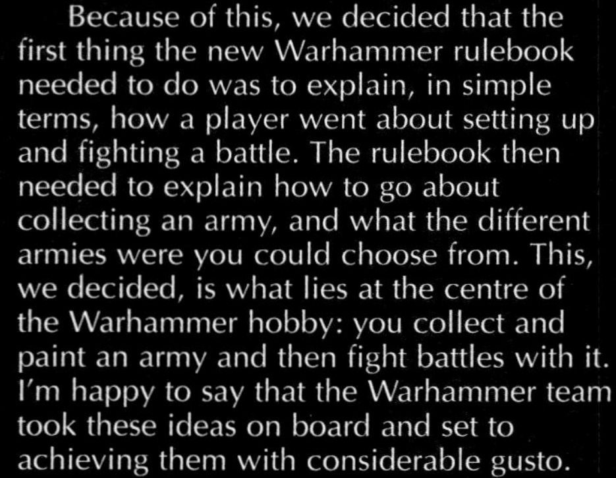

Because of this, we decided that the first thing the new Warhammer rulebook needed to do was to explain, in simple terms, how a player went about setting up and fighting a battle. The rulebook then needed to explain how to go about collecting an army, and what the different armies were you could choose from. This, we decided, is what lies at the centre of the Warhammer hobby: you collect and paint an army and then fight battles with it. I'm happy to say that the Warhammer team took these ideas on board and set to achieving them with considerable gusto.

Probably the best example of how this changed the format of the book is what happened to the rules for setting up a game of Warhammer. In the last edition this was tucked away at the back of the book along with a selection of different scenarios. In the new edition, how to set up the battlefield and your troops is explained first of all, before we explain how to move and fight with your troops. This means that the rules section explains everything you need to know in order to fight a Warhammer battle, right from setting up the table and deploying your army, through moving, fighting and magic to how you decide the winner of the game.

Warhammer in full splendour

By now some you will be saying "Hold on Johnson, does that mean that there is only one way to play Warhammer now?", or words to that effect anyway. The answer is, of course, a resounding "no". There are still just as many ways to explore the Warhammer hobby as there ever were. The difference is that the Warhammer rulebook now provides the foundation upon which that larger hobby is built. And while we know that the majority of players will be happy just collecting an army and fighting battles with it, we're going to make sure that we show the wider aspects of the hobby here in White Dwarf, on our website and in future published expansions to the core Warhammer rules. The Warhammer hobby is a broad church, and we want to show all aspects of it!

All in all, then, the new edition of Warhammer will be the most focussed and well-balanced version of the game so far.

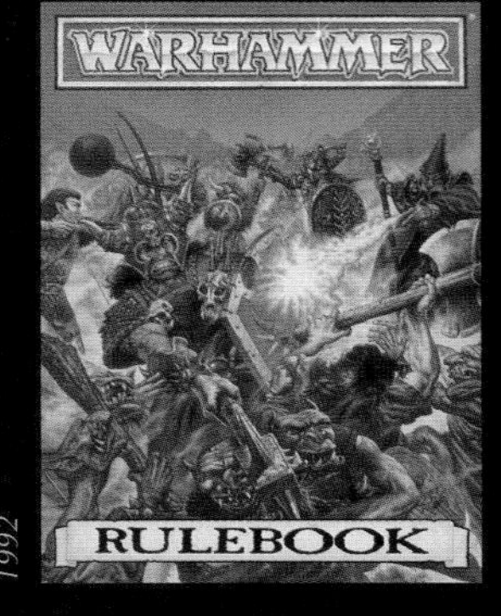

1992

1987

1984

1983

"The new edition is the start of something really big... There's never been a better time to try Warhammer!"

What's more, we're going to build on the really solid foundation the new rulebook provides by making the Army Books equally strongly focussed, and by bringing out a range of expansions that will allow you to explore different ways of playing Warhammer, but in a way that doesn't interfere with or change the 'core' game.

Warhammer Day

I think the new edition is going to be the start of something really big for Warhammer, and I can say with confidence that there really was never a better time to try the game out if you haven't done so already. On the other hand, if like me you already know and love Warhammer, then I think you're going to be over the moon with this edition of our premier game; I really think it is the best version yet.

And it's not just me that thinks that – everyone at the Studio and throughout Games Workshop is just as excited about the new edition of Warhammer. So excited in fact that we've decided to turn the release day of 9th September into a worldwide celebration of the Warhammer hobby. Games Workshop stores and stockists across the globe will be running special events and generally doing everything they can to ensure that the launch of the new edition of Warhammer is a really special and unique occasion. Trust me, you don't want to miss out on the fun, so ask at your local store what they have planned and how you can join in.

Just think, by the time you are reading the next edition of this column in a month's time, Warhammer will be out – I can hardly wait!

AMMER®
WARHAMMER
THE GAME OF FANTASY BATTLES
BATTLE
WARHAMMER
BATTLE FOR SKULL PASS
HIS FIRST
CITADEL MINIATURES®
GAMES WORKSHOP®

FORCES OF LUSTRIA

The Lizardmen are the servants of long-extinct creatures, whose power still affects all who dwell in the Warhammer world. With the release of the new edition of Warhammer looming, we take a look at this ever-popular force.

Saurus Warriors
Strongest among the Old Ones' soldiery, the Saurus form a solid core to any Lizardmen army. Tough, strong and brutal, they excel in both defensive and attacking roles.

Slann Mage-priests

The Slann are unimaginably old, creatures of astounding magical power and great intellect, who served the Old Ones during their time in the world.

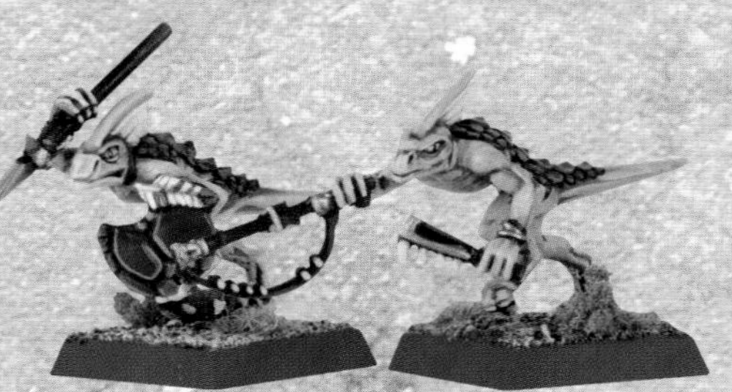

Skinks

Most numerous of the Lizardmen, the Skinks are skirmishers extraordinaire. They move with stealth and speed through even the most difficult terrain, harassing the enemy with poisoned attacks from their deadly blowpipes.

Chameleon Skinks

Some Skink spawnings bear the powers of the chameleon, allowing them to blend in with their surroundings and strike without warning!

Getting Started

At just £50 the Lizardmen Battalion box set makes an excellent starting point for any aspiring Lustrian general, and a good source of reinforcements for veteran scar-leaders. With 24 Saurus Warriors, 24 Skinks and 8 Saurus Cold One cavalry, your scaly host has some serious stopping power right from the start.

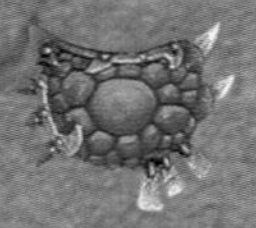

ARMIES OF THE ANCIENTS

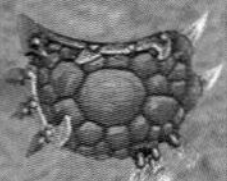

TWO APPROACHES TO COLLECTING A LIZARDMEN ARMY

Army List

Skink Priest *Level 2; 2 dispel scrolls*	**150 points**
Skink Priest *Level 2; mark of the Old Ones*	**135 points**
Skink Priest *Level 2*	**100 points**
Skink Priest *Level 2*	**100 points**
10 Skinks	**60 points**
10 Skinks	**60 points**
10 Skinks	**60 points**
10 Skinks	**60 points**
10 Skink scouts	**70 points**
2 Jungle Swarms	**120 points**
3 Kroxigor *Kroxigor Ancient*	**194 points**
3 Kroxigor *Kroxigor Ancient*	**194 points**
3 Terradons *Skink Brave*	**115 points**
10 Chameleon Skinks	**150 points**
3 Salamanders	**195 points**
Stegadon	**235 points**

www.games-workshop.co.uk /store/amphibioushorde/

Eavy Metal painter and renowned Lizardmen player Pete Foley put together this army list, which contains lots of Skink skirmishers and big, scary monsters! This type of army can be incredibly frustrating for an opponent, so using it frequently in friendly games could make those decidedly unfriendly! However, as a tournament army it is surprisingly effective. The army contains four Level 2 Skink Shamans, one of whom has the Mark of the Old Ones to counter any miscasts he may roll. Though none of the magic users are individually powerful, this army is no pushover in the Magic phase. Also, with 50 Skink skirmishers and 10 Chameleon Skinks, you'll pose some serious problems to shooty armies – who simply can't hit the sprightly lizards – and to combat armies, who can't get to grips with them. In fact, the only solid opponents the latter foe can usually charge are the very creatures they want to avoid – Kroxigors and a Stegadon.

A key feature of this army is its poisoned attacks, coming from the Skinks (including the Terradon riders and Stegadon crew) and Jungle Swarms – a massive bonus when fighting against high-Toughness foes.

The most common tactic for this army is to use the horde of Skinks and the Terradons, to outflank, outshoot and generally annoy the enemy. If they're charged, they can flee merrily away across the nearest river or swamp where the opposition cannot follow. Their primary aim is to pepper the foe with poisoned attacks, with a potential 60 shots a turn!

A deadly Kroxigor.

THERE ARE A VARIETY OF LETHAL ARMY COMBINATIONS THAT LIZARDMEN PLAYERS CAN EMPLOY. HERE, WE ASK TWO VETERAN PLAYERS FOR THEIR SUGGESTIONS.

POWER OF THE ANCIENTS

1,998 Points

This list was drawn up by Mark Havener, who's a strong advocate of hitting the enemy hard. Mark began his selection with a Fourth Generation Slann Mage-Priest, and armed this centrepiece model to the teeth. As he is the General, best Wizard in the army, and the Battle Standard Bearer all rolled into one, it is vital this model is protected. To make the Slann even safer, Mark put it in a unit of Temple Guard with a War Banner. These mighty warriors are going nowhere in a hurry, cause Fear due to the Totem of Prophecy, and can take on the best your opponent can offer.

The Saurus Scar-Veterans provide serious hitting power. Mark uses the one with the Charm of the Jaguar Warrior in a unit of Saurus Warriors, which can be ferried about the battlefield as long as the Slann has the Steed of Shadows spell. At a moment's notice, the Scar-Veteran can charge from his unit up to 18", to take out vulnerable enemy characters or even chariots! The other Scar-Veteran works very well in the Temple Guard unit, but this really does put all your proverbial eggs in one basket. Still, it's very handy having such a powerful hero around to accept challenges and present yet another deterrent to potential chargers.

The Skinks provide skirmish screens for the Kroxigors, and work closely with these big hitters. Kroxigors come with great weapons, meaning that chariots are swiftly reduced to so much kindling, while their Fear-causing presence works well in tandem with the Temple Guard. The Skink Priest is there mainly to allow the Slann Mage-Priest to cast spells remotely – though his extra casting dice comes in handy too.

Skink Priests add some extra magical zing!

Army List

Slann Mage-Priest *4th Generation; Plaque of Tepok, Totem of Prophecy, Diadem of Power*	**515 points**
Scar-Veteran *Light Armour, Quetzl, Enchanted Shield, Burning Blade of Chotec*	**137 points**
Scar-Veteran *Tepok spawning, Quetzl spawning, Charm of the Jaguar Warrior, Great Weapon, Light Armour, Shield.*	**148 points**
Skink Priest *Magic Level 1*	**65 points**
14 Temple Guard *Halberds, Shields, Standard with War Banner, Musician, Revered Guardian*	**315 points**
3 Kroxigors *Great weapon*	**174 points**
3 Kroxigors *Great weapon*	**174 points**
10 Skinks *Javelins, shields*	**60 points**
11 Skinks *Javelins, shields*	**66 points**
10 Skink Scouts *Javelins, shields*	**70 points**
19 Saurus Warriors *Standard, Spawning Champion, Musician*	**258 points**

WARHAMMER 40,000

DEATH STALKS MACHAVIUS

The ruined settlements on the outskirts of Machavius Hive are desolate wastes, scarred by the battles between the Necrons and the Ultramarines. However, in the ruins something stirs – the Necrons rise again!

GAME STATISTICS

Scenario
Urban Assault (Cities of Death, Gamma-level scenario)

Location
Machavius Minoris

Forces
Ultramarines vs. Necrons

Points
1500

Players
Alessio Cavatore and Matt Hutson

Timeline
The closing years of the 41st millennium

Machavius Hive has been hotly contested since Van Grothe's Rapidity first stirred the sleeping Necrons into action. Having seemingly scoured the surrounding cities of any Necron presence, the combined force of Ultramarines and Vostroyans pulled out of the area, leaving only a skeleton defence and a series of command posts to continue surveillance. Now, it seems that the Necrons have returned, or perhaps never left. These deathly automata seem unstoppable – whenever they appear to have been defeated, they return to their terrifying half-life, a menace that can never truly be stopped.

The Necrons have infested several structures in the subsidiary city of Machavius Minoris, their dark machinery generating massive amounts of power for unknown ends, and are marching upon the nearest Ultramarines command node. As the alarms sound, a small strike force of the Emperor's finest answers the call to arms, but can even they put down this ancient, unkillable evil?

++ 493 M5-UG 6795/OXI ++
++ENCRYPTION BETA 8 ++

FROM: Astartes Command Node Adornus

TO: Strike Force Morpheus

++ MACHAVIUS MINORIS PERIMETER BREACH ++ SECURITY LEVEL GAMMA ++ MASSIVE POWER SURGE DETECTED IN NORTHERN QUADRANT OF CITY ++ THE XENOS APPEAR TO BE CONSTRUCTING SOME KIND OF ENERGY BEACON OF UNKNOWN DESIGNATION ++ REQUEST URGENT FIRE SUPPORT IMMEDIATELY ++ THE NECRONTYR XENOS MUST BE PURGED FROM MACHAVIUS ++

++ end despatch ++
++ 493 M5-UG 6796/OXI ++

ULTRAMARINES

STRIKE FORCE MORPHEUS

1500 Points

HQ

Captain Morpheus
135 points
with power fist and bolt pistol.

Fast Attack

Land Raider *258 points*
with lascannons, heavy bolter, extra armour and smoke launchers.

Elites

Terminator Squad Quiescor *240 points*
with storm bolters and 2 assault cannons.

Terminator Assault Squad Obdormior *200 points*
2 with lightning claws, 3 with thunder hammers and storm shields.

HQ

Chaplain Somnus *135 points*
with crozius arcannum, rosarius, teleport homer and bike.

Fast Attack

Landspeeder Tornado 'Vexor' *80 points*
with assault cannon and heavy bolter.

Troops

Tactical Squad Cubilis *155 points*
Sgt. with Terminator Honours and power fist; meltagun and missile launcher.

Elites

Dreadnought 'Idaeus' *113 points*
with assault cannon, power fist, storm bolter, extra armour and smoke launchers.

Troops

Tactical Squad Lectus *233 points*
Sgt. with Terminator Honours and power fist; meltagun; Rhino with extra armour and smoke launchers.

Models 40%, Land Raider 35%

Alessio Cavatore is the custodian of our rules systems. The only thing this tabletop general likes better than playing Warhammer 40,000 is winning games of Warhammer 40,000!

Crush the xenos!

Starting with my Troops and HQ, I first picked a tactical squad and a Rhino, together with a Captain. This Rhino-borne close-attack team contained one meltagun and two power fists – all weapons that are perfectly suited to dropping Necrons and to convince most of them to stay down (unless, of course, there is a Resurrection Orb nearby). My other Troops choice was designed to defend my command node. They probably wouldn't need to move much, so I gave them a missile launcher, but with a meltagun and power fist for 'close encounters'.

I then concentrated on the attack. For a start I bought a Master of Sanctity on bike. My plan revolved around his teleport homer, and a Terminator squad. The plan was for the Chaplain to turbo-boost his way as far forward as possible, making the teleportation of the Terminator squad very precise. A plan fraught with ifs and buts, I know, but a very nice one if it worked…

I then wanted something that could take on the inevitable Monolith, and I opted for a Land Raider. Once the Monolith had been disabled, the plan was for the Land Raider to charge forward and disgorge my second squad of Terminators into the objective. The image of a Terminator Assault squad charging out of a Land Raider was just too appealing!

I spent what few points I had left on a Dreadnought sporting an assault cannon and, more importantly, a Strength 10 close combat weapon.

Finally, I picked a Tornado to bolster my anti-personnel firepower and give me a fast reserve that I could quickly redeploy if the enemy managed to outflank me with their dirty teleporting tricks.

THE NECRONTYR

ARMY OF THE STORM LORD

1500 Points

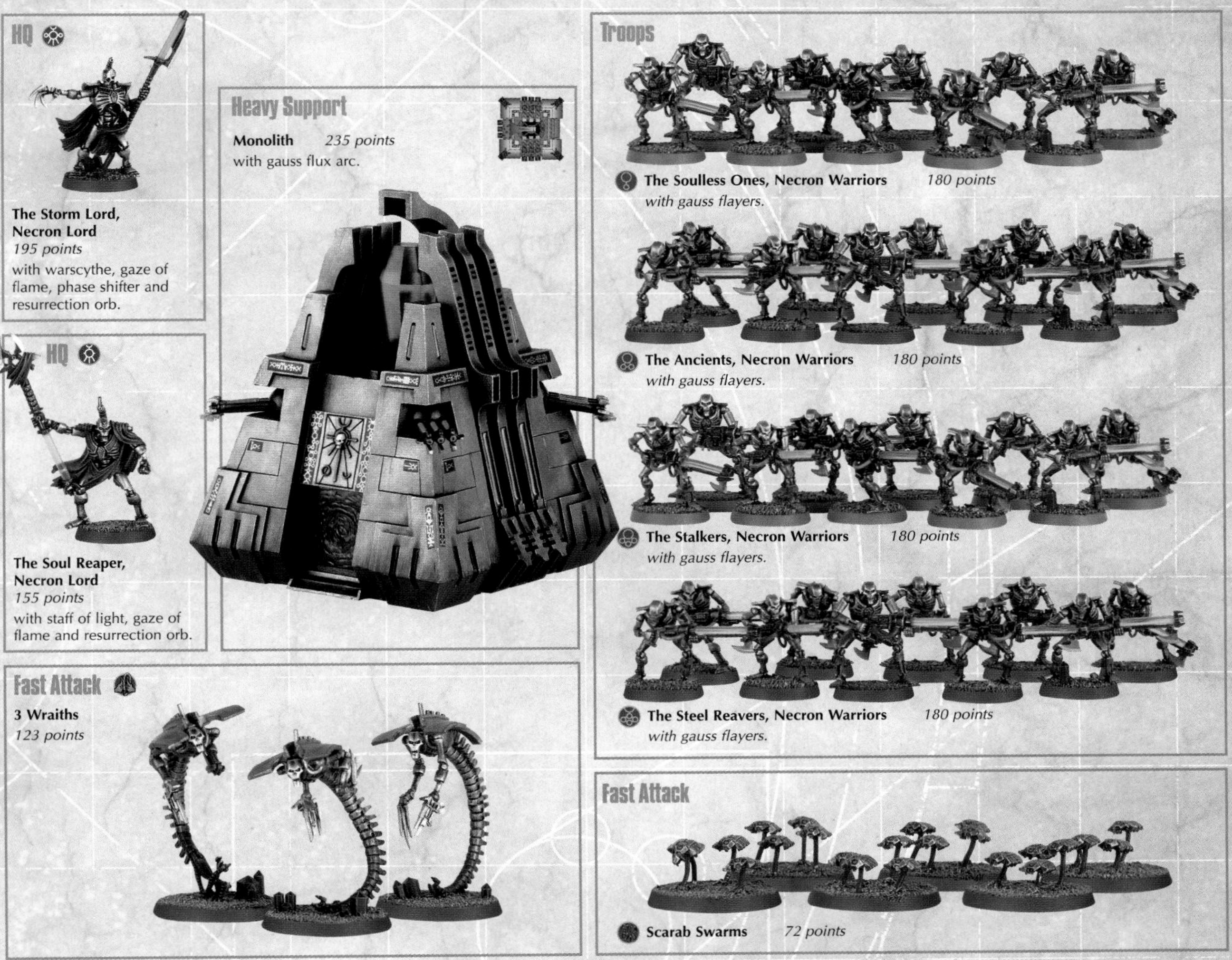

Models 40% Monolith 30%

The flesh is weak

I've been using a Necron force in the Studio Cities of Death campaign, and it's become apparent to me that large infantry-based armies that have plenty of point-scoring units are very effective at taking objectives in the rubble-strewn streets.

This force is based around four units of 10 Necrons, which pack a huge amount of firepower, perfectly capable of taking down anything from swathes of infantry to Land Raiders thanks to their gauss weapons.

To increase their survivability I've chosen two Necron Lords, each armed with a Resurrection Orb. For me, this piece of kit is a must, allowing Necrons to use their 'We'll be back' rule, even against Instant Death and power weapon attacks. I equipped each with the gaze of flame – this denies your opponent their attack bonus when assaulting the Necron Lord .

With the core force picked, it was time to add some spice! First up was the Monolith. This ominous vehicle is a steal at 235 points – it's near-impervious to all but the most concentrated heavy weapons fire, while it can redeploy a unit of Necrons that are within 18" of it using its portal. I was sure that Alessio would take a lot of assault troops, so the portal would allow me to pluck a Necron unit out of close combat, leaving their opponents stranded while I unleashed those 40 rapid-firing gauss flayers on them.

Next on the list were three Wraiths. These flying Necrons move like jetbikes, ignore all difficult terrain, and are pretty nifty in an assault. I also took six Scarab Swarms to tie up fast moving enemies. Lastly, my stratagems – Power Generator and Booby Traps – would further help intensify my firepower.

Matt has worked on more issues of White Dwarf than any man alive – that's scientific fact. He's one of the clever guys responsible for laying out much of the magazine.

CLEANSE AND BURN! Turns 1-3

Rapid Response

The Chaplain's teleport homer allowed Alessio to choose the exact placement of Terminator Squad Quiescor. With two assault cannons amongst their armament, these elite warriors were well placed to open up on the objective building.

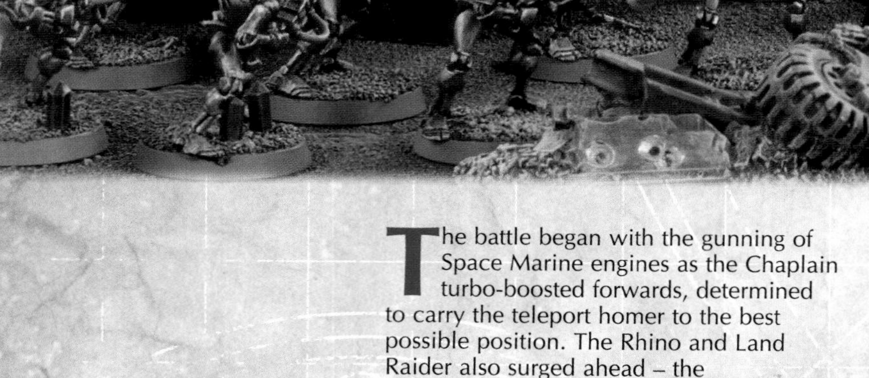

The battle began with the gunning of Space Marine engines as the Chaplain turbo-boosted forwards, determined to carry the teleport homer to the best possible position. The Rhino and Land Raider also surged ahead – the Ultramarines were taking the fight to the enemy! Realising the Chaplain's intent, the Wraiths moved to intercept him, while the four squads of Necron Warriors took up firing positions ready to unleash a deadly fusillade of gauss-fire at the first enemy that presented itself. The Shooting phase saw four Necrons fall to assault-cannon fire, while the Chaplain took a wound thanks to the Necrons' Power Generator stratagem. The Wraiths charged into the Chaplain, wounding him but failing to deliver the crushing blow, while the Chaplain's crozius arcanum cleaved one of the metallic monstrosities into so much scrap.

> "The Chaplain's crozius arcanum cleaved one of the metallic monstrosities into so much scrap."

In turn 2, four Necrons clambered back to their feet, but this only increased the Ultramarines' resolve. The Chaplain activated the teleport homer, and five Terminators stepped forth from the ether next to the Necrons' defences. Alessio disembarked his Captain and Tactical Squad nearby, and sent the Land Raider into a position from which the Terminator Assault squad could charge into combat. The Space Marines' shooting phase saw seven Necron Warriors fall to bolter rounds, causing The Steel Reavers to fall

back, before the Terminator Assault squad moved into combat, and the Dreadnought charged the Wraiths to support the beleaguered Chaplain. The Assault phase saw another Wraith fall to the Chaplain's crozius, though he was cut down in return, leaving the Dreadnought to fend for itself. The Assault Terminators forced The Stalkers to fall back but, at the start of the Necron turn, six Warriors reanimated!

Three of The Stalkers who had got back to their feet joined the nearest squad, as their own unit had fled, and took up firing positions against the Land Raider. The remaining Stalkers promptly rallied and consolidated into rapid fire range, levelling their guns at the Ultramarines. The Scarabs turbo-boosted towards the Space Marine command node, with Matt hoping that they could dislodge the Adeptus Astartes guarding it. The Stalkers, Steel Reavers and Monolith wiped out the Terminator Assault squad in spectacular fashion. The Soulless Ones and Ancients poured twenty shots into the Land Raider, blowing off both side-sponsons and immobilising the vehicle. In all, Matt fired over forty gauss shots this turn, sowing destruction amongst the Ultramarines' ranks.

Turn 3 opened with Terminator Squad Quiescor and Tactical Squad Lectus charging into the objective building, while the Captain hot-footed it back to help the Dreadnought. Five Necrons fell, but at the start of Matt's turn, four stood up again! Matt used the Monolith to teleport the Ancients away from the combat. They opened fire on the surprised Marines, supported by the Monolith, felling three of Squad Cubilis and two Terminators. However, the Ultramarines stood firm and the objective was theirs, for now.

Big Moment

***Matt*: The coolest part of the opening turns for me was in turn 2. The rapid-firing gauss flayers, combined with a devastating six-hit volley from the Monolith's flux arc, dispatched the Terminator Assault squad in short order. Alessio failed four armour saves, sealing the fate of the expensive unit.**

COLD STEEL

Turns 4-6

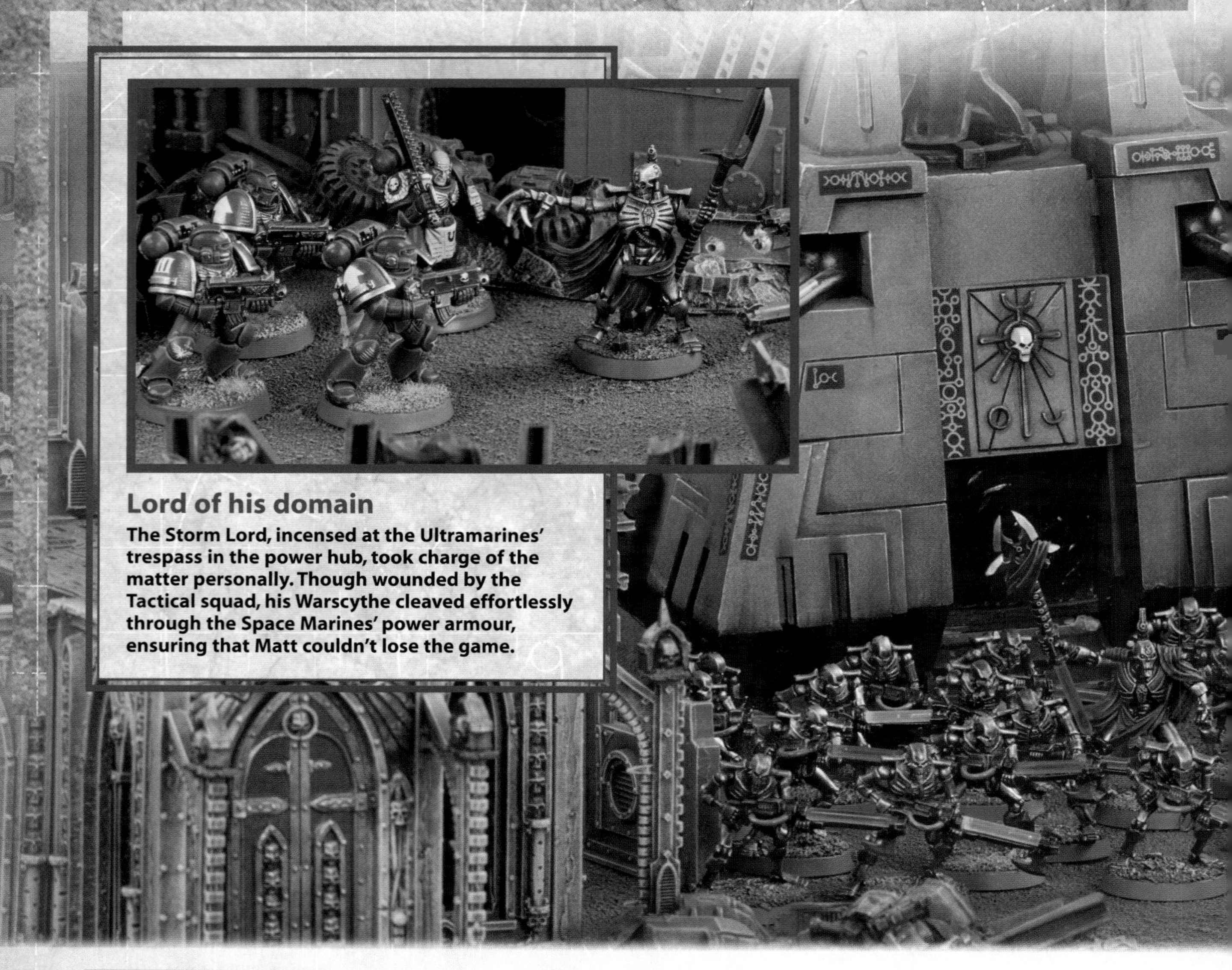

Lord of his domain

The Storm Lord, incensed at the Ultramarines' trespass in the power hub, took charge of the matter personally. Though wounded by the Tactical squad, his Warscythe cleaved effortlessly through the Space Marines' power armour, ensuring that Matt couldn't lose the game.

Big Moment

***Alessio*: With only one Terminator remaining from Squad Quiescor, I threw caution to the wind. The bold veteran cut through the objective building and charged into the Ancients, power fist swinging! Though he was ultimately doomed, he managed to see off this squad of Necron Warriors single-handed.**

The last remaining Terminator of Squad Quiescor charged into The Ancients alone. The Tactical Squad pulled away from the main thrust of the fighting and ran to the rear of the building – Alessio realised that with only four models left, he needed them all to claim the objective, so running out of range of those gauss guns seemed like the best plan. In the Assault phase, the Terminator got the better of the Necron Warrior squad, while Captain Morpheus and the Dreadnought finally wiped out the Wraiths.

In Matt's turn, the Monolith stirred again, and the lone Terminator was left punching thin air as the metal warriors phased out. The Ancients, plus the Monolith opened up on the Terminator, yet his tactical dreadnought armour protected him and he emerged unscathed. The Storm Lord ordered his warriors back into the assault, before personally cutting down the last member of Terminator Squad Quiescor and consolidating into the objective building, determined to take it back from the Space Marines.

Seeing the Necron Lord alone in the objective building, Tactical Squad Lectus charged into him, hoping to take his Orb of Resurrection out of the equation. Throwing caution to the wind, the Captain and Dreadnought each charged a unit of Necron Warriors, killing one each. The Squad Lectus caused 2 Wounds on the Lord, but failed to put him down. In Matt's turn 5, the Stalkers, who were fighting Captain Morpheus, teleported away, before rapid firing their gauss guns at the Space Marine leader. With so many shots brought to bear, the Captain was shot to ribbons! In the same Shooting phase, the Land Raider was destroyed by a withering hail of gauss

To the wire... Almost

The Scarabs had done little during the battle, largely due to Matt's indecisiveness. However, in the final turn Matt tried a desperate gambit with these tiny metal constructs. Alessio had rolled unnaturally poor dice for the entire game – and he almost failed to score the one wound he needed to beat the Scarabs, despite being armed with a power fist. Luckily for him, however, he caused the wound by the narrowest of margins. However, the result was irrelevant – Swarms cannot hold objectives, something Matt forgot!

END OF TURN FIVE

NECRONS
- The Storm Lord
- The Soul Reaver
- Soulless Ones
- The Ancients
- The Stalkers
- Steel Reavers
- Scarabs

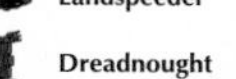
Monolith

ULTRAMARINES
- Captain Morpheus
- Squad Lectus
- Squad Cubilis
- Landspeeder
- Dreadnought

Objective

Objective

shots. Elsewhere, the Scarabs, who had so far been out of the game, skimmed into cover near to the Ultramarines' defences, ready for a spiteful last assault on the Space Marines' objective.

The final turn began with the tide of Necrons advancing grimly towards the Ultramarines' command node. The Scarabs swooped into the building and assaulted Tactical Squad Cubilis, whose missile launcher had been a constant threat throughout the battle. The outcome of the game would be decided by two assaults – one in each objective building.

Over in the command node, the Scarabs and Marines fought to a standstill, the Ultramarines had held their building. Victory would be decided in the Necron power hub, the remaining Tactical Marines battled bravely, but the Necron Lord was simply too powerful. With his Warscythe crackling with energy, he won the assault and reduced the squad to below quarter strength – they could no longer contest the objective. The Necrons too had held their Power Generator, and their nefarious plans could progress unhindered...

The result

By the slimmest of margins, and thanks to some outrageous fortune on both sides, the game was a draw, with both sides failing to take the other's building. For the few remaining Ultramarines looking out at a city full of Necrons, this was small comfort. The order was given to fall back, and under heavy fire, the Emperor's warriors retreated...

NECRONS	IMPERIUM
DEFENDED OBJECTIVE	DEFENDED OBJECTIVE

STALEMATE

MAN OF THE MATCH:

I think the last man of my Terminators performed admirably. For a while it looked like he could single-handedly hold back the Necron tide that was trying to recapture the objective, but alas! He eventually fell to the Necron Lord.

Fought to a standstill

Alessio: I hate Resurrection Orbs, especially when combined with a player like Matt who simply cannot roll bad dice (seriously, the man consistently rolled above average for the entire game, making a mockery of statistics). At the end of several turns I thought I had done a good job of killing Necrons, but then so many simply stood back up again that killing them always felt like wasted effort!

I have to admit that I made quite a few mistakes, and my Ammo Dump and Fortifications stratagems played little part. I think I should have kept the Land Raider back, bombarding the Monolith, out of range of the deadly gauss flayers of the Necron Warriors (or perhaps I should not have taken any vehicles against Necrons – their gauss weapons deadly against them, my Land Speeder, for example, was quickly stripped of its guns).

I charged the Necrons building too soon. Being inside the building made me visible to the entire enemy army, allowing them to rapid fire at my squads. I should have sheltered behind the building and then rushed in at the end of the game. Matt played the Necrons very well, as the combination of a lot of Warriors with two (two!) Resurrection Orbs makes it very difficult to get the army to phase out.

The Monolith was vital to Matt's tactics, allowing his Warriors to teleport out of combat and riddle my squads with gauss fire. The only weakness I could perceive in Matt's army was its lack of mobility, as my building never felt under serious threat. What I would have done is omit the Scarabs and Wraiths, bought more Warriors, and given one of my Lords a Veil of Darkness. This would have allowed me to Deep Strike with the Warriors, giving me a more aggressive army. Oh, and I would have kept both Resurrection Orbs, even though I really, really hate them (did I mention that already?).

> **"Their gauss weapons are great against anything with an armour value."**

ANCIENT WAR ENGINE OF THE MATCH:

Without it I would never had been able to hold off the assaulting Ultramarines and the game would have been over on turn 2. My whole tactic revolved around it... Maybe next time I'll take two.

Victory denied!

Matt: Blimey! Necrons can really take some punishment. Their high Toughness, 3+ Armour Save and 'We'll be back' rule makes them very hard to kill. This makes them ideal at winning fire-fights, which is especially useful in this mission.

Overall I think I played too defensively. I concentrated too much on defending my own building than attacking Alessio's, and wasted my most mobile units by getting them killed quite early in the game. I should never have used the Wraiths to attack the Chaplain, instead using them to threaten Alessio's building. I didn't exploit their ability to ignore difficult terrain at all. It would have been far better holding off with them and attacking in the later stages of the game. Likewise, I got the Scarabs shot up far too early, losing their nuisance potential.

What worked well for me was the tactic of combining the Necrons' vast amount of firepower with the Monolith's ability to teleport units out of close combat, which came as a shock to Alessio. The Terminators fell quickly to this tactic, which stalled his attack. 40 Necrons with gauss flayers pack a mighty punch!

Overall, Alessio's plan was sound. His assault-heavy army and aggressive plan kept me in my table quarter, making it very hard for me to achieve my objective.

Although I eventually managed to overwhelm his force, it was too late in the game for me to cover the ground to his building with anything that could hold it.

If I had been the Ultramarines, I'd have dropped the Land Raider in favour of a Devastator squad to take out the Monolith. If I had lost this awesome vehicle I wouldn't have been able to deal with Alessio's assault, and the outcome of the game would have been very different.

A draw, but a great game – the Medusa V setting really helps tell a cool story. Now it's time to post the result on the website!

> **"The Terminators fell very quickly to my tactics, which stalled Alessio's attack."**

SIGN UP! JOIN IN!

MEDUSAV.GAMES-WORKSHOP.COM

The website is open NOW!

Register!

1. Log on to the Medusa V website.
2. Register.
3. GET PLAYING!
4. Post results.
5. When the campaign ends, sit back and await news of your faction's victory.

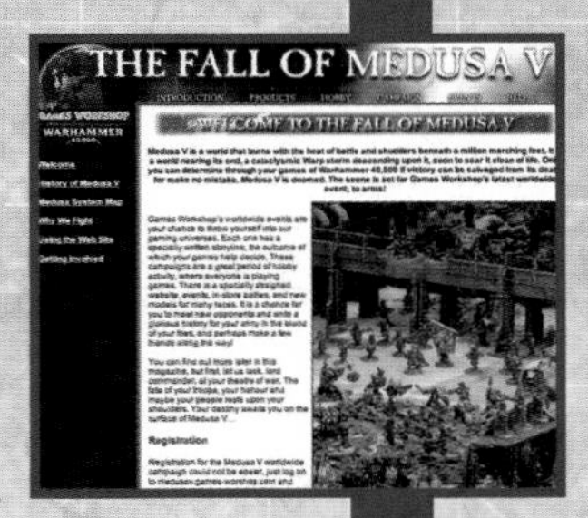

Website Features

- Service record
  Tally your triumphs and defeats.
- Unique battlefields
  Battle over spaceports, ruined cities, agri-complexes, ice wastes and more.
- Leader boards
  Measure your might against the rest of the world.
- Scenario ideas and objectives
  More ways to play.
- Hobby section
  Comprehensive modelling and painting guides.

+++CAMPAIGN ENDS 30/08/06 +++ RESULTS POSTED 01/09/06 +++

HONOUR 

RESEARCH 

HOLD 

CORRUPT 

WAAAGH! 

PRESERVE 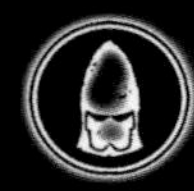

ENSLAVE 

DEVOUR 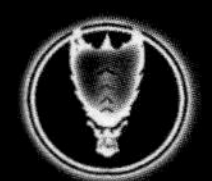

HARVEST 

WARHAM
COLLECTORS' EDITION
Special Collectors' Edition
£60
• Numbered limited edition of 4,000 copies.
• Textured tapestry hard cover.
• Heavy weight parchment coloured pages.
• Copper blocked edges.
• Warhammer embossed presentation box with magnetic catches.
• Coloured cloth headband and bookmark.
PRE-ORDER
NOW

AMMER®
WARHAMMER
RULE BOOK
WARHAMMER
The Game of Fan
WARHAMMER
GAMES WORKSHOP
Special Gamers' Edition £60
• Hardback rulebook.
• Small format rulebook.
• Special edition Warhammer dice (8 D6, Scatter and artillery dice, plus pouch).
• Special edition Warhammer templates.
• Warhammer counter set – get these game and spell effect counters two months before general release.
• Exclusive satchel with three pockets, velcro release fastenings and shoulder strap, embroidered with the Warhammer logo.

'EAVY METAL

ELVES OF ULTHUAN

Tyrion, Defender of Ulthuan

The High Elf prince Tyrion is one of the greatest warriors in all the world, and it is said by some that he is Aenarion come again. Mounted upon the steed Malhandir, Tyrion makes a fine general for a High Elf army. Painting such a magnificent Citadel miniature is a reward in itself – save him as a treat for when you've finished 30 Spearmen!

Tyrion's gold armour was painted Shining Gold over a basecoat of Dwarf Bronze. Mithril Silver was added to the gold for the highlights.

Dark red and grey contrast well with High Elf blues and whites.

Teclis, High Loremaster of the White Tower

Teclis is the twin of Tyrion, and although frail in body he is the greatest living practitioner of the magic arts. Rules for both brothers can be found in the High Elf army book.

There is a reference list of runes, like those above, in the High Elf army book.

The Teclis model is covered with fine detail.

Eltharion, Warden of Yvresse

Blinded by Malekith the Witch King, Eltharion is nonetheless still a ferocious warrior and expert swordsman.

Fine lines are a good way of adding extra detail to otherwise plain areas of cloth.

High Elves tend to be blond. Start with a light brown and highlight up to Skull White.

WARHAMMER

The 'Eavy Metal team is the most talented group of professional miniatures painters in the world. This month, we look at their work on High Elves.

High Elf Lord

The Lords of the High Elves are noble, if arrogant, creatures, inheritors of a martial tradition going back thousands of years. These are fine models, as each High Elf Lord is possessed of the best wargear Elven craft can create. A Citadel Fine Detail Brush is a must here.

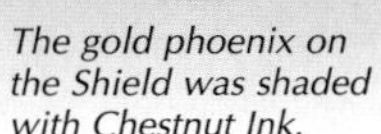

The gold phoenix on the Shield was shaded with Chestnut Ink.

Purple is another good contrast to the mainly white robes worn by most High Elves.

High Elf Lord

Many of the metal Lords come in several parts. Care must be taken when cleaning them prior to assembly, as the pieces, such as this Lord's axe, can be slender.

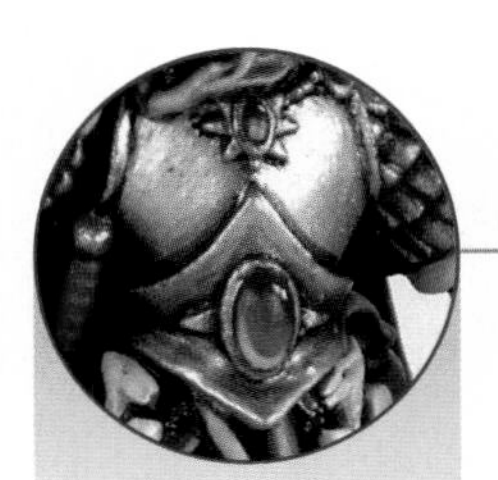

Our Elves wear Mithril Silver armour that has been carefully shaded with Blue Ink.

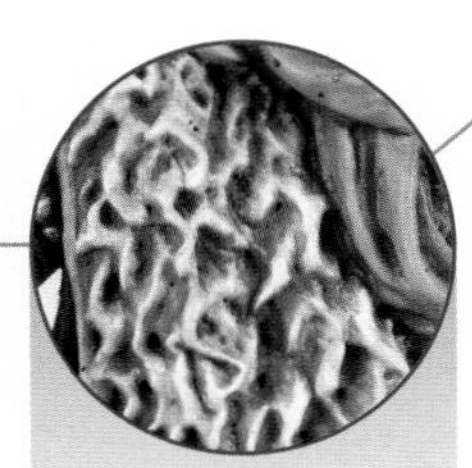

The lion pelts worn by Elves are pale cream. Snakebite Leather forms the basecoat.

Painting Gems

High Elf models are decorated with precious gems and jewels. This is the painting method that the 'Eavy Metal team use.

From a Chaos Black undercoat, paint 3/4 of the gem Red Gore.

Paint half the gemstone Blood Red

Paint a crescent moon of Fiery Orange in the bottom corner of the gemstone.

Paint a small stripe of Skull White at the top of the black area to create the illusion of light catching the gem.

A simple alternative for painting gems is to apply several coats of Red Ink over a white basecoat.

Another alternative is to paint the gem red and add a white spot to the top as a highlight.

Colours of Ulthuan

The Elves of Ulthuan dress, as a rule, in white and blue. Other colours may be used to offset this (the red below is given as an example), with strong, darker shades being especially good contrasts. Other details, such as wood, skin and hair, should be pale tones that complement white.

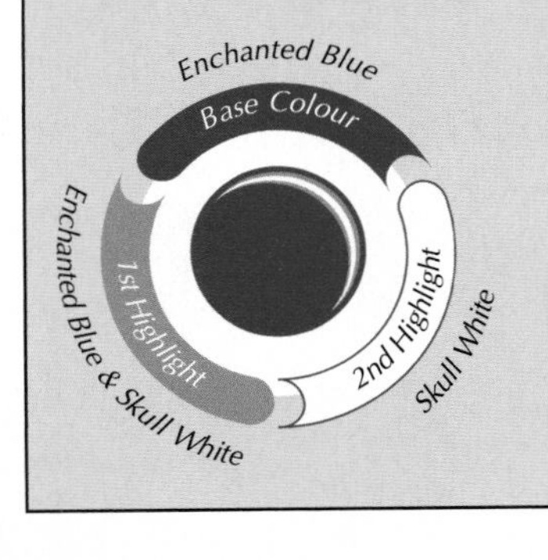

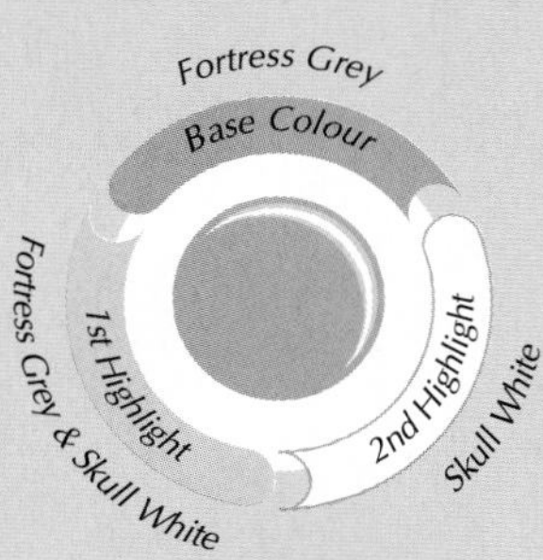

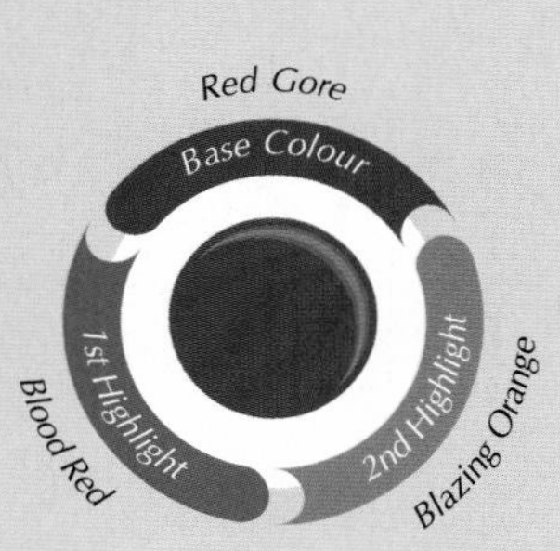

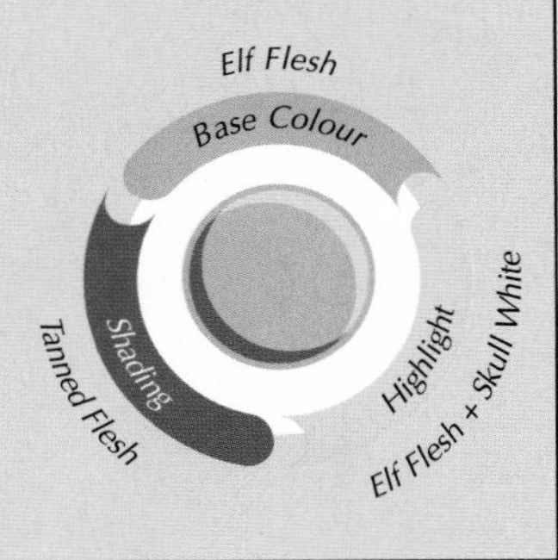

Imrik, Dragon Prince of Caledor

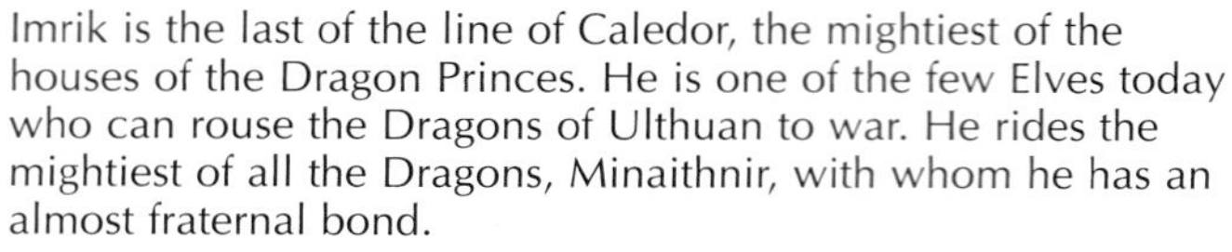

Imrik is the last of the line of Caledor, the mightiest of the houses of the Dragon Princes. He is one of the few Elves today who can rouse the Dragons of Ulthuan to war. He rides the mightiest of all the Dragons, Minaithnir, with whom he has an almost fraternal bond.

The light blue pattern on the cloak makes a subtle yet vivid contrast with the dark blue.

Designs like this are relatively easy to paint onto cloth if you use a Fine Detail Brush.

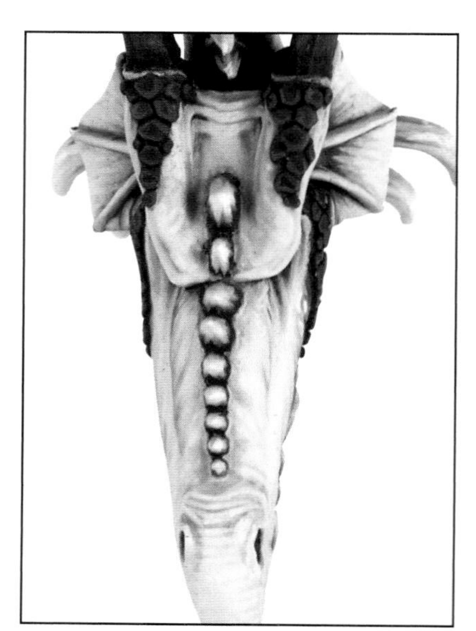

Banner Designs

Like High Elf clothes, banners are usually white, and can be either simple (left) or relatively complicated (right). Animals and monsters that the Elves have a particular affinity with, such as Unicorns, Dragons and horses; and icons from Elven mythology, such as the Phoenix, the heart and sword, the horned moon and the crossed swords; feature prominently. For more examples of Elven heraldry see Games Workshop Online and the High Elf Army book.

Shield Designs

The shields of the High Elves are tall and kite shaped, providing cover to much of a warrior's body. Their curved steel surfaces offer plenty of space for Elven artisans (and human Hobbyists) to create bold designs. Despite the long and bitter enmity between the two races, the common roots of High Elf and Dark Elf culture can be glimpsed in the similarity in symbols both Elven kindreds apply to their wargear.

1. *The star and flames are common motifs, and are often used to represent Isha and Asuryan respectively.*
2. *The sword and heart are associated with Khaine.*
3. *Emblems such as this are used by the horse clans of Ellyrion.*
4. *Sea Dragons feature prominently on the arms of Lothern.*
5. *The Elves of Caledor favour Dragons.*

***Right**: A wide selection of model High Elf shields and banners, painted by the 'Eavy Metal Team.*

DOK BUTCHA'S CONVERSHUN KLINIC

Dis munf we've got a lizzard for youse lot to look at, all big and bitey. I'd like to get hold of a head like dat for some eksperimunts, I could stick it on Gitfang's neck. I bet dat'd make him dead killy. Course, I'd 'ave to wait until he woz asleep – he likes da head he's got.

HIGH ELF MERWYRM

Contributed by gamer Eric van den Broek

No model exists for the Merwyrm from the Elf Sea Patrol list, so I had the perfect opportunity to make a cool centerpiece for my army based on Imrik's Dragon.

I changed the foot to make it look like it is grasping the base **(1)** by cutting it in half and sticking it to the rock, filling the gap with Greenstuff. It's longer than the other now, but you don't really notice. I also filled in the gaps between the spikes on the spine with Greenstuff to create a fin **(2)** to make the dragon look aquatic. Thankfully you can't see my fingerprints under the paint!

The other thing I did was to gently bend the tail **(3)**, and add a fin to it.

1

2

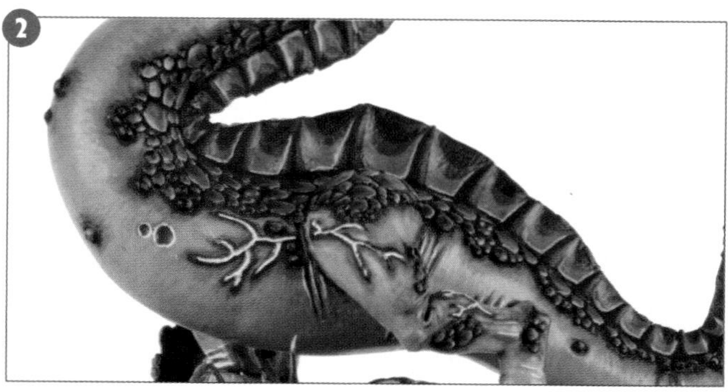

3

Eldar Rangers

From the lectures of Lord Inquisitor Eusebius Nomandes, Ordo Xenos.

Eldar Rangers are a shadowy sect of covert warriors, outcasts, pathfinders and expert marksmen. Rarely seen by their enemies, these Eldar represent a silent and deadly threat.

Life for an Eldar is strict and disciplined, and the confinement of their Craftworld homes can become oppressive. There have been many over the millennia that have tired of this existence and left their Craftworld seeking excitement, but even for these discontented souls, the Eldar Path offers forms of release. Some may follow the path of the starfarer for several human lifetimes, joining the crews of Craftworld or pirate fleets in search of adventure. Others are lonely figures, travellers who leave Eldar society altogether and wander amongst the worlds of men, treading the dangerous Path of the Outcast. A few survive to exorcise their wanderlust, rejoin their Craftworld and settle down to gentler ways, but most do not return. Many are killed, others abandon the Eldar Path entirely, falling from grace and becoming consumed by their dark passions. These tormented beings die far from home, alone with their secret anguish, their spirit stones drifting forever in the darkness of space, or lying buried on far-flung, forgotten worlds.

These adventurers are the only Eldar likely to be encountered by men except on the battlefield. They are haunted figures, torn between the love of their Craftworld homes and the glories of the forbidden universe. Their instincts lead them to lives of danger, rooting out the hidden threat of Chaos, and visiting the ancient Exodite clans on the far rim of the galaxy.

Eldar Rangers are resilient, world-weary, independent warriors, used to looking after themselves. When a Craftworld is threatened, its Rangers may hear its call, taking up their weapons and going to war once more.

Though by no means the most overtly destructive of Eldar units, Rangers are quite capable of inflicting serious losses on any force fighting them. They are armed with powerful sniper rifles, with which they can pick out weak points in their enemy's armour. It has been known for a single band of Eldar Rangers to hold up an entire column of Imperial Guard. Standard Imperial procedure is therefore to fall back and call for heavy artillery support.

Clearance Alpha
Subject:007/a2-b8
'Eldar'/Outcast
++Genotype:
Class 2 proto anthropoid
++Primary features:
superior psionic potential; metaphrenic technology base
++Capture date:
0937993.M41
++Date of Interrogation:
0005994.M41
++Autopsy Date:
0173994.M41
++Date of Psychic Interrogation:
NECROLOGUE UNSUCCESSFUL
++Attending Explicator:
Nillo Deaaris

Standing Order 2830/x/Wa – for dissemination to all front line units.

++ ACTIONS TO BE TAKEN WHEN CONFRONTED BY ELDAR SNIPERS. ++

Upon attack from an enemy sniper of the xenotype 'Eldar', all units are ordered to perform a Reconnaissance by Fire. No further actions are sanctioned, by pain of administrative punishment or death, as determined by the Commissariat or duly appointed Regimental Provost.

Orbital bombardment: A single, well-placed orbit-to-surface munition will destroy any enemy sniper. In addition, any surviving xenos will be cowed sufficiently that further aggressive acts are likely to be forestalled. Furthermore, much of the cover from which any further attacks might be launched will be destroyed.

Superheavy ordnance: Titans and superheavy tanks make ideal counter-sniping units. Upon receiving fire, notify the masters of any such vehicles within range and let them rain the Emperor's vengeance upon your foes!

Battlecannon: A single round from a Leman Russ is capable of levelling any cover, and of destroying most enemies no matter their skill at fieldcraft.

Heavy weapons: Squad support weapons such as heavy bolters and missile launchers, as well as higher-level mortars and other indirect firing weapons are ideal for engaging cowardly enemy snipers. Use them to direct holy fury at any location in which the pernicious xenos may lurk.

Small arms: Squad leaders should identify all possible locations in which the enemy may be hiding, and communicate these to his warriors. Upon his word, all troopers should shoot at their designated target, deluging the enemy with fire and scouring him from his hide. By the power of the las-gun might all foes be defeated!

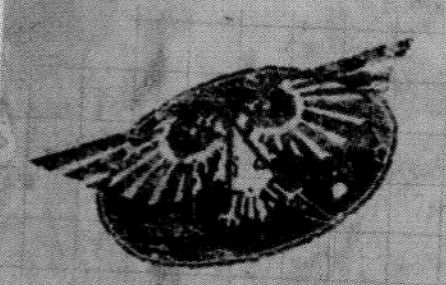

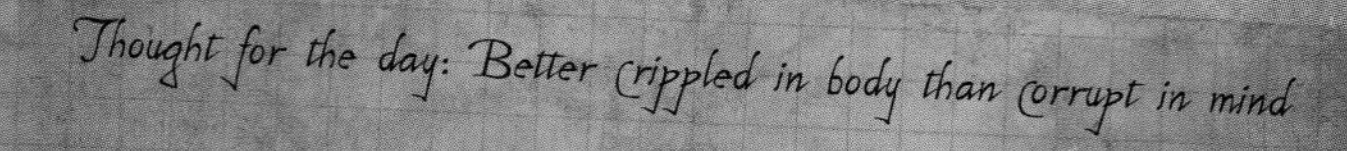

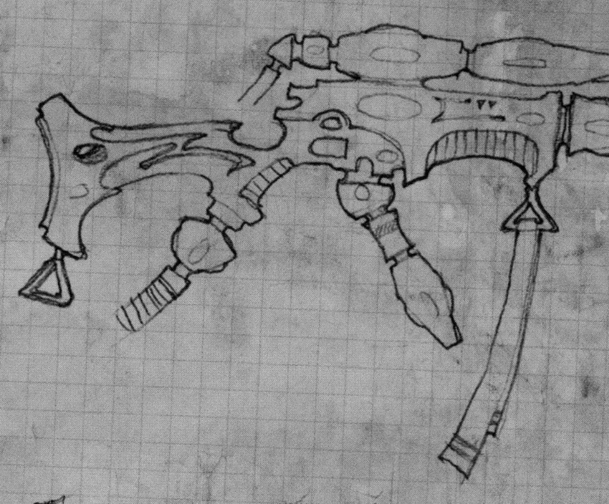

Rifle

High-energy impulse sends monomolecular ammunition at high velocity, modulated by high frequency laser carrier beam. ADEPT'S NOTE: Though functionally similar to human equivalents, this weapon is manufactured to extreme tolerances and is capable of highly energetic impact.

Sensor Spike

Unknown device carried by many captured Ranger specimens. Appears to contain some manner of psychotelemetric receiver. ADEPT'S NOTE: Remote viewing? Perhaps this device allows the Ranger to spy the land ahead, perhaps through a webway portal. If so, this means it is possible for the Eldar to discern our actions in the vicinity of a portal even when they are within the webway. The strategic ramifications of this are huge.

++ Pict-capture of Eldar Ranger Xenos, Hive Sybilla Tertius ++

Ordo Xenos

Message Decryption Simulacrum

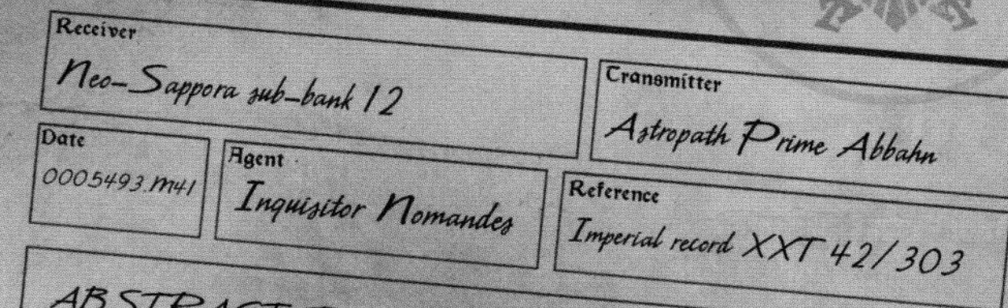

Receiver	Transmitter
Neo-Sappora sub-bank 12	Astropath Prime Abbahn

Date	Agent	Reference
0005493.M41	Inquisitor Nomandes	Imperial record XXT 42/303

ABSTRACT: There follows a summary of pertinent data regarding the xeno sub-type Eldar Ranger. These data to be cross-checked with your subject and any deviation whatsoever to be reported through my staff as a matter of highest priority. Eldar Ranger activity has increased exponentially in the Medusa system in recent weeks, and collating intelligence on their actions is vital to achieving our own aims there.

ITEMS:

Helmet

- Psychoplastic engineered armour, containing advanced sensor suite, communications and life support systems.

Armour

- Eldar carapace plates over flexible mesh inner body suit. Provides limited protection against ballistic and energy attack. ADEPT'S NOTE: This puny armour offers no protection against the blessed weapons of the Astartes.

Cameleoline cloak

- Adaptive camouflage weave refracts light around wearer, resulting in a blending effect with surroundings. ADEPT'S NOTE: Camouflage effect substantially increased in low light conditions.

Biel-tan

Thanks to the dazzling array of Aspect Warriors found in a Biel-tan army, its Ranger squads are often foolishly overlooked by ignorant foes. A key component in a Biel-tn attack force, Eldar Rangers direct the fury of the Swordwind against the enemy, silently scouting out enemy positions in preparation for the main assault. The Rangers shown here wear a dark woodland camouflage scheme of the type described by the survivors of the Twyfed Gorge Massacre.

Saim-hann

Saim-hann is famed for its mighty Wild Rider Hosts, composed of scores of sleek and deadly jetbikes and skimmers. Unlike the other members of their Craftworld, the Eldar Rangers of Saim-hann do not ride headlong into battle, instead utilising stealth and cunning to approach the enemy unseen. When a Wild Rider Host goes to war its Eldar Rangers scout ahead, ascertaining the lie of the land and neutralising immediate threats.

"When the Eldar make their attack, the enemy will already be half-defeated, having spent days or even weeks chasing the shadows of the Rangers."

– Inquisitor Nomandes

Alaitoc

Of all the Eldar Craftworlds, Alaitoc adheres most stringently to the Path of the Eldar. This zealous attitude has caused many of the Alaitoc Eldar to live the life of outcasts and become Rangers. As a result of this, when Alaitoc goes to war it falls to the Rangers to return to protect their Craftworld. Currently an Alaitoc Ranger force of unequalled size operates on Medusa V, severing enemy communications and preparing the way for larger Eldar armies to attack.

Telennar

The cordial relations between Alaitoc and Telennar have brought the forces of this small Craftworld to Medusa V, where its warriors battle to protect the Webway from the coming Warp storm. These Rangers wear the livery of those sited to the north of Battlezone Tisiphone. Small bands of Telennar Rangers have staged devastating ambushes against the Ork buggy gangs patrolling around Nazdreg's ruined space hulk, hampering the greenskin scavenging efforts at every turn.

Never shopped online before? Here's why you should!

THE ONLINE STORE

Fast, secure and direct!

Exclusive Models

WARHAMMER 40,000

WARHAMMER

THE LORD OF THE RINGS STRATEGY BATTLE GAME

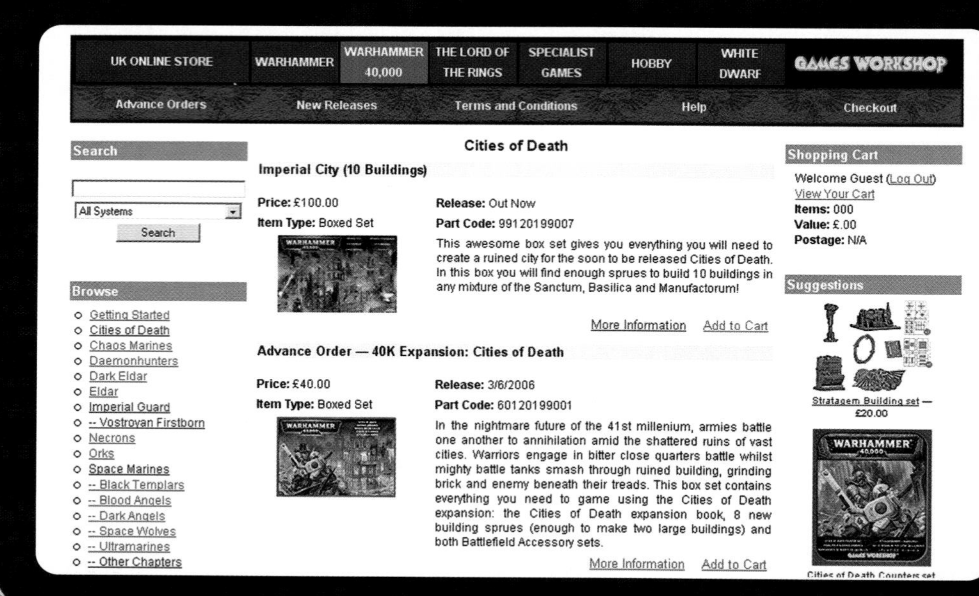

The UK Online Store keeps getting better and better. It's a great place to get your miniatures, and it's so easy to use!

- **EASY:** The Online Store has never been easier to use; with straightforward navigation categorised by game, you will be able to find everything that you want.
- **SAFE:** We use Verisign 128-bit encryption which, put simply, means that the Online Store is 100% safe to use.
- **STRAIGHT TO YOUR DOOR:** Your models are delivered wherever you want. You won't even have to go out!
- **CONVENIENT:** It doesn't get much easier to buy something new than to log onto the Online Store and place an order – you don't even need to get out of your pyjamas to do it!
- **CHEAP:** When you take a trip into town – paying for your bus fare, petrol, parking, a coffee and a bite to eat, the costs can rapidly rack up. By using the Online Store you could be spending a lot less money and saving time too!
- **THE HUMAN TOUCH:** If you want help using the Online Store, the Hobby Specialists are available Mon-Sat 10:00-18:00 and Sunday 11:00-17:30 on 0115 9140000. They will be able to talk you through any aspect of using the store.

+++DIRECT EXCLUSIVE+++
SKAVEN WARLORD 2
9947020607403 **£6.00**

+++DIRECT EXCLUSIVE+++
SPACE MARINE TECHMARINE
99060101313 **£9.00**

www.games-workshop.co.uk\store

The Complete Range

Everything in store and a lot more! The Online Store carries everything a traditional Hobby Centre does, plus a lot more that you just can't get anywhere else. We also have huge stock levels and if an item is out of stock it is probably in the warehouse so we can get it back for you within a few days.

Battleforces and Battalions

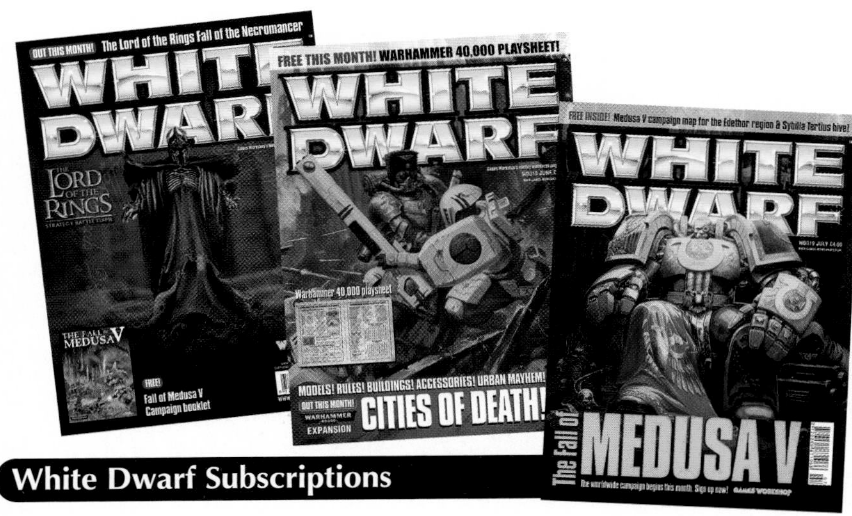

White Dwarf Subscriptions

Games Day 2006 tickets

FREE! POST OFFER

Never tried the Online Store before - then now is the perfect time to give it a try!

Every order placed between 12pm on Friday 28th of July and 10am Monday 31st July over the amount of £18 (that's the price of a regiment box set) through the UK Online Store will be delivered straight to your door without paying a penny in postage costs!

Offer only available to orders being delivered to the United Kingdom and Northern Ireland and on our standard 'Royal Mail Express' postage.

All orders placed after 10am on Monday the 31st of July will be charged postage at our usual rate.

BE AMONG THE FIRST TO PLAY

From the 19th of August every Games Workshop Hobby Centre will be running Warhammer introductory games, three weeks before the launch of the game! An advanced copy of the rules has been secretly delivered to each of our Hobby Centres. Be among the first to see what's inside! Find out what's new, what's changed and what's remained the same!

BE AMONG THE FIRST TO...

- See fantastic miniatures from the new boxed game –Battle for Skull Pass!
- Field test the new rules!

Don't be late! Get in-store to see for yourselves and earn yourself some valuable bragging rights!

To find your nearest Games Workshop Hobby Centre turn to page 116 or go online to:

www.games-workshop.co.uk/storefinder

ne.games-workshop.com/shopping

AMMER®

THE NEW EDITION!

PREPARE FOR WAR!

Saturday 26th August

Try the new rules with your Warhammer army at this special event! Bring down a 500 point force on Saturday 26th August to any UK Hobby Centre and have a game against one of the armies from the new Warhammer boxed game – Battle for Skull Pass. Remember, your existing army book is valid under the new rules. Call your nearest UK Hobby Centre for details on this great event!

WARHAMMER® The Art of Games Workshop

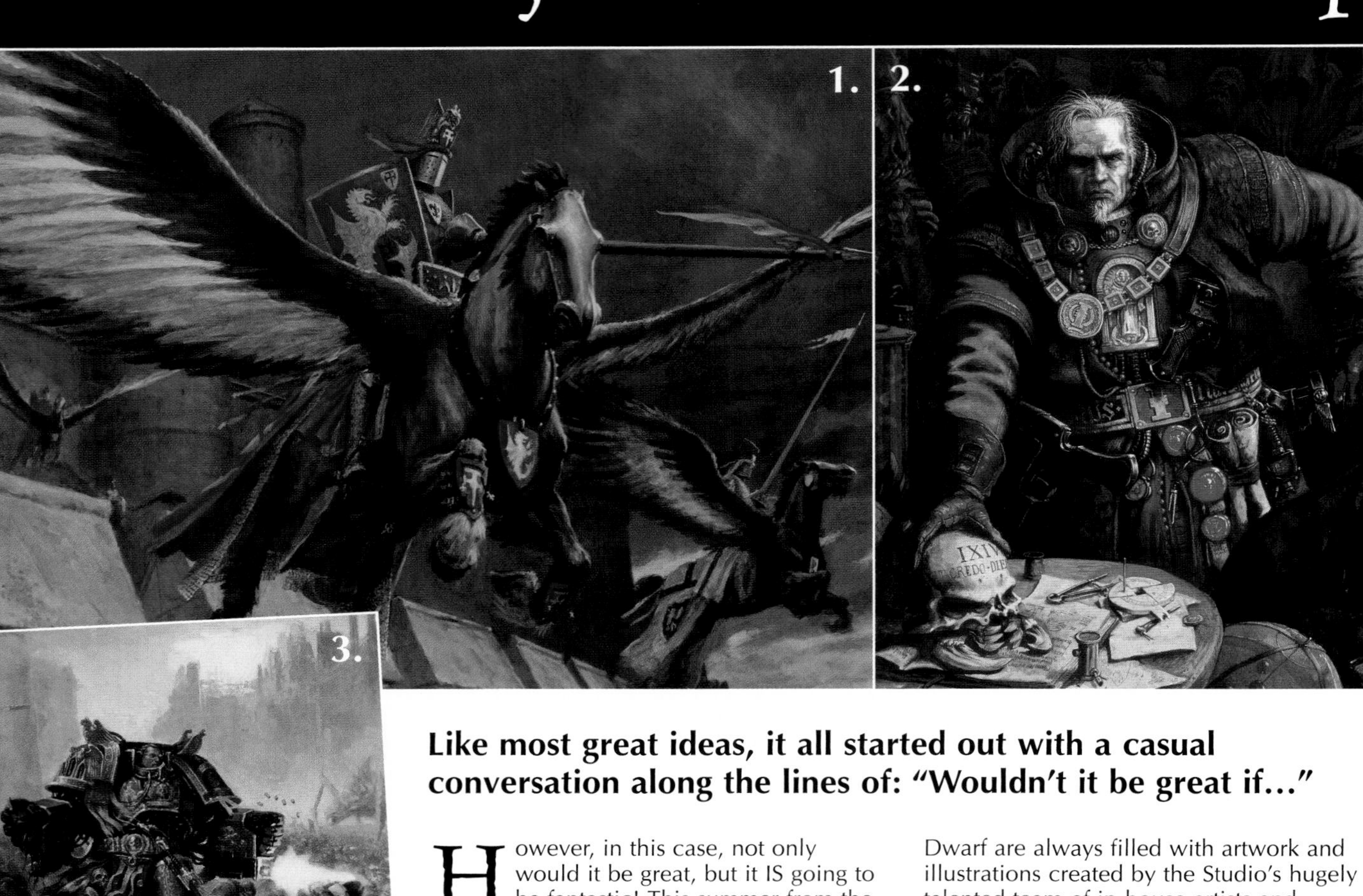

ABOVE
1. Pegasus Knights: Paul Dainton.
2. Inquisitor: Dave Gallagher.
3. Space Marines: Karl Kopinski.

Like most great ideas, it all started out with a casual conversation along the lines of: "Wouldn't it be great if..."

However, in this case, not only would it be great, but it IS going to be fantastic! This summer from the 15th July to the 24th September, Nottingham Castle will be hosting a unique exhibition entitled "Warhammer – The Art of Games Workshop."

For almost thirty years, Games Workshop has been creating, sculpting and illustrating the imaginary worlds of Warhammer and Warhammer 40,000 to the delight of hundreds of thousands of gamers, model makers and fantasy enthusiasts from around the world. Now, for the first time, the original artwork, miniatures, sculptures and drawings will be brought together to showcase the creative arts of Games Workshop.

What's most exciting about this event is that, with one or two exceptions, none of this art has ever been seen in its original form. We're all very used to seeing fantastical images illustrating our game boxes and books and the pages of White Dwarf are always filled with artwork and illustrations created by the Studio's hugely talented team of in-house artists and freelancers. However, despite this familiarity, very few people outside of the Design Studio have ever seen the original works.

Until recently the same principle also applied to the thousands of beautifully painted models and miniatures created by the 'Eavy Metal team. However, last year, with the opening of the Citadel Miniatures Hall we took our entire collection and put it on public display to a phenomenal reaction from fans and visitors. Since opening the miniatures gallery at Lenton just over a year ago we've had more than 50,000 visitors come to Warhammer World to gaze at and enjoy these models in person.

Inspired by this response, we wondered whether we could do something similar with our art collection. Since the advent of digital scanning, once a piece of artwork or

illustration has been scanned, it is catalogued and then safely stored in plan chests in our art archive. Sometimes, one of the artists might ask if they can have a particular piece to hang on the wall at home, and on occasion, staff members have been given a piece of original art, but on the whole the collection has largely remained unseen.

Part of the problem lay in the fact that we simply didn't have any space at Lenton where these pieces of art could be put on display in anything close to a gallery setting. It was at this point in the story that Nottingham Castle stepped in. Sharon Cooke, the woman responsible for archiving and storing our artwork had a friend, Jim Waters, who was the Exhibition Officer at Nottingham Castle. She and Jim were talking about their respective jobs and he asked whether we'd ever thought of mounting an exhibition. Well, one thing led to another and the idea for "Warhammer – the Art of Games Workshop" was born.

One of the remarkable things about this collection and exhibition is how coherent the artwork and images are. Although they represent work by many different artists drawn from more than twenty years' worth of artwork and illustration, there is a freshness and vitality about these images that initially makes them appear to be the work of only one or two painters and artists.

Early on in the history of the company, Games Workshop succeeded in establishing a very strong 'house' style, that has influenced our artwork ever since. In no small part this style was inspired by the personal work and approach of Nottingham painter and illustrator John Blanche who, for the last fifteen years, has worked as Games Workshop's Art Director. Back in 1989, John gave the following list of influences: "My favourite artists are many and varied; a full list would fill a page and I am still discovering more, but Grunwald, Dürer, Albrecht Altdorfer, Friedrich, the pre-Raphaelites, Casper, Géricault and Gerome immediately spring to mind."

John continued: "I did my first illustration job for White Dwarf magazine in about 1978, I think, which grew steadily from a part-time position to a full-time one. We then developed what became the single most important facet of Games Workshop's take on fantasy art, the application of the Northern European art heritage against the dominant, clean, classical version of fantasy imagery that existed at the time. The first big publication we tackled in this way was Warhammer 40,000 where nearly all the art was commissioned by me from freelance artists. During the next twenty years, as we built our in-house illustration department, the art developed into a body of work that stands alongside any other, but the vision never changed."

It's this focus on Northern European mediaeval, romantic, neo-classical and heroic art that has allowed Games Workshop to develop its own distinctive style which John now calls Games Workshop Gothic!

John again: "Gothic means lots of things. You have the architectural style from the Early Middle Ages, which was then re-invented by the Victorians. They applied it to all sorts of stuff, and we now

5.

6.

ABOVE
***4.** Storm of Chaos: Alex Boyd.*
***5.** Space Marines: Dave Gallagher.*
***6.** Witchhunters: Paul Dainton.*

"John: my favourite artists are many and varied; a full list would fill a page and I am still discovering more"

BELOW
7. Sigmar on his throne: Karl Kopinski.
8. Emperor versus Horus: Adrian Smith.
9. Dark Mechanicus Lord: John Blanche.

7.

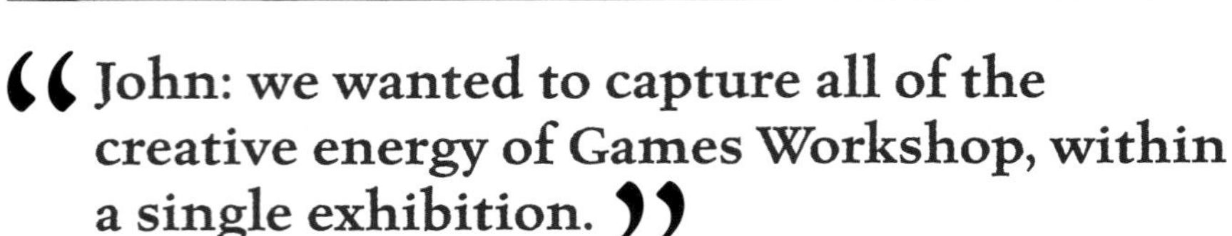

have modern gothic, which is inspired by yet is none of these things. Its internal Games Workshop meaning is typified by the robust, bellicose, often archaic and bleak view of the fantasy and science fiction genres you can see in our artwork and images."

What is clear, is that visitors to the exhibition will be astounded not only by the range of artwork, imagery and artefacts on show, but by the juxtaposition of concept sketches and other preliminary work with the two and three-dimensional artworks they finally become.

As John explains: "We wanted to capture all of the creative energy of Games Workshop within a single exhibition, from concepts and sketchbooks through to fully painted miniatures and models. This was never really going to happen and selecting the individual pieces and models that would make it into the exhibition was a difficult task. However, at the end of the day, we are pretty pleased and we hope that visitors will leave the exhibition both excited and inspired."

In addition to the artworks, throughout the exhibition, Nottingham Castle will be hosting a range of special events, from miniature painting demonstrations by some of the top 'Eavy Metal painters, through to one-off guided tours of the show by some of Games Workshop's top artists and designers. These events will be strictly limited and places can be booked through Nottingham Castle on: *0115 915 3651*.

The show runs at Nottingham Castle from the 15th July until the 24th September.

8.

9.

ARMING FOR MEDUSA

Part 3: Waaagh!

Paul Evans from our Manchester Hobby Centre show us his immense Ork Speed Freek army and how he, and his store, are prepared for the Medusa V campaign!

ORK SPEED FREEKS

Kult of Speed Rules

- **Mount Up!**
  All infantry in transports.
- **Fast Response**
  Reserves from turn 1.
- **Mobbing Up**
  Squads mob up on transports.

Paul: Mad Mek Git Stix is one of Warlord Nazdreg's most notorious Meks. He caught Nazdreg's eye when, while working with the teleport maintenance crews, he somehow got the equipment to "beam up" half an enemy platoon – the top half. His fixation for building things, bigger, shootier, faster or louder, was evident even then, but back in these early days his designs were often ridiculed by conventional Mek Boyz. Eventually, he obtained the rank of Big Mek, a promotion gained quickly after the rest of his crew were accidentally teleported into the molten core of a nearby planet.

His first construction was a massive "Kustom Job" Cybork Body, commissioned by one of Nazdreg's Warbosses. However, in an unfortunate case of mistaken identity, the Mad Dok performing the operation attached the Cybork Body to Git Stix instead, unintentionally boosting his physical stature to match that of the most powerful Warbosses. Furthermore, before the mistake could be rectified, the unlucky Warboss was tragically sucked out of a malfunctioning air lock. Since then Git Stix has thrived at the head of his own warband and is never short of a volunteer or two for his latest project.

Shortly after their arrival on Medusa V, Nazdreg tasked Git Stix with a mission of his own. While the Orks gather the materials they need to

continued on page 102

Warboss: Cybork body, bionik bonce, 'eavy armour, power claw, attack Squig, kombi weapon: shoota/rokkit launcha, kustom job: more dakka, shootier, blasta
5 Nobz: Mega armour, kustom job: more dakka, shootier, blasta
Battlewagon: 2x Twin-linked rokkit launcha, zzap gun, armour plates, Grot riggers, armoured top, krusher 600pts

Big Mek: Cybork body, bionik arm, burna, power claw, mekboy's tools
Mekboy 1: Kustom force field, bionik arm. mekboy's tools
Mekboy 2: Bionik arm, burna, mekboy's tools, waaagh banner (carried by Grot)
Mekboy 3: Super stikkbomz, burna, bionik arm, mekboy's tools
Mekboy 4: Kustom mega-blasta, mekboy's tools
Battlewagon: 2x Twin-linked rokkit launcha, zzap gun, armour plates, Grot riggers, force field 405pts

9 Skarboyz: slugga and choppa, 3 burnas, frag stikkbombz, Nob with power claw.
Wartrukk: Grot riggers, armour plates, rokkit launcha, red paint job 211pts

10 Skarboyz: slugga and choppa, 3 burnas, frag stikkbombz, Nob with power claw.
Wartrukk: Grot riggers, armour plates, bolt-on shoota, red paint job 224pts

Alternative HQ

Warboss: bike, powerclaw, 'eavy armour, bionic bonce
Nobz Warbike Mob: 3 slugga and choppas, 1 choppa and power claw 366pts

Warbuggy: Grot riggers, Twin-linked rokkit launcha 42pts
Warbuggy: Grot riggers, Twin-linked rokkit launcha 42pts
Warbuggy: Grot riggers, Twin-linked rokkit launcha 42pts

10 Trukk Boyz: shootas, 1 burna, Nob with power claw,
Wartrukk: Grot riggers, big shoota, bolt on big Shoota, Armour plates 181pts

4 Warbikes: Nob with choppa and power claw 167pts

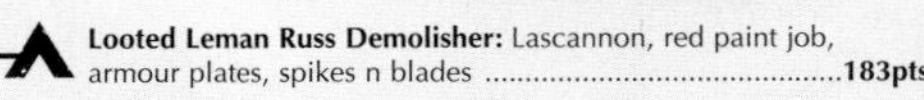

Looted Leman Russ Demolisher: Lascannon, red paint job, armour plates, spikes n blades 183pts

Deth Kopta Squadron: Mek with burna 50pts
Deth Kopta Squadron: Mek with burna 50pts
Deth Koptas Squadron: 2 boyz, Mek with burna 120pts

Ork Bomma: 2 Grot bombs, 2 rokkits 2 bombs, 3 twin-linked big shootas 228pts

TOTAL: 2537 pts

PAINTING SPEED FREEKS

Metal
- Tin Bitz
- Boltgun Metal
- Blue Ink
- Chestnut Ink
- Chainmail

Skin
- Dark Angels Green
- Dwarf Flesh
- Chestnut Ink
- Rotting Flesh

Red Armour Plates
- Dark Flesh
- Blood Red

Yellow Armour Plates
- Desert Yellow
- Bubonic Brown
- Sunburst Yellow

Military Greens and Greys
- Catachan Green
- Shadow Grey
- Chaos Black
- Kommando Khaki

Paul uses the new Ork Kommandos as Skarboyz

continued from page 100

rebuild their Hulk, Git Stix must secure a energy source large enough to power it.

His plan is a typically ambitious one that involves breaching the Hives defences, placing teleport beacons around the primary reactor, launching "Da Killa-Tun Mega-Rokkit" at the Greater Sybilla Gate and destroying a Warlord Titan to boot.

Arming for Cities of Death

As I thought about the best way to use my Speed Freek army in Cities of Death, it was apparent that I had a bit of a problem. A round peg (my current army) and a square hole (the Cityfighting missions).

My thoughts turned towards the idea of building a Footslogging Ork army, it would allow me to replace my fast vehicles with walkers and take the more tactically sound units without the need for all of the vehicles. So armed with my trusty Codex Orks, I began to plan the foundations for my new army. I started to write but began to notice that the niggling uneasy feeling that had originated in the pit of my stomach, was now climbing it's way up my spine and wrestling for my attention. It resolved itself as a mental picture of an Ork Warboss, faced with the challenge of a round peg and a square hole. Would an Ork Warboss look around for a more suitable peg? No, I didn't think so either. The Ork would make the peg fit, regardless of it's size or shape, and the only thing the Ork would look for is something big and heavy to whack it in with! So Speed Freeks it was. Though that did leave me with just one last little dilemma, as Speed Freeks can't take Kommandos, what was I going to use these fantastic new models as?

Now, if like me, you feel the need to drive your Ork army, full throttle, into an urban war zone, there are one or two pearls, (or at least, shiny trinkets) of wisdom I can pass on.

First: Deth Koptas

The compact terrain doesn't slow them down and when armed with a Burna, they make the perfect weapon for incinerating enemy sniper teams, melting through the rear armour of an unsuspecting tank or performing that last minute Turbo boost onto the mission objective. Next on my list of must-haves is the looted Demolisher. With its strength 10 Ordnance weapon, the tank was designed for this style of warfare and any general passing up the opportunity to field one needs his "'ead lookin' at". Other recent additions to my army include the Mega Armoured Nobz and a second unit of Skarboyz, for which I am using the new Kommando models.

Second: tank and trap

Just two, small, innocent looking words, harmless really. Do not be fooled! If your opponent is switched on enough to choose the Tank Traps Stratagem, (which of course, after reading this article, all of mine now will be!) you will come to hate them. But do not despair, you may not be able to get rid of the Tank Traps, but arm your Demolisher with the specialist Siege shells and you can just blast a path through the buildings instead! Use in conjunction with the Demolition Stratagem, both to minimise the effectiveness of the Tank Traps and make the biggest bang!

Booby trap stratagem markers

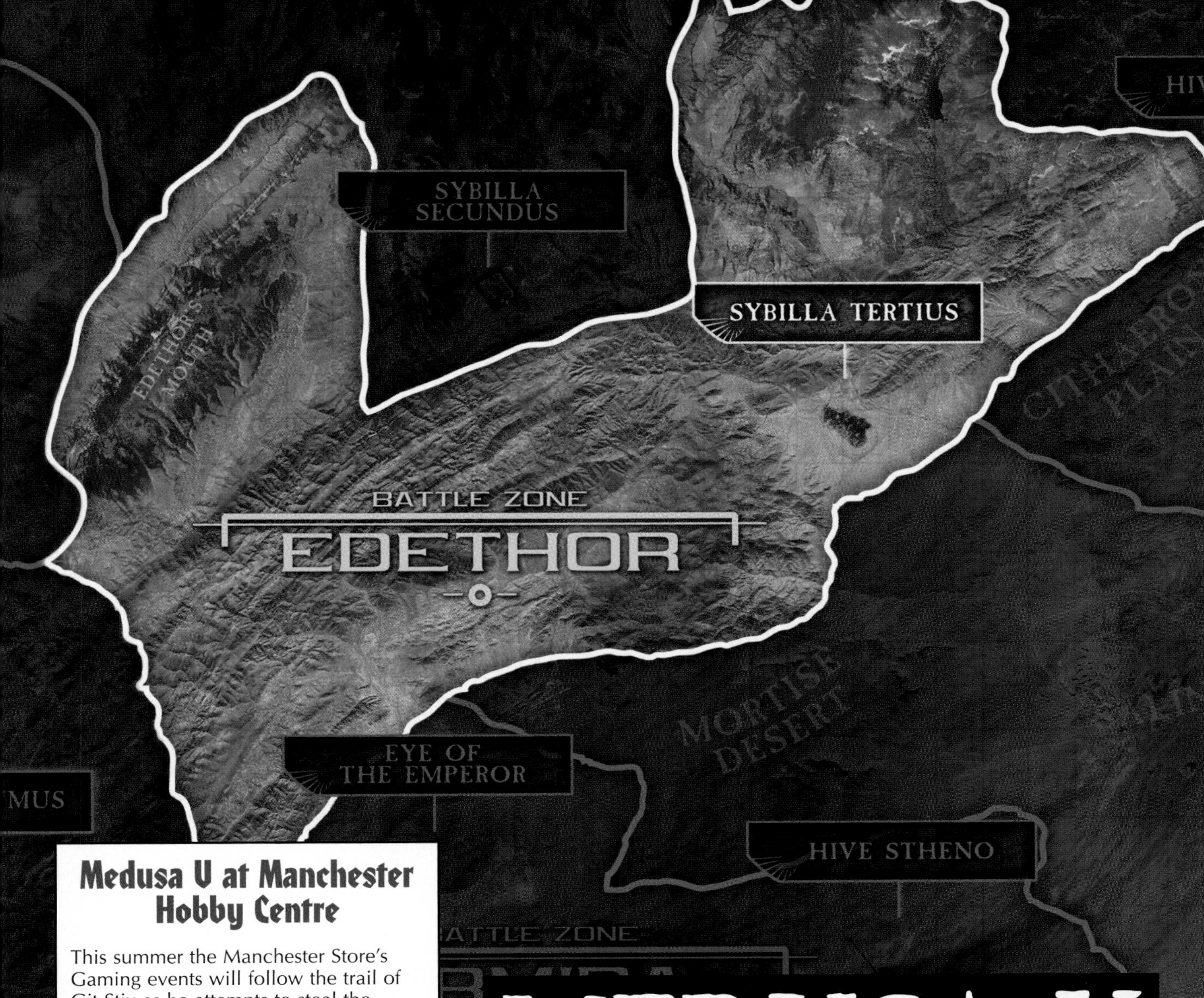

Medusa V at Manchester Hobby Centre

This summer the Manchester Store's Gaming events will follow the trail of Git Stix as he attempts to steal the fusion reactor that currently supplies power to the Sybilla Tertius Hive.

- **Saturday 5th August 10am start – "Da Big Dig."**
  The "Fighta-Tunullas" are deployed to place Tellyporta beacons onto the Hive's Reactor.
- **Saturday 12th August 8pm start – "The Battle for the Epsylion Gate"**
  Your chance to be a part of this 250,000 point Mega Battle!
- **Saturday 19th August 10am start – "Deuscide"**
  "Da Stelf-Bommas" spearhead an assault against the Warlord Titan.
- **Saturday 26th August 10am start – "The Battle for Norden's Bunker"**
  Will the Orks get their reactor? This is the one were we find out!

Call: *0161 834 6871* to get involved!

MEDUSA V

SYBILLA TERTIUS HIVE

THIS SUMMER YOU CAN HELP DECIDE HOW A WORLD WILL DIE.

Games Workshop Hobby Centres across the UK will be battling in the depths of the Sybilla Tertius hive, the primary hive of the region.

Each store will be running its own campaigns and activities, so don't miss out.

Sign up in-store now and be a part of history.

DEATH FROM ABOVE

Winner of Best Painted Army at Heat Three of the Warhammer 40,000 Grand Tournament, Nicola Taylor's Tyranid army, Hive Fleet *Apophis*, gets the White Dwarf treatment, for all those who didn't get to see it at the event.

This isn't the first time Nicola has collected Tyranids, in fact her first army was the gribblies from outer space, so she's no stranger to all those mandibles and scything talons.

"I'm a big fan of non-Human armies and these guys aren't even Humanoid," she says of her motivation for the creatures of the Great Devourer.

"The models are so interesting and there are so many ways that I could personalise them." With all the conversions and winged beasties in the army, Nicola has certainly achieved that. It's a good lesson for anyone who has aspirations to win a similar award – well-painted, strongly themed and distinctive armies tend to get the prizes.

1,500 Points

Buy this army from the Online Store:
www.games-workshop.co.uk/store/deathfromabove

WINGED WARRIORS

"I used the Morathi Dark Pegasus wings from the Warhammer Dark Elf range for the Winged Warriors. The ones in flight are mounted on lengths of brass rod to get them at different heights."

Fast and Deadly

Nicola's army is one meant for a tournament and as such it's an effective gaming force as well as an aesthetic treat.

"My force is very fast and heavily close combat based – once it hits the enemy front line it's very difficult to dislodge."

Her tactics revolve around the outnumbering potential inherent in the army, "The sheer weight of numbers means I can distract dangerous enemy units with the little guys, until the slightly slower big-hitters can get there." This is made possible by Nicola's stringent policy of 'no upgrades' for most of the army, "I use the points to get more bodies on the table, as I find that upgraded, expensive Gaunts die just as easily to a boltgun as cheaper ones!"

Another feature of the Hive Fleet *Apophis* is its disdain for armoured elites, "I have so much rending capability in my army that power armour isn't really a problem." And in summary, "My force is a hybrid of speed, close combat power and numbers – so it's flexible and adaptive."

Alien Markings

With this heftily sized army to paint, Nicola, like all good army painters, had a strategy to completing it. "I painted it in Brood blocks, seeing one through to completion and then starting over with the next one."

As for the scheme she used, it harked back to her original Tyranid army, "It's an evolution of the older force, which had red carapace and purple skin." Though for this incarnation, Nicola has gone for a slightly darker scheme to make it more 'sinister'. "I also added hive fleet markings. Yellow and black are nature's danger colours, so it seemed a fitting choice."

The Invasion deepens

Now she's played some games with the force, Nicola has plans to iron out the last few rough edges and make Hive Fleet *Apophis* even deadlier... "I'll drop the Lictor – he is rarely effective in this army – and add a couple of Raveners, instead," she says, "A Zoanthrope could provide some valuable anti-tank shooting power (Nicola struggles against armoured companies) but I've discovered these tend to catch the attention of too many heavy weapons and are rather slow. Most of my army can move over 6" a turn, and a floating brain just doesn't fit! That said, a Carnifex with the ability to actually shoot something, other than spinebanks, might be useful..."

The dreaded Carnifex, tooled up for maximum destruction!

Requirements

- 1,500 point Warhammer 40,000 force using the standard force organisation chart.
- There will be six games across the weekend.
- Qualifiers from the heats will receive free entry into the Grand Final in March 2007.
- Event includes two lunches, and evening meal on the Saturday.
- Tea & coffee available both mornings with doughnuts on Saturday morning.
- Ticket price £50.
- Ticket on sale for all heats, 8th July 2006, by calling *0115 91 40000.*

www.games-workshop.co.uk/tournaments

On display throughout August at:
The Citadel Miniatures Hall

GAMESDAY & GOLDEN DEMON 2006

September is around the corner and that means Games Day will once again take over the Birmingham NEC, so we decided to have a preview of all the day's action.

It was over six months ago that the first whisperings of Games Day 2006 started to filter around the office and slowly the ideas started coming together that will culminate in Games Day 2006 at the Birmingham NEC on September 24th. Most of you will have your tickets by now, and will be anticipating the activities, personalities and cool stuff you'll see within the three halls at the NEC this year.

THE FORUM

Pre-release Miniatures

The sales stands will be here for you to get your hands on a variety of pre-release miniatures from the new Orcs & Goblins (you can see the fantastic cover art for the new army book on the next page). There will also be miniatures from our current ranges for you to add to your armies.

Hobby Area

Want to win the coveted Scrap Demon in the conversion competition by trying your hand at making a plastic conversion? Want to see just how easy it is to make a piece of scatter scenery? Or maybe you just want to put together your new miniatures bought

10am to 4pm on Sunday 24th September 2006. Birmingham National Exhibition Centre (NEC). Ticket price £25.

Tickets on sale for White Dwarf subscribers from 22nd May 2006, and general release from 1st July 2006. Order yours by calling 0115 91 40000 (Golden Demon entry forms also available).

from the sales stands? All of this is possible in the Hobby Area at Games Day.

Art Competition
Also in the Forum will be the Artwork competition. Budding artists are challenged to bring along a piece of A4 drawn or painted art to put on display and be judged by one of our Studio artists. Entries will be sorted into two age categories with category winners receiving an award at the end of the day.

Bring & Battle
This area was introduced last year and became a resounding success. Not wanting to disappoint, it returns again this year providing the perfect opportunity to meet and play against other gamers from all over the UK. Bring dice and a tape measure, along with a small force of Border Patrol, Combat Patrol or War Party size, and you can get gaming. Once again, there will be tables for Warhammer, Warhammer 40,000 and The Lord of The Rings, so no matter what you play, you should get a game.

THE ARENA

Participation Games and Mega Battles
The whole Arena floor will be covered with participation games this year. Games Workshop Hobby Centres and Independent Clubs from across the UK have made some excellent themed tables and painted miniatures. You could join massed forces of Dwarfs to fight off an Orc & Goblin horde, or deal with the machine menace of the Necrons using the armies of the Imperium; all you need to do is turn up & play.

Stage & Screen
Once again the stage and screen will be in the Arena Hall giving us a grandstand finish to the event with the awards ceremony. Make sure you take your seats in plenty of time to see the big screen display images of the winning Golden Demon entries as the awards are declared.

THE PAVILION

Golden Demon
Golden Demon entrants can register here. The Pavilion is also where all the entries for the painting competition will be displayed. As well as viewing the miniatures 'in the flesh' you can admire some of the best entries close up with the help of the plasma screens at each end of the Golden Demon stand. Good luck to all the competitors vying for the coveted Golden Demon Slayer Sword!

The Gaming Club Network (GCN)
This network of independent gaming clubs grows from strength to strength with members all across the UK. They are supporting Games Day this year with a number of participation games in the Arena Hall. In addition they have an assembly area in the Pavilion where they are on hand to discuss the benefits of starting a club in your area and joining the GCN. They have also thrown down a challenge to anyone who wants to bring an army along for a game.

Design Studio
This year the Design Studio is pulling out all the stops to provide you with a snapshot of the design process. This will include the presence of around 40 members of the Design Studio as well as representatives from our Pre-production Studio and GW Tooling. If you ever wondered how we get from concept art sketches to 'Eavy Metal painted miniatures to boxed sets in our stores, now's your chance to find out. You'll also have the chance to meet artists, games

▲ The Scrap Demon, prize for the best conversion.

▼ The cover art from the Orcs & Goblins Army book, the unique prize for the art competition.

▲ *The Hobby Area is a flurry of conversions.*

developers, miniatures sculptors, 'Eavy Metal painters and scenery makers, so if there's any question about our games and miniatures that you want to ask, this is where to do it!

The Archive
Each year we like to remind you about some of the bygone products that Games Workshop has developed. Come and see how the Warhammer Fantasy Battle game has developed over the years.

White Dwarf
White Dwarf will be around again this year, taking pictures, conducting interviews and generally wandering about the event. In addition, we have given them their own area so you can approach them to ask questions about past articles, future issues or anything White Dwarf related. We're also hoping to persuade previous White Dwarf Editors to make an appearance to autograph your favourite issues.

NOT TO BE MISSED...
Games Day is the showcase event in our event calendar. It encompasses painting, gaming and modelling in a vast, one-day event. However, the day would be nothing without the participation of the thousands of hobbyists who come to share in the enjoyment of the hobby. So join us to make this year's Games Day special.

If you like the sound of all the activities going on at this year's Games Day, then get yourself a ticket. Most Games Workshop Hobby Centres will be providing a coach for the day, (make enquiries at your local Hobby Centre for details of this) but there is on-site parking and access from the station and airport as well.

Tickets are available right now. Make sure you don't miss out.

◀ *Only available at Games Day or through buying a ticket, the Troll Slayer on Golden Demon head is a truly unique and amazing model. The Troll Slayer is detachable so can be put on a 25mm base for use in your Warhammer armies.*

BL PUBLISHING www.blacklibrary.com

Black Library Merchandise
Earlier this year Warp Artefacts came to an end, but only to be replaced by Black Library Merchandise! Black Library Merchandise is the place you will now find all your iconic jewellery and clothing from the worlds of Warhammer and Warhammer 40K plus lots more!

Games Day 2006 for BL merchandise will be big! Exclusively this year you will find badges, t-shirts and posters complimenting the re-release of Warhammer! Remember you'll not find these particular items anywhere else!

Along with these exclusive items you'll find all the classic, high quality merchandise items ranging from Black Templars to High Elves!

Black Library
The return of Gotrek & Felix! The Old World's most notorious duo are back in the action-packed novel *Orcslayer*, and what's more, author Nathan Long will be there signing copies!

Galaxy in Flames is the third book in the Black Library's hot new Horus Heresy series. Ben Counter takes up the reigns and turns the action dial up to 100!

Dan Abnett will be on hand to sign copies of the latest Gaunt's Ghosts novel *The Armour of Contempt*. It's high-octane adventure all the way as Gaunt and his men attempt to liberate a Chaos held planet!

Warhammer Historical
Warhammer Historical will have participation games including Legends of the Old West and Warhammer Ancient Battles. There's sure to be some Warmaster Ancients gaming going on too, showcasing the forthcoming Warmaster Ancient Armies supplement release.

Make sure you head over to the Warhammer Historical retail stand and check out the full range of games and dioramas. You can pick up the latest releases including the new Warhammer Ancient Battles supplement *"The Art of War"* which lets you bring the mighty Terracotta army to the table top as you strive to match the feats of the First Emperor of China.

LAST YEAR'S GAMES DAY

Wondering what you missed out at last year's Games Day? WD asked Jonathan Carter to tell us all about it...

Jonathan: As another English summer approaches, strawberries and cream make their appearance once again, the playing fields of England echo to the sounds of leather on willow, and it once again falls to me to take a nostalgic look at last year's Games Day.

Anyone who has had the misfortune to read one of my previous reviews of Games Day (your mug shot alone is scary – Grombrindal) will know that I am on a 15 year quest to obtain a little statue, the Golden Demon. Last year's event wasn't the first time I had tried to get my hands on one of these (but I won't bore you with that again). However, it was the first time I had helped White Dwarf as a volunteer photographer and, more importantly, a first for Games Day itself. To everyone's delight, the event got a whole lot bigger and a whole lot easier to get to – just off the M42!

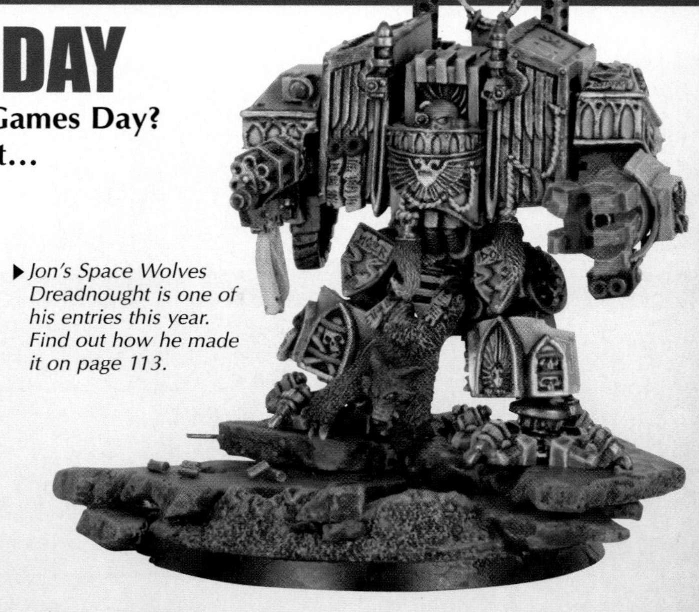

▶ *Jon's Space Wolves Dreadnought is one of his entries this year. Find out how he made it on page 113.*

The larger venue meant that the participation games could be expanded, with the different Hobby Centres from around the country and the Gaming Club Network producing some great tables to play on. Games Workshop also expanded the gaming element of the event by beginning the 'Bring and Battle' games (I feel a Blue Peter badge coming on). These were warmly welcomed as it allowed players to play against other hobbyists from around the country, which added to the spirit of the event. Inevitably though, just like there weren't enough hours in the day for Dan Abnett to sign all the books thrust in front of him, so there weren't enough tables to go round for all the eager players!

If you tired of all the gaming stuff, you could take a break and survey the latest in Games Workshop inspired games in the computer area. Although playing the newly revealed Dawn of War expansion, Winter Assault, is still 'gaming', it could be argued it's a totally different experience to the tabletop version. Alas, it's not how my wife views it!

The Golden Demons were easier to access owing to the fact that they were located in the centre of a large hall called the Pavilion. This allowed everyone a better view of the models and ended the long queues that were plagued previous years.

More space meant more room for new models to buy, which included loads of pre-release Wood Elves and Close Combat Terminators – seems like old news now, doesn't it! Forge World brought their designers and were showing off their massive Tau Manta which certainly turned a few heads! They also managed to bring along the Anphelion Base from the then-unreleased Imperial Armour 4, including a custom-built board which was later photographed for the book.

▲ *Jon will need his cat to stop drinking his paint water if he has any hope of completing his models for Golden Demon 2006.*

For the Black Library, all this extra space to spread out was quickly taken up with people trying to get their hands on the special pre-release books, such as *His Last Command*, and then to join the ever-growing line of people patiently waiting to get their new purchases signed by the author. This year these queues will be much greater, I am sure; with the release of the great new Horus Heresy series, Dan Abnett, Graham McNeill and Ben Counter's pens will definitely be smoking after signing all of the requested autographs!

One of the parts of the weekend which is of interest to all hobbyists is the chance to have a sneak-peak at the plans and proposed new release models. Last year it was Black Templars and Dwarfs, two and three months before release. It is always interesting to meet the designers and have a chat with them about their designs.

I'll leave you now, as I skulk off to my painting room and contemplate trying to produce a model to enter this year. I've already been busy and have managed to finish one entry, a Venerable Dreadnought. I do have lots of other ideas but I'm afraid they're not publishable at the moment. I can't have anyone pinching my ideas now can I? It is 16th time lucky after all! If I can stop the cat drinking my paint water I might actually have a chance; if not, perhaps it might be time for me to have a crack at winning one of the Scrap Demons in the Hobby Area – these are awarded to the best converted model produced at the competition on one of the special tables neatly (!) arranged with a plethora of parts, materials and tools for us all to play with. For anyone attending next year's event, I'll probably see you around and about – look for me under a pile of sprues in the construction area.

But, make sure you grab your tickets fast or you won't be seeing anything at Games Day 2006!

Want to know more?

You can read about Jon's Golden Demon experiences at Games Day 2005 online, at:

www.games-workshop.co.uk/gamesday

Store and Community news

FRONTLINE UK

NEW!

Independent Stockists

Wargames Workshop
7 Mill Road
Cranfield
Bedford
MK43 OJG
01234 757878

GAMES WORKSHOP Old Faithful Southhampton gets a Makeover

One of Games Workshop's oldest stores, Southampton, had the Techpriests down recently to give it a refit. The Hobby Centre will be ready for war this summer, as the forces of order and disorder battle it out in the Edethor region of Medusa V.

**23 East Street,
Southampton, Hampshire, SO14 1HG
Tel: 02380 331962**

NEW!

Five new clubs join the GCN

Royal Guild of Minted Boards (Cheshire)
Contact: Christopher Fry
Phone: *07976 878732*
E-mail:*Chris_Fry@Fryup Films.com*

York Garrison (York)
Contact: Robey Jenkins
Phone: *07967 277994*
E-mail:
garrison_wargaming@ yahoo.com

BRBBA (Bognor Regis)
Contact: Mr Frank Hill
Phone: *07896 319 683*
E-mail:
mrfrankhill@yahoo.com

Mitcham Marauders (Mitcham)
Contact: Jason Fowler
Phone: *07766 340 3472*
E-mail: *Mitcham-marauders@yahoo.co.uk*

Hammer N Ales (Southsea)
Contact: Daniel Few
Phone: *0781 688 9028*
E-mail:
sonofsmy@hotmail.com

GCN Gaming Club Network

COPENHAGEN BATTLE BUNKER

The clash of dice upon flocked gaming board is heard night after night, as armies battle for supremacy in the Battle Bunker located in Partnership store Faraos Cigarer in central Copenhagen. Play when it suits you, as the Battle Bunker gaming room is open Monday through Saturday, with Monday nights reserved especially for veterans. With 10 gaming tables, fantastic terrain, outstanding artwork on the walls it all adds to a fantastic atmosphere!

The Battle Bunker is having lots of exciting events, including campaigns, leagues and weekend tournaments. Logon to the Northern Europe website for more information on upcoming events!
http://ne.games-workshop.com/events/diary

Opening hours:
Mon – Tue: ....11.00 – 23.00
Wed – Thur:..........................11.00 – 17.30
Friday: ....11.00 – 18.00
Saturday: ....10.00 – 19:00

**COPENHAGEN BATTLE BUNKER
Faraos Cigarer
Skindergade 27
1159 Copenhagen
Telephone: 33 32 22 11**

**TICKETS AVAILABLE ONLINE NOW AT:
www.games-workshop.co.uk/goldendemon**

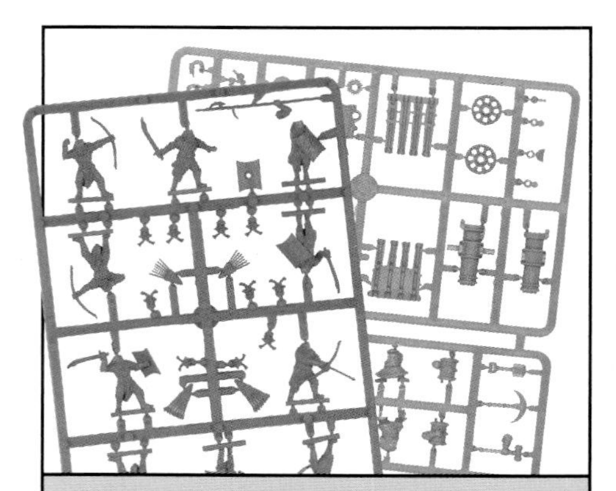

RECYCLE YOUR PLASTIC SPRUES

Wondering what to do with all those plastic sprues you have left over after assembling your latest game winning unit? Now's your chance to do your bit for the environment and recycle them! All events run at Warhammer World and also Games Day will have recycling points. Just pop all your unwanted plastic bits (no painted, metal or glued models please) in a carrier bag and bring them with you.

GOBSTYKS CORRECTION

Apologies to Gobstyks for a few incorrect details in WD317 on their club. Their Bloodbowl trophy is called the Gobstykup not the Gobstyka, gold membership is awarded after five years not three, and the Presidents are Mike Purvis and Tony Burgess not Will Platten. Summary execution of the reading Gnoblars has been performed.

WHITE DWARF ONLINE

The highlights this month...

RELATED ARTICLES
All the magazine-related articles...

Two Towers Masterclass
Find out expert ways to paint some of the key characters from the Two Towers journey who were at Helm's Deep, including the defenders of the fortress and the some of the key Uruk-hai characters attacking them.

Uruk-hai Army Building
With the new plastic Uruk-hai Scouts, Legion of the White Host battlehost, Feral Uruk-hai and Legions of the White Hand army list in the Legions of Middle-earth expansion, we thought it would be a great chance to look at collecting, modelling, painting and a splash of gaming with a force of Uruk-hai.

Space Wolves Venerable Dreadnought
In this month's Games Day article, volunteer reporter Jonathan Carter shows us his latest entry for Golden Demon – a Space Wolves Venerable Dreadnought. We show you how he painted and modelled his mighty miniature, from concept to varnish, online.
See the model on page 111.

HOBBY ARTICLES
...and everything else to fuel your hobby.

Eastern Empire
The Eastern Fringe is home to the emerging Tau Empire. Australian hobbyist Sebastian Stuart has collected a unique Tau army over the last few years. Here we ask Sebastian to take us on a tour of his Tau Cadre and give us a few pointers on how he painted them.

Ollie Gray's Dark Elves
You'd think Ollie Gray was preparing an invasion of Ulthuan, such is the size of his Dark Elf army. He regularly takes to the field with it at Games Workshop Lincoln, where he is the manager, although in smaller, more game-sized, chunks. He also has many interesting conversions which this article takes a look at.

Pursued By Wolves
Based upon the scenario of Arwen's perilous flight to the Bruinen Ford, this scenario by Adam Troke features Sam Gamgee's beloved pack-animal. Can Bill escape the ravening pack of Wargs, or will he find himself a feast for the hounds of Sauron?

What is WD Online?
White Dwarf Online is our free weekly online newsletter by the UK White Dwarf team. Every issue is packed with exciting articles and features that keep you up-to-date with what's going on in the hobby.

Why subscribe?

- **Read forthcoming hobby articles first!**
- **See the latest new releases and advanced orders!**
- **Sneak peeks delivered direct early, to your inbox!**
- **Exclusive editorial content and articles!**
- **Absolutely free!**

Subscribe now, IT'S FREE!

www.games-workshop.co.uk/wdonline

Check out this month's Store & Club finder as well as the Events Diary

THE EVENTS DIARY

All the latest from the UK and Northern Europe events scene.

Upcoming Events

Are you a Hobby Centre, Independent Stockist, GCN or WPS club that's running an event? If you want to advertise it for free in this fine publication simply drop us an e-mail at:

whitedwarf@games-workshop.co.uk

The closing dates for receiving details for publication in the following issues are:

- 1st August ....WD323 (Nov)
- 1st September....WD324 (Dec)
- 1st October ....WD325 (Jan)

Please note all dates and details are correct at the time of going to print but are subject to change.

Events diary abbreviation guide

WH ....Warhammer
40K ....Warhammer 40,000
BB ....Blood Bowl
WAB....Warhammer Ancient Battles
WPS....Warhammer Players' Society
WECW Warhammer English Civil War
Epic................Epic Armageddon
LOTR ......The Lord of The Rings
GW................Games Workshop
GT................Grand Tournament

AUGUST

Games Workshop presents:

DA BIG DIG

Date: Saturday 5th August, 2006
Venue: Manchester Hobby Centre
Details: The "Fighta-Tunullas" are deployed to place Tellyporta beacons onto the Hive's Reactor. This summer the Manchester Store's Gaming events will follow the trail of Git Stix as he attempts to steal the fusion reactor that currently supplies power to the Sybilla Tertius Hive. 10am start.
Contact: 0161 834 6871
Website: www.games-workshop.co.uk/events

Games Workshop presents:

WARHAMMER CAMPAIGN

Date: Sunday 6th August, 2006
Venue: Gaming Workshop Wakefield
Details: The thawing snows in the Black Mountains have opened the passes and the trade routes to the East. Can you protect the passes from the hordes of Orcs, Skaven and Ogres that live high in the mountains? You will need a 2,000 points army and a 500 points Combat Patrol force to take part. Tickets cost £15 including lunch on the day.
Contact: 0114 243 4633
Website: www.games-workshop.co.uk/events

Games Workshop presents:

The Battle for Epsylion Gate

Date: Saturday 12th August, 2006
Venue: Manchester Hobby Centre
Details: Your chance to be a part of this 250,000 point Mega Battle! This summer the Manchester Store's Gaming events will follow the trail of Git Stix as he attempts to steal the fusion reactor that currently supplies power to the Sybilla Tertius Hive. Starts 8pm.
Contact: 0161 834 6871
Website: www.games-workshop.co.uk/events

Games Workshop presents:

DEUSCIDE

Date: Saturday 19th August, 2006
Venue: Manchester Hobby Centre
Details: Da Stelf-Bommas" spearhead an assault against the Warlord Titan. This summer the Manchester Store's Gaming events will follow the trail of Git Stix as he attempts to steal the fusion reactor that currently supplies power to the Sybilla Tertius Hive. 10am start.
Contact: 0161 834 6871
Website: www.games-workshop.co.uk/events

Games Workshop presents:

THE BATTLE FOR NORDEN'S BUNKER

Date: Saturday 26th August, 2006
Venue: Manchester Hobby Centre
Details: Will the Orks get their reactor? This is the one were we find out!This summer the Manchester Store's Gaming events will follow the trail of Git Stix as he attempts to steal the fusion reactor that currently supplies power to the Sybilla Tertius Hive. Starts 10am.
Contact: 0161 834 6871
Website:
www.games-workshop.co.uk/events

Games Workshop presents:

FALL OF THE NECROMANCER

Date: Sunday 20th August, 2006
Venue: Gaming Workshop Wakefield
Details: Deep in Mirkwood lies the stronghold of the Necromancer. His shadow is growing over the Elven realm. Can the forces of Good rid the woods of this evil menace or will the Necromancer's power continue to expand? To take part in this The Lord of The Rings campaign you will need a 500 point force.
Tickets cost £15 including lunch on the day.
Contact: 0114 243 4633
Website:
www.games-workshop.co.uk/events

GCN presents:

MEDUSA V: END GAME
GCN Campaign Weekend

Date: 19th - 20th August 2006
Venue: Warhammer World, Nottingham
Ticket Price: £45. This covers seven games across two days, lunch on both days, and an evening meal on Saturday. There will only be 14 tickets available for each race (Chaos, Orks, Necrons, Tyranids, Tau, Eldar or Dark Eldar) and 28 Imperial tickets, so book early to avoid disappointment!
Details: see attached advert
Contact: Steve Nolan on 07793 198516
Website: events@gcnm.org.uk

SEPTEMBER

Games Workshop presents:

The Lord of The Rings DOUBLES TOURNAMENT

Date: Sunday 17th September, 2006
Venue: Gaming Workshop Wakefield
Details: Pair up with a friend to battle against others in this competition of deadly duos. To play you will need two warbands of 300 points and a friend to play with. Full details sent with the event pack. Tickets cost £20, including lunch.
Contact: 0114 243 4633
Website: www.games-workshop.co.uk/events

Games Workshop presents:

Date: Sunday 24th September 2006
Venue: Birmingham NEC
Details: Tickets cost £25.
Website: www.games-workshop.co.uk /gamesday

OCTOBER

SLAYER DAY: From the Ashes

Date: Sunday 1st October, 2006
Venue: The Pemberton Centre, H.E Bates Way, Rushden, Northamptonshire.
Details: 4-a-side team tournament; 2 x 1,500 points Warhammer singles and 2 x 1,500 points 40K singles. Prizes for the winners. Trade stands, participation and open play tables, plus the 'Slayer Day Axe' painting competition. Tickets cost £40.00 per team.
Contact: Carl King on 07979 281 350 or Darrell Lee on 01933 411559

Games Workshop presents:

Heat One: GRAND TOURNAMENT WARHAMMER

Date: 7th – 8th October, 2006
Venue: Warhammer World
Details: This is the first heat in the new Warhammer Grand Tournament season. You will require a 2,000 point force designed around the restrictions listed in the tournament pack. Tickets cost £50 and include lunches on both days and an evening meal on Saturday. Qualifiers from this heat will receive free entry into the Grand Final in February 2007.
Website: www.games-workshop.co.uk/events

Games Workshop presents:

Dutch Grand Tournament: WARHAMMER 40,000

Date: 14th - 15th October 2006
Venue: Sporthal UvT, Tilburg
Age: 16+
Details: The annual Dutch Warhammer 40,000 Grand Tournament returns for the sixth year. Tickets go on sale through Northern Europe Mail Order about two months before the event.
Contact: NEGT@games-workshop.co.uk
Website: http://ne.games-workshop.com

Games Workshop presents:

Heat One: GRAND TOURNAMENT WARHAMMER 40,000

Date: 14th – 15th October, 2006
Venue: Warhammer World
Details: First heat in the new Warhammer 40,000 Grand Tournament season. You will require a 1,500 point force designed around the restrictions listed in the tournament pack. Tickets cost £50 and includes lunch on both days and an evening meal on Saturday. Qualifiers from this heat will receive free entry into the Grand Final in March 2007.
Website: www.games-workshop.co.uk/events

Games Workshop presents:

WARHAMMER Doubles Tournament

Date: Sunday 15th October, 2006
Venue: Gaming Workshop Wakefield
Details: Pair up with a friend to battle others in this competition of deadly duos. To play you will need two Border Patrol forces of 500 points and a friend to play with. Full details sent with the event pack.
Tickets cost £20 including lunch on the day.
Contact: 0114 243 4633
Website: www.games-workshop.co.uk/events

Games Workshop presents:

WARHAMMER 40,000 Doubles Tournament

Date: Sunday 22nd October, 2006
Venue: Gaming Workshop Wakefield
Details: To play you will need two Combat Patrol forces of 500 points and a friend to play with. Full details of the rules will be sent with the event pack.
Tickets cost £20 including lunch on the day.
Contact: 0114 243 4633
Website: www.games-workshop.co.uk/events

WPS Grand Tournament WARHAMMER 40,000

Date: 21st – 22nd October, 2006
Venue: Warhammer World
Details: The WPS Warhammer 40,000 Grand Tournament. Tickets cost £35 including lunch on both days.
Website: conrad.gonsalves@players-society.com

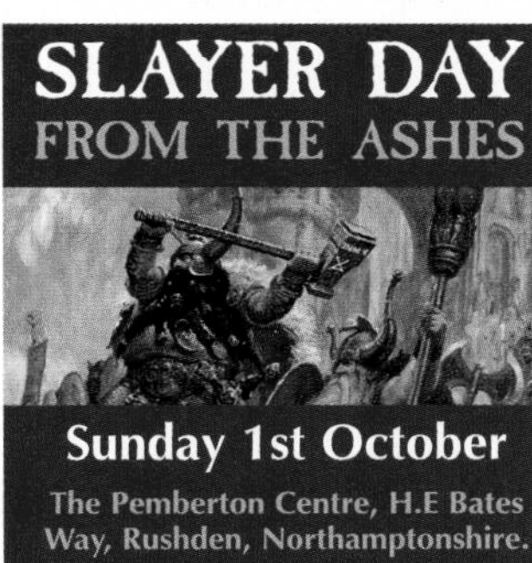

MEDUSA V
END GAME
GCN CAMPAIGN WEEKEND
19th & 20th August 2006,
Warhammer World

The end is nigh...the Tau must extract their forces from the planet, having gathered valuable intelligence. Imperial, Ork and heretic forces seek to prevent them from escaping. Meanwhile, in the Sybilla Quarantine Zone, all hell has broken loose! Eldar forces must keep the Imperials, Tyranids and Necrons at bay long enough to complete their mission on Medusa V.

events@gcnm.org.uk

STORE & CLUB FINDER

All the Games Workshop stores, independent stockists and GCN clubs, at your fingertips

Our Gaming Club allows you to find independent clubs that are a part of the Gaming Club Network. The clubs listed on page 121 all have:

- A committee of at least three members to run their affairs openly.
- Public liability insurance to protect the members against accident.
- A good standard of club rules and a club constitution.
- A child protection policy.
- A policy of submitting the committee for CRB Disclosure.

As part of our commitment to customer service and safety we do not promote any club outside of the Gaming Club Network.

look it up online at:
www.gcnm.org.uk

GAMES WORKSHOP Hobby Centres

OPENING TIMES

Monday - Friday:	**12pm – 6pm**
Saturday:	**10am – 6pm**
Sunday:	**11am – 5pm**

Except for:

- **Stores in shopping centres still open and close according to shopping centre times.**
- **Some stores are not open every day. Please ring the relevant store for details.**

- **FULL RANGE OF PRODUCTS**
  All our centres stock a full range of Warhammer 40,000, Warhammer and The Lord of The Rings games and models as well as all the hobby materials you need to collect, build and paint your armies.

- **IN-STORE ORDER POINT**
  All of our stores have a Direct in-store order point which you can use to get your hands on all of our Specialist Games products, plus many exclusive miniatures, components and classic models with which to customise your Warhammer, Warhammer 40,000 and The Lord of The Rings forces.

- **FREE PAINTING & MODELLING ADVICE**
  No matter what your level of painting or modelling skill, if you spend 30 minutes with one of our members of staff you will see those skills improved and might find out something you never knew!

- **FREE GAMING & TACTICS ADVICE**
  All our staff are experienced gamers (after all it's what they do for a living!). They can give you sound tactical advice, help you build battle-winning armies and clear up most of your rules queries.

- **FREE BEGINNERS PROGRAMME**
  Our special Beginners' programme teaches you how to play and helps you take your first steps into the Games Workshop hobby. The programme runs on Sundays, but there is also one night during the week when you can indulge in more gaming too. All you need to do is come along!

- **GAMING ROOMS**
  Like regular Hobby Centres, all Gaming Rooms provide the full range of Games Workshop services. However they are larger than a normal Hobby Centre and have many tables, which makes them perfect for meeting fellow hobbyists.

Locating stores & independent stockists ▸▸

Games Workshop products are sold by a large number of shops in 16 different countries across the world. What follows is a listing of all the stores that sell Games Workshop products across the UK, parts of Europe, South Africa and the Middle East. Games Workshops are open seven days a week, with gaming into the evening on certain nights. Call your local Hobby Centre for more details.

You can find a full list of our UK retail outlets on our website:
www.games-workshop.co.uk/storefinder.

If you're unsure where your nearest stockist is located, then call GW Direct on:
0115 91 40000

STOREFINDER KEY

GW Store	*(•) Indicates Gaming Room facilities.*
UK Elite Store	*Stocks an extensive range products.*
NE Elite Store	*Stocks the complete Games Workshop range.*
NE Partner Store	*Stocks most of the Games Workshop range.**
ALTRINCHAM, The Gaming Crypt: 44 Greenwood Street, WA14 1RZ Tel: 0161 929 9919	*New Store opening.*

**To be exactly sure they have what you want in stock, we recommend calling the store first.*

Store directory

AVON
GW BRISTOL (CENTRAL):
13 Broadweir. Tel: 0117 925 1533
GW BRISTOL (CRIBBS CAUSEWAY):
Unit 129, The Mall. Tel: 0117 959 2528
BRISTOL, Area 51:
Tel: 0117 9244655
PORTISHEAD, Makit:
Tel: 01275 844751

BEDFORDSHIRE
GW BEDFORD:
10 Greyfriars. Tel: 0123 427 3663
LUTON, Final Fantasy
45 New Bedford Road, Tel: 01582 729001
LUTON, Ottakers:
Tel: 01582 486999
CRANFIELD, Wargames Workshop:
Tel: 01234 757878

BERKSHIRE
• GW MAIDENHEAD:
Unit 2, 17 Market Street. Tel: 0162 863 1747
GW READING:
29 Oxford Road, Tel: 0118 959 8693
NEWBURY, Miniature Merchants:
3 Weavers Walk, Tel: 01635 528176
BRACKNELL, Ottakers:
Tel: 01344 488124
BRACKNELL, Toy Planet:
Tel: 01344 426262
SANDHURST, Toyworld:
Tel: 01252 873350
WINDSOR, Ottaker's Bookshops Windsor:
Tel: 01753 856456
WINDSOR, WJ Daniels:
Tel: 01753 862106

BIRMINGHAM AREA
GW BIRMINGHAM:
Unit L16, Bullring Link. Tel: 0121 633 7193
GW DUDLEY:
Unit 36, Merry Hill Centre. Tel: 0138 448 1818
GW SOLIHULL:
690 Warwick Road. Tel: 0121 705 7997
• GW SUTTON COLDFIELD:
45-47 Birmingham Road. Tel: 0121 354 3174
GW WOLVERHAMPTON:
9 King Street. Tel: 0190 231 0466
GW WALSALL:
Unit 27, Old Square Shopping Centre.
Tel: 0192 272 5207
BIRMINGHAM, Console Games:
1159 Bristol Road South, Northfield, B31 2SL
Tel: 0121 477 0022
GREAT BARR, Gaming Crypt:
Tel: 0121 360 5080
RUBERY, Roy's Hobbies & Toys:
Tel: 0121 453 3280
SUTTON COLDFIELD, Digital Dragons:
Tel: 07941 637793

BUCKINGHAMSHIRE
GW HIGH WYCOMBE:
Unit 29, The Octagon Centre. Tel: 0149 453 1494
GW MILTON KEYNES:
Unit 2,West End Extension, 502 Silbury Boulevard, Shopping Centre. Tel: 0190 869 0477
AYLESBURY, Bear Necessities:
8 The Cloisters, Great Western Street, HP20 2PU
Tel: 01296 421098
BUCKINGHAM, Abacus Toys:
Tel: 01280 821815
GERARDS CROSS, Howard Marshall:
Tel: 01753 882952
PRINCES RISBOROUGH, Treats:
Tel: 01844 344354

CAMBRIDGESHIRE
• GW CAMBRIDGE:
54 Regent Street. Tel: 0122 331 3350
GW PETERBOROUGH:
3 Wentworth Street. Tel: 01733 890 052
ELY, City Cycle Centre:
Tel: 01353 663131
HUNTINGDON, Sports & Fashions:
Tel: 01480 454541
PETERBOROUGH, Westgate Department Store:
Tel: 01733 563151
ST NEOTS, First Computer Games:
Tel: 01480 386638
ST NEOTS, Westgate Department Store:
Tel: 01480 473242
WISBECH, Westgate Department Store:
Tel: 01536 203525

CHANNEL ISLANDS
JERSEY, ST. HELIER, The Little Shop:
Tel: 01534 732187
GUERNSEY, ST. PETERS PORT, Carousel:
Tel: 01481 721721
ST. HELIER, Bambola Ltd:
Tel: 0604 29828

CHESHIRE
GW ALTRINCHAM:
Unit 1, 19 Grafton Street. Tel: 0161 929 9896
• GW CHESTER:
112 Foregate Street. Tel: 0124 431 1967
• GW MACCLESFIELD:
Unit 38, Chestergate Mall, Grosvenor Centre.
Tel: 0162 561 9020
GW STOCKPORT:
32 Mersey Square. Tel: 0161 474 1427
GW WARRINGTON:
Unit 20, Time Square. Tel: 0192 565 1984
ALTRINCHAM, The Gaming Crypt:
44 Greenwood Street, WA14 1RZ
Tel: 0161 929 9919
ALTRINCHAM, Altrincham Gaming Ltd:
Tel: 0161 9294708
CHEADLE, Fantasia:
Tel: 0161 491 1130
CONGLETON, Deans Toys & Cycles:
Tel: 0126 0273277
CREWE, ABC Model Sport:
Tel: 01270 505 048
CREWE, Potters Model World:
Tel: 01270 250 038
MACCLESFIELD, Jac in a Box:
Tel: 01625 502 221
NANTWICH, Funfayre:
Tel: 01270 626 346
NESTON, Carousel:
Tel: 0151 336 621
NORTHWICH, Level 1:
Tel: 01606 45053
NORTHWICH, The Model Shop:
Tel: 01606 826 346
STALYBRIDGE, Hardcastles:
Tel: 0161 3038528
STALYBRIDGE, KMV Models:
Tel: 0161 304 8700
STOCKPORT, Goslings Toymaster:
Tel: 0161 427 2099
WARRINGTON, Steve Webb Models & Hobbies:
Tel: 01928 735 225
WIDNES, The Hobby Shop:
Tel: 01514 241 947

CLEVELAND
• GW MIDDLESBROUGH:
Unit 33, 39 Dundas Street. Tel: 0164 225 4091
HARTLEPOOL, Illusions:
Tel: 01429 233 199
HARTLEPOOL, Westgate Department Store:
Tel: 01429 244 337

CORNWALL
GW TRURO:
Unit 1, Bridge House, New Bridge Street.
Tel: 0187 232 0047
BODMIN, Bricknells:
Tel: 01208 77088
BUDE, Nitro RC:
Tel: 01288 353 388
BUDE, More Value:
Tel: 01288 352 362
FALMOUTH, Wonderland Falmouth:
Tel:01326 312 571
HAYLE, Blewetts of Hayle:
Tel: 01736 753 012
HELSTON, Eddy & Son:
Tel: 01326 572 787
NEWQUAY, Planet Hobbywood:
Tel: 01637 859 941
ST AUSTELL, Adeba Toys:
Tel: 01726 73125
ST AUSTELL, Mad for Miniatures:
Tel: 01726 72259
ST IVES, Dragon's Hoard:
Tel: 01736 79848
TRURO, Toymaster:
Tel: 01872 272 452

COUNTY DURHAM
• GW DURHAM:
64 North Road. Tel: 0191 374 1062
GW DARLINGTON:
78 Skinnergate. Tel: 0132 538 2463
BISHOP AUCKLAND, Windsock Models:
Tel: 01388 609 766
CONSETT, Kwikpart:
Consett, Tel: 01207 581 024
DARLINGTON, Lamb's:
Tel: 01325 466 042
SEAHAM, Games of War:
Tel: 01915 817 118
TEESDALE, Toy Shop:
Tel: 01833 637 396

CUMBRIA
• GW CARLISLE:
Unit 2, Earls Lane. Tel: 0122 859 8216
KENDAL, North West Warriors:
10 Kent Street, Tel: 01539 731666
BARROW-IN-FURNESS, Heaths:
Tel: 01229 820 435
BOWNESS-ON-WINDERMERE, Ernest Atkinson & Sons:
Tel: 01539 443 047
COCKERMOUTH, Playtimes:
Tel: 01900 829 299
COCKERMOUTH, The Toy Shop:
Tel: 01900 825 855
KENDAL, O'loughlins':
Tel: 01539 723 264
KESWICK, J B Dixon Ltd:
Tel: 01768 772 381
KESWICK, Lakeland Toys and Hobbies:
Tel: 01768 775 275
PENRITH, Harpers Cycles:
Tel: 01768 864 475
ULVERSTON, Sawdust 'n Stitches:
Tel: 01229 582 284
WIGTON, Jacksons Diecast Models:
Tel: 01697 342 557
WORKINGTON, KSA Models and Hobbies:
Tel: 01900 873 338

DERBYSHIRE
GW DERBY:
42 Sadler Gate. Tel: 0133 237 1657
BELPER, Frearsons:
Tel: 01773 823 244
BUXTON, D&E Knowles & Sons:
Tel: 0129 824 203
CHESTERFIELD, Chesterfield Department Store:
Tel: 01246 220 200
CHESTERFIELD, Model Trader:
Tel: 07951 947736
CHESTERFIELD, Peak Bookstore:
Tel: 01246 224 666
GLOSSOP, Glossop Craft and Model Centre:
Tel: 01457 863 559
GLOSSOP, Wain Services:
Tel: 01457 853 548
ILKESTON, Ilkeston Co-op:
Tel: 01159 327 777
MATLOCK, Shawes:
Tel: 01629 582 482

DEVON
• GW EXETER:
31a Sidwell Street. Tel: 0139 249 0305
GW PLYMOUTH:
84 Cornwall Street. Tel: 0175 225 4121
GW TORQUAY:
12 Market Street. Tel: 0180 320 1036
BARNSTAPLE, The Battlezone:
Tel: 01271 321 344
DARTMOUTH, WG Pillar & Co:
Tel: 01803 832 139
EXMOUTH, Gamezone Models:
Tel: 01395 267 733
HOLSWORTHY, Bazaar:
Tel: 01409 243892
HONITON, Honiton Toy Shop:
Tel: 01404 43741
KINGSBRIDGE, The Trading Post:
Tel: 01548 852 923
NEWTON ABBOT, Austins:
Tel: 01626 333 444
PLYMOUTH, Model Shop:
Tel: 01752 221 851
TAVISTOCK, Kaleidoscope:
Tel: 01822 615 236
TEIGNMOUTH, Jackmans Toybox T/A:
Tel: 01626 778 260
TIVERTON, Wings 'N' Wheels:
Tel: 01884 242 819
TORRINGTON, Angling Pastimes:
Tel: 01805 625 888

DORSET
GW BOURNEMOUTH:
24 Post Office Road. Tel: 0120 231 9292
• GW POOLE:
Unit 12 Towngate Centre. Tel: 0120 268 5634
BOURNEMOUTH, Battle-Scar:
Tel: 01202 258 194
BOURNEMOUTH, Roberts Toys & Games:
Tel: 01202 482 031
BRIDPORT, Frosts Toymaster:
Tel: 01308 422 296
DORCHESTER, Dorchester Toys:
Tel: 01305 261 152
EASTBOURNE, Phantasia:
Tel: 01323 723 388
SHAFTESBURY, Hardings:
Tel: 01747 852 156
SHERBOURNE, The Corner House:
Tel: 01935 815 615
SWANAGE, Leonards:
Tel: 01929 426 096
WEYMOUTH, Razzamataz:
Tel: 01305 780 601

ESSEX
GW CHELMSFORD:
Unit 4C, The Meadows Centre.
Tel: 0124 549 0048
GW COLCHESTER:
2 Short Wyre Street. Tel: 0120 676 7279
GW SOUTHEND:
12 Southchurch Road. Tel: 0170 246 1251
GW THURROCK:
Unit 415B, Level 3, Lakeside Shopping Centre.
Tel: 0170 886 7133
SAFFRON WALDEN, Game On:
30 High Street, Tel: 01799 506 070
BRENTWOOD, B&M Cycles:
Tel: 01277 214 342
CHADWELL HEATH, Atomic Comics:
Tel: 0208 597 547
CHELMSFORD - The Meadows Shopping Centre, Toymaster Kingdom:
Tel: 01245 493 355
CLACTON ON SEA, Clacton Art & Craft Centre:
Tel: 01255 436 346
HARLOW, Marquee Models:
Tel: 01279 423 334
HOCKLEY, Hobbiton:
Tel: 01702 200 180
LEIGH-ON-SEA, Caliver Books:
Tel: 01702 473 986
MALDON, Colin Bliss Models:
Tel: 01621 851 327
RAYLEIGH, Toys N Tuck:
Tel: 01268 775 501

GLOUCESTERSHIRE
GW CHELTENHAM:
16 Pittville Street. Tel: 0124 222 8419
GW GLOUCESTER:
35 Clarence Street. Tel: 0145 250 5033
CHELTENNAM, Toywizz:
Unit 1a Regent's Arcade, Tel: 01242 222 325
BOURTON ON THE WATER, Bourton Model Railway:
Tel: 01451 820 686
STROUD, Antics:
Tel: 01453 764 487
STROUD, Psisoft Games:
Tel: 0870 242 7428
TEWKESBURY, Toy Zone:
Tel: 01684 295 776

HAMPSHIRE
GW BASINGSTOKE:
3 Potters Walk. Tel: 0125 646 6050
GW PORTSMOUTH:
34 Arundel Street. Tel: 0239 287 6266
GW SOUTHAMPTON:
23 East Street. Tel: 0238 033 1962
GW WINCHESTER:
6 St Georges Street. Tel: 0196 286 0199
ALDERSHOT, The Game Shop:
Tel: 01252 311 443
ALTON, Alton Model Centre:
Tel: 01420 542 244
ANDOVER, Hoggosaurus Toymaster:
Tel: 01264 352 263
FAREHAM, Fareham Toys and Hobbies:
Tel: 01329 282 183
FLEET, Fleet Toys:
Tel: 0125 261 3949
GOSPORT, JC Books:
Tel: 02392 580 931
MILFORD ON SEA, Milford Models and Hobbies:
Tel: 01590 642 112
NEW MILTON, Toys of New Milton:
Tel: 01425 617 805
PETERSFIELD, Folly Models:
Tel: 01730 267 932
PETERSFIELD, Fun for All:
Tel: 01730 267 271
PORTCHESTER, Wicor Models:
Tel: 02392 351 160
RINGWOOD, Toys of Ringwood:
Tel: 01425 479 444
ROMSEY, Roundabout:
Tel: 01794 512 145
SOUTHHAMPTON, Hidden Fortress Ltd:
Tel: 02380 710 550
SOUTHSEA, Southsea Models:
Tel: 02392 733 208
WATERLOOVILLE, Forever Toys Ltd:
Tel: 02392 266 253
WATERLOOVILLE, Paul's Hobby Shop:
Tel: 01705 259 186

HEREFORDSHIRE
HEREFORD, Hereford Model Shop:
Tel: 01432 352 809
LEOMINSTER, Martin's Models & Crafts:
Tel: 01568 613 782
ROSS ON WYE, Revolutions:
Tel: 01989 562 639

HERTFORDSHIRE
GW HEMEL HEMPSTEAD:
16 Bridge Street. Tel: 0144 224 9752
GW ST ALBANS:
18 Heritage Close, off High Street.
Tel: 0172 786 1193
HERTFORD, Game On:
29 Maidenhead Street SG13 1DW.
Tel: 01992 537 774
BERKHAMSTED, Hamlins:
Tel: 01442 864 642
BISHOP'S STORTFORD, Boardmans:
Tel: 01279 654 033
BISHOP'S STORTFORD, Play Mode:
Tel: 01279 755 988
COCKFOSTERS, Murray & Brand:
Tel: 02084 490 827
HARPENDEN, Felicitations:
Tel: 01582 767 811
HERTFORD, Marquee Models:
Tel: 01992 504718
HITCHIN, Mainly Models:
Tel: 01462 422 204
LETCHWORTH, Model Images:
Tel: 01462 684 859
ROYSTON, Toyshop:
Tel: 01763 243 270
ST ALBANS, E Rider and Son:
Tel: 01727 854 638
STEVENAGE, KS Models:
Tel: 01438 746 616
WELWYN GARDEN CITY, Toys Toys Toys:
Tel: 01707 391 319

ISLE OF MAN
DOUGLAS, Toymaster:
Tel: 01624 622 154

ISLE OF WIGHT
COWES, Chivertons Newsagents:
Tel: 01983 292 013
NEWPORT, Battalion:
Tel: 01983 533 222
NEWPORT, Toy & Models:
Tel: 01983 528 258
RYDE, The Sports & Model Shop:
Tel: 01983 862 454
RYDE, Fun, Fact and Fantasy:
Tel: 01983 617 323

KENT
GW BLUEWATER:
Unit 052B, Upper Thames Walk, Bluewater, Greenhithe, Kent. Tel: 0132 242 7880
GW CANTERBURY:
Unit 5, Iron Bar Lane. Tel: 0122 745 2880
GW MAIDSTONE:
7a Pudding Lane. Tel: 0162 267 7435
GW TUNBRIDGE WELLS:
4A Camden Street. Tel: 0189 252 5783
ASHFORD, GZ Computers Ltd:
28 Country Square, Tel: 0123 366 3996
ASHFORD, Wide Eyes:
44 Osbourne Road, Willesborough, TN24 0EF
Tel: 01233 636600
BEXLEY HEATH, Kit Krazy:
Tel: 0208 298 7177
BROADSTAIRS, Time & Space:
Tel: 01843 866 006
CHATHAM, Maynes:
Tel: 01634 400 031
DOVER, Turners Models:
Tel: 01304 203 711
FAVERSHAM, Abacus Toys:
Tel: 01795 591 203
GRAVESEND, Steve's Collectables and Models:
Tel: 01474 564 465
GRAVESEND, The Stamp Centre:
Tel: 01474 534 166
HERNE BAY, Spearings:
Tel: 01227 374 049
MARGATE, Toymaster Kingdom:
Tel: 01843 225 400
RAMSGATE, The Giggling Goblin, Games Emporium:
Tel: 01843 594 884
SEVENOAKS, JH Lorimer:
Tel: 01732 452 840
SEVENOAKS, Manklows:
Tel: 01732 454 952
SITTINGBOURNE, AJ Blundell & Son:
Tel: 01795 424 371
TONBRIDGE, Kids Stuff:
Tel: 01732 353 186
WOODCHURCH, The Model Shop:
Tel: 01233 860 008

LANCASHIRE

GW BLACKPOOL:
8 Birley Street. Tel: 0125 375 2056
GW BOLTON:
Unit 27, 36 Acresfield Mall. Tel: 0120 436 2131
GW PRESTON:
15 Miller Arcade. Tel: 0177 282 1855
ASHTON UNDER LYNE, Roundabout Toys:
Tel: 01613 432 344
BLACKBURN, Batcave:
Tel: 01254 667 488
BLACKBURN, Mercer & Sons:
Tel: 0125 458 700
BURNLEY, Arthur Benn:
Tel: 01282 422 546
BURY, Conways Toymaster:
Tel: 01617 616 209
CHORLEY, A & B Games:
Tel: 01257 261 833
CHORLEY, Hampsons Toys & Nursery World:
Tel: 01257 263 045
CLITHEROE, Cowgills of Clitheroe Ltd:
Tel: 01200 423 587
KIRKHAM, RK Boyes:
Tel: 01772 671 900
LANCASTER, Lawsons Toymaster:
Tel: 0152 464 518
LANCASTER, Micro Markets:
Tel: 01524 840 486
LEIGH, Toymaster:
Tel: 01942 671 116
MORECAMBE, Micro Markets:
Tel: 01524 416 306
OLDHAM, Ottakers:
Tel: 01616 205 543
POULTEN LE FYLDE, Aabas bookstore:
Tel: 01253 851 116
PRESTON, Conways Toymaster:
Tel: 01772 887 799
ROCHDALE, Microshack:
Tel: 01706 715 938
ROSSENDALE, Rossendale Models:
Tel: 01706 250 007
THORNTON-CLEVELYS, Toy2save Collectables:
Tel: 01253 855 905
WIGAN, Wigan Model Centre:
Tel: 01942 245 683

LEICESTERSHIRE

GW LEICESTER:
Unit 2,16/20 Silver Street. Tel: 0116 253 0510
GW LOUGHBOROUGH:
22 Biggin Street. Tel: 0150 923 8107
ASHBY-DE-LA-ZOUCH, Steve's Models:
Tel: 01530 416 827
COALVILLE, Geoffs Toymaster:
Tel: 01530 832 795
HINCKLEY, Punctilio Model Spot:
Tel: 01455 230 952

LINCOLNSHIRE AREA

GW GRIMSBY:
9 West St Mary's Gate. Tel: 0147 234 7757
GW LINCOLN:
Unit SUA, Saltergate (on outside of Waterside Centre). Tel: 0152 254 8027
BOSTON, Models and Computers:
Tel: 01205 365 102
GRANTHAM, Access Models:
Tel: 01636 673 116
GRANTHAM, Arbon & Watts:
Tel: 01664 855 030
GRANTHAM, Portprince Models and Hobbies Ltd:
Tel: 01476 592 001
LOUTH, Castaline:
Tel: 01507 602 149
MABLETHORPE, Belas Toymaster:
Tel: 01507 473 328
QUADRING, MS Sturgess:
Tel: 01775 821 967
SCUNTHORPE, Shermans Model Shop:
Tel: 01724 842 439
SKEGNESS, The Model Shop:
Tel: 01754 763 429
SPALDING, Mason's Models:
Tel: 01775 722 456

LONDON

GW BRENT CROSS:
Unit F9, Lower Mall (near Fenwicks), Brent Cross Shopping Centre. Tel: 0208 202 4979
• GW BROMLEY:
Unit 24, The Mall, Bromley. Tel: 0208 466 0678
GW COVENT GARDEN:
Unit 33, The Market. Tel: 0207 240 5106
GW CROYDON:
Unit 35, Drummond Centre (outside the back of the centre), Keeley Road. Tel: 0208 680 4600
GW ENFIELD:
3/5 Genotin Road. Tel: 0208 363 3238
GW HAMMERSMITH:
161 King Street.Tel: 0208 846 9744
GW HARROW:
296 Station Street. Tel: 0208 861 2350
GW KENSINGTON:
Shop 7, Lancer Square, Kensington Church Street. Tel: 0207 937 7011
GW KINGSTON ON THAMES
33 Fife Road. Tel: 0208 549 5224
GW LONDON (OXFORD ST):
Unit F10, The Plaza Shopping Centre, 1st Floor,116-128 Oxford Street. Tel: 0207 436 0839
GW RICHMOND:
Unit 8, Westminster House, Kew Road. Tel: 0208 948 6122
GW ROMFORD:
12 Quadrant Arcade. Tel: 01708 742 140
GW STAINES:
8 Clarence Street. Tel: 0178 446 0675
GW SUTTON:
Unit 26, Times Square Shopping Centre. Tel: 0208 770 9454
• GW UXBRIDGE:
Unit 32, Chequers Mall, The Pavilions Shopping Centre. 0189 525 2800
GW WATFORD:
Unit Q, 1A Queen Street, Harlequin Centre. Tel: 0192 324 5388
BLACKHEATH, 2nd Impressions:
Tel: 0208 852 6192
CHINGFORD, Hobby Stop:
Tel: 0208 529 7377
CHINGFORD, Rossis of London:
Tel: 0208 529 1920
CLAPHAM JUNCTION, Toystop:
Tel: 0207 228 9079
DULWICH, The Art Stationers:
Tel: 0208 693 5938
EALING, And So It Begins:
Tel: 0208 579 2244
FINCHLEY, Leisure Games:
Tel: 0208 346 2327
HAMPSTEAD, Happy Returns:
Tel: 0207 435 2431
HERNE HILL, Just Williams:
18 Half Moon Lane, SE24 9HU,
Tel: 0207 733 9955
KNIGHTSBRIDGE, Harrods:
Tel: 0207 730 1234
LONDON, Just Games:
Tel: 0207 323 3080
LONDON, Russ:
Tel: 0207 228 6319
PUTNEY, Toystop:
Tel: 0208 785 9555
RUISLIP, John Sanders:
Tel: 01895 634 848
WIMBLEDON, Elys:
Tel: 0208 946 9191
WOOD GREEN SHOPPING CENTRE, Toy City:
Tel: 0208 881 0770

MANCHESTER AREA

GW MANCHESTER (central):
Unit R35, Marsden Way South, Arndale Centre. Tel: 0161 834 6871
GW TRAFFORD CENTRE:
Unit L40c Trafford Centre. Tel: 0161 755 0065
ECCLES, Amazon Miniatures:
Tel: 0161 788 7650
MANCHESTER, Waterstones:
Tel: 0161 832 1992

MERSEYSIDE AREA

• GW LIVERPOOL:
13b Central Shopping Centre, Raneleigh.
Tel: 0151 703 0963
GW SOUTHPORT:
Unit K2, Marble Place Shopping Centre.
Tel: 0170 450 1255
ST HELENS, Wargames World:
22 Cooper Street, Tel: 01744 285 00
SOUTHPORT, Claymore Games:
Tel: 01704 545349

MIDDLESEX

EAST SHEEN, Play Inside Out:
Tel: 02088 765 229
EAST SHEEN, Pandemonium:
Tel: 02088 780 866
ENFIELD, Jennings Stores:
Tel: 0208 804 1804

NORFOLK

GW NORWICH:
12-14 Exchange Street. Tel: 0160 376 7656
DISS, Toymaster:
Tel: 01379 641 743
DEREHAM, Starlings Toymaster:
Tel: 01362 697 769
EAST DEREHAM, Youngsters World:
Tel: 01788 562 372
FAKENHAM, Lou Lous Toys and Gifts:
Tel: 01328 853 118
GORLESTON, Toy King:
Tel: 01493 443 097
HOLT, Starlings-Toymaster:
Tel: 01263 713 101
HUNSTANTON, Hunstanton Models:
Tel: 01485 533 325
KINGS LYNN, Empire:
Tel: 01553 765 174
KINGS LYNN, Westgate Department Store:
Tel: 01553 760 981
NORTH WALSHAM, Games N Fun:
Tel: 07851 031 246
NORWICH, Battlenet:
Tel: 01603 765 595
NORWICH, Kerrisons:
Tel: 01603 494008
NORWICH, Langleys, Rackheath industrial estate: Tel: 01603 621959
NORWICH, Toys Plus, Norwich airport industrial estate: Tel: 01223 837 839
SHERINGHAM, Starlings-Toymaster:
Tel: 01263 822 368
TAVERHAM, Norvic Models Ltd:
Unit 2, Taverham Garden Centre, NR8 6HT
Tel: 01603 865213
WROXHAM, Point House Toyshop:
Tel: 01603 706 804

NORTHAMPTONSHIRE

• GW NORTHAMPTON:
24-26 Abington Square. Tel: 01604 636 687
CORBY, Westgate Department Store:
Tel: 01536 203 525
KETTERING, Battlemaster Games Ltd:
Tel: 01536 414 880
KETTERING, Green Angel Cards & Games:
Tel: 01536 359 248
KETTERING, Toymaster Kingdom:
Tel: 01536 512 507
OUNDEL, Oundel News:
Tel: 01832 273 518
RUSHDEN, Osborne Sports & Toys:
Tel: 01933 312 415
WELLINGBOROUGH, Software Seller:
Tel: 01933 440 861

NORTHUMBERLAND

BERWICK UPON TWEED, Berwick Computer Games and DVDs:
Tel: 01289 309 551
HEXHAM, Fairplay:
Tel: 01434 606 678
HEXHAM, Robbs Department Store:
Tel: 01434 602 151
MORPETH, TG Allan:
Tel: 01670 515 136

NOTTINGHAMSHIRE

GW NOTTINGHAM (central):
34a Friar Lane. Tel: 0115 948 0651
GW WARHAMMER WORLD:
Willow Road, Lenton. Tel: 0115 916 8410
MANSFIELD, The Games Emporium:
Tel: 01623 640 022
NEWARK, Access Models:
Tel: 01636 673 116
SUTTON-IN-ASHFIELD, Big Boys Toys:
Tel: 01623 557 812
WORKSOP, Model Base:
Tel: 01909 501 752

OXFORDSHIRE

GW OXFORD:
1A Bush House, New Inn, Hall Street. Tel: 01865 242 182
ABINGDON, Just Toys:
Tel: 01235 524 333
BANBURY, Trinder Bros:
Tel: 01295 262 546
BICESTER, Dentons:
Tel: 01869 323 946
CARTERTON, Giles Sports:
Tel: 01993 842 396
COWLEY, Dentons:
Tel: 01865 749 746
DIDCOT, Dentons:
Tel: 01235 816 566
OXFORD, Boswells Toymaster:
Tel: 01865 241 244
THAME, Pied Pedaller:
Tel: 01844 260 022
WALLINGFORD, Pettits of Wallingford:
Tel: 01491 835 253
WITNEY, Romkrish:
Tel: 01993 704 979

SHROPSHIRE

• GW SHREWSBURY:
6 Market Street. Tel: 0174 336 2007
TELFORD, Sanda Games:
4 Albert Place, Donnington, Tel: 01952 676 722
BRIDGENORTH, Hobby Horse:
Tel: 0174 6 766 659
OSWESTRY, Funfayre:
Tel: 01691 670 646
TELFORD, Questing Knight Games:
Tel: 01952 417 747

SOMERSET

• GW BATH:
5-10 Westgate Buildings, Avon Street.
Tel: 0122 533 4044
BRIDGEWATER, Games Mart:
Tel: 0127 8 433 677
BURNHAM ON SEA, GW Hurley:
Tel: 01278 789 281
CHARD, Games Wizard:
Tel: 01460 239 090
CHEDDAR GORGE, Class Creations Ltd:
The Lippiatt, BS27 3QP, Tel: 01934 749 240
CLEVEDON, JJ Toymaster:
Tel: 01275 341 819
FROME, The Ellenbray Press:
Tel: 01373 462 139
FROME, Frome Model Centre:
Tel: 01373 465295
GLASTONBURY, Pedalers Toymaster:
Tel: 01458 834 562
MINEHEAD, Minehead Toys & Models:
Tel: 01643 705 550
TAUNTON, Krackers:
Tel: 01823 335 057
WELLS, Wells Models:
Tel: 01749 675 262
WESTON SUPER-MARE, Griffins Games:
Tel: 01934 429 799
WESTON SUPER-MARE, JJ Toys:
Tel: 01934 418 151
YEOVIL, Yeovil Collectors Centre:
Tel: 01935 433 739
YEOVIL, Witch Engine:
Tel: 01935 47978

STAFFORDSHIRE

• GW BURTON ON TRENT:
Unit 8, Union Court, Union Street.
Tel: 0128 353 5865
GW STOKE:
27 Stafford St. Tel: 0178 220 5287
COCKERMOUTH, The Toy Shop:
Tel: 01900 825 855
LEEK, Chapter 1:
Tel: 01538 399 885
NEWCASTLE UNDER LYME, Sundowner Models:
Tel: 01782 610 606
STAFFORD, Stafford Games:
1E Paul Reynolds Centre, Foregate Street, ST16 2PJ
Tel: 01785 255577
STAFFORD, Too Fat Goblinz:
Tel: 01785 244 499
STOKE-ON-TRENT, Alsager Toys and Models:
Tel: 01270 882 871
STOKE-ON-TRENT, Battlezone Games & Collectables:
Tel: 01782 833 633
TAMWORTH, Geoff's Toys:
Tel: 01530 832 795
UTTOXETER, The Toybox:
Tel: 01889 565 357

SUFFOLK

• GW IPSWICH:
49 Buttermarket. Tel: 01473 210 031
BECCLES, Toy Box:
Tel: 01502 712 785
BURY ST. EDMUNDS, Model Junction:
Tel: 01284 753 456
BURY ST. EDMUNDS, Toymaster Kingdom:
Tel: 01284 761 646
FELIXSTOWE, Wizards Taxis:
Tel: 01394 275 555
HALESWORTH, Halesworth Toy Shop:
Tel: 01986 874 270
HAVERHILL, Baby Connexion:
Tel: 01440 706 292
IPSWICH, Galaxy Models & Hobbies Ltd:
Tel: 01473 729 279
IPSWICH, Toyworld Ipswich:
Tel: 01473 728 535
LOWESTOFT, Toymaster Kingdom:
Tel: 01502 565 688
NEWMARKET, Moons Toyland:
Tel: 01638 663 147
STOWMARKET, D J Collectables:
Tel: 01449 771 015
STOWMARKET, Simpson & Sons:
Tel: 01449 612 914
SUDBURY, CXG Computers:
Tel: 0870 922 1313
SUDBURY, FT Games:
Tel: 01787 466 060
SUDBURY, Toymaster Kingdom:
Tel: 01787 372 238
SUDBURY, Toy Connexion:
Tel: 01787 888 002
WOODBRIDGE, Toytown:
Tel: 01394 383 170

SURREY

GW GUILDFORD:
Unit 1, 9/12 Tunsgate. Tel: 0148 345 1793
GW WOKING:
Unit 3 Cleary Court. Tel: 0148 377 1675
CAMBERLEY, Morningstar:
6 Beitegheim Way, Tel: 01276 685 160
COULSDEN, Taylors Toys and Sports:
Tel: 0208 666 00710
CRANLEIGH, David Mann:
Tel: 01483 273 777
DORKING, Dorking Models:
Tel: 01306 881 747
EPSOM, Ottakers:
Tel: 01372 742 533
EPSOM, Treehouse Toys:
Tel: 01932 252 272
FARNHAM, Darkstar:
Tel: 01252 820 324
OXTED, JH Lorimer Ltd:
Tel: 0208 656 6625
PURLEY, JH Lorimer Ltd:
Tel: 0181 660 9716
REDHILL, Gamers Guild:
Tel: 01737 789 123
REIGATE, The Toy Shop:
Tel: 01737 245 300
WALTON ON THAMES, Treehouse Toys:
Tel: 01932 252 272

SUSSEX AREA

GW BRIGHTON:
Unit 7, Nile Pavilions. Tel: 0127 320 3333
GW CRAWLEY:
11 Broadway. Tel: 0129 355 2072
GW EASTBOURNE:
13 Terminus Road.Tel: 0132 364 1423
BOGNOR REGIS, Trains Models and Hobbies:
Tel: 01243 864 727
BURGESS HILL, Kid's Stuff:
Tel: 01444 257 724
CHICHESTER, Chichester Toys:
Tel: 01243 788 055
EAST GRINSTEAD, Ready To Run Models
Tel: 01342 300 917
HAYWARDS HEATH, 4JRIN Ltd:
Tel: 01444 455 993
HORSHAM, Gentle Gallery:
Tel: 01403 258 567
HORSHAM, Ottakers:
Tel: 01403 268 088
SEAFORD, Big Kids Toy Shop:
Tel: 01323 899 099
SOUTHWICK, The Dragons Tears:
52 Highdown, BN42 4QS
Tel: 01273 595418
STEYNING, Gentle Gallery:
Tel: 01903 812 933
UCKFIELD, Kid's Stuff:
Tel: 01825 768 398
WORTHING, KC's Games Shop:
Tel: 01903 237 983

TYNE AND WEAR AREA

• GW NEWCASTLE (Central):
Unit 6A, Newgate Shopping Centre
Tel: 0191 232 2418
GW METRO (METRO CENTRE):
Unit 2, First Floor, The Arcade (near the Mediterranean Village). Tel: 0191 461 0950
NEWCASTLE, Fenwick Ltd:
Tel: 0191 232 5100
NORTH SHIELDS, SR Gladston & Son:
Tel: 01912 570 335
SUNDERLAND, Joplings:
Tel: 01915 102 105
WHITLEY BAY, T&G Allan:
Tel: 01912 531 564

WARWICKSHIRE

GW COVENTRY:
Unit 39, Upper Level, Cathedral Lanes Shopping Centre. Tel: 0247 622 7311
GW LEAMINGTON SPA:
32 Regent Street. Tel: TBC
BEDWORTH, Railway & Modellers Junction:
Tel: 02476 316 285
KENILWORTH, Abacraft Arts & Pictures:
Tel: 01926 511 294
LEAMINGTON SPA, Trinders Toy Town Ltd:
Tel: 01926 470 501
NUNEATON, Nuneaton Bookshop:
Tel: 02476 342 000
RUGBY, Joto Railways & Models:
Tel: 01788 562 372
STRATFORD-UPON-AVON, 3 Windsor Place:
Tel: 01789 295 850

WILTSHIRE

GW SALISBURY:
1B Winchester Street. Tel: 0172 233 0955
GW SWINDON:
50 Fleet Street. Tel: 0179 343 6036
CALNE, SPS Stationary:
Tel: 01249 813 560
DEVIZES, Hoggosaurus Toymaster:
Tel: 01380 723 841
MALMESBURY, SPS Stationary:
Tel: 01666 824 440
MARLBOROUGH, H Duck:
Tel: 01672 512 170
MELKSHAM, The Toyshop:
Tel: 01225 768 415
SWINDON, Spot On Models:
Tel: 01793 522 098
TROWBRIDGE, The Toy Shop:
Tel: 01225 768 415

WORCESTERSHIRE

• GW WORCESTER:
23 Lychgate Mall, Cathedral Plaza.
Tel: 0190 561 6707
DROITWITCH, Look-rite Ltd T/A Toyworld:
Tel: 01905 772 403
EVESHAM, Battle Honours UK:
Tel: 0138 645 875
STOURPORT ON SEVERN, TP Activity Toys:
Tel: 01299 872 800

YORKSHIRE

GW BRADFORD:
4 Piccadilly, Bradford. Tel: 0127 473 9430
GW DONCASTER:
Unit 10, The Colonnades. Tel: 0130 232 0535
GW HARROGATE:
53 Station Parade. Tel: 0142 356 4310
GW HULL:
30 Paragon Street. Tel: 0148 258 9576
GW LEEDS (central):
12-16 Central Road. Tel: 0113 242 0834
GW LEEDS (WHITE ROSE):
Unit 28D, White Rose Centre. Tel: 0113 272 3470
GW SHEFFIELD (central):
16 Fitzwilliam Gate. Tel: 0114 275 0114
GW SHEFFIELD (MEADOWHALL CENTRE):
Unit 91B, High Street, Upper Mall (next to entrance near Boots). Tel: 0114 256 9836
• GW WAKEFIELD:
96 Kirkgate, the Ridings Centre. Tel: 0192 436 9431
GW YORK:
13A Lendal. Tel: 0190 462 8014
RICHMOND, Anything Goes:
Bridge Garage, Gatherley Road, Tel: 01748 810 135
BEVERLEY, Mayfair Toymaster:
Tel: 01482 862 777
BRIDLINGTON, Croppers:
Tel: 01262 677 727
HALIFAX, Halifax Modellers World:
Tel: 01422 349 157
HALIFAX, Magazine World:
Tel: 01422 330 547
HUDDERSFIELD, Games Emporium:
Tel: 01484 532 838
HUDDERSFIELD, Something Wicked:
Tel: 01484 559 226
HULL, Mayfair Toymaster:
Tel: 01482 862 777
KEIGHLEY, Conways Toymaster:
Tel: 01535 604 045
LEEDS, Royal Armouries Museum:
Tel: 01132 201 999
LEEDS, Toyworld:
Tel: 01132 439 800
NORTHALLERTON, T & FM Grover Ltd:
Tel: 01609 773 334
OTLEY, Conways Toymaster:
Tel: 01943 462 065
PICKERING, Puffers of Pickering:
Tel: 01751 472 762
POCKLINGTON, Chylds Play:
Tel: 01759 306 041
SCARBOROUGH, Maison Militaire:
Tel: 01723 362 257
SCARBOROUGH, Space, Myth and Magic:
Tel: 08456 441 113
SELBY, A1 Sports and Toys:
Tel: 01757 705 115
SHEFFIELD, Wargames Emporium:
Tel: 01142 754 826
WAKEFIELD, Model and Craft Centre:
Tel: 01924 374 097
WHITBY, John Anderson - Toymaster:
Tel: 01947 602 213
WHITBY, Models and Movie Props Ltd:
Tel: 01947 603 123

WALES

GW CARDIFF:
31 High Street. Tel: 0292 064 4917
• GW NEWPORT:
25 Skinner Street, Tel: 0163 325 6295
GW SWANSEA:
45 Princess Way, Tel: 0179 246 3969
CARDIGAN, Helm's Deep:
Royal Buildings Priory Street, Tel: 01239 614 080
ABERGAVENNY, Richards of Abergavenny:
Tel: 01873 852 466
ABERYSTWYTH, Albatross:
Tel: 01970 617 836
BANCHORY, Banchory Toy & Gift shop:
Tel: 01330 825 586
BANGOR, ACME Computers:
Tel: 01248 371 457
BRECON, J Clark Toys & Gifts:
Tel: 01874 622 865
BRIDGEND, Joust for Fun:
Tel: 01656 767 680
CARMARTHEN, Good News:
Tel: 01267 237 789
CARMARTHEN, Hardings:
Tel: 01267 237 774
CHEPSTOW, Artists Corner:
Tel: 01291 627 393
DYFED, Clarice Toys:
Tel: 01834 843 493
GWYNEDD, LT Leisure:
Tel: 01341 281 402
LLANELLI, AM Frost:
Tel: 01554 777 277
LLANDRINDOD WELLS, Corven Arts:
Tel: 08700 664 904
LLANDUDNO, Dibs Toymaster:
Tel: 01978 758 451
LLANTWIT MAJOR, Rainbow Plaza:
Tel: 01446 794 118
MILFORD HAVEN, Foster Powell Ltd:
Tel: 01646 697 111
NEWPORT, Battle On:
Tel: 01983 533 222
PORTHCAWL, Game It:
Tel: 01656 784 428
PEMBROKE, Dragon Alley:
Tel: 01646 621 456
RHYL, Lightfoot Models & Toys:
Tel: 01745 331 564
SWANSEA, Comix Shoppe:
Tel: 01792 642 097
SWANSEA, West Coast Games Ltd:
6 High Street Arcade, SA1 1LE
Tel: 01792 648 007
WREXHAM, Brite Ideas:
Tel: 01978 758 451

SCOTLAND

• GW ABERDEEN:
Unit 1, 12-14 Upper Kirkgate.
Tel: 0122 464 9779
GW AYR:
10 Arran Mall. Tel: 0129 261 0673
GW BRAEHEAD:
115 Braehead Shopping Centre, Kings Inch Road.
Tel: 0141 885 9440
• GW DUMFRIES:
44 High Street. Tel: 0138 724 9702
GW DUNDEE:
110 Commercial Street. Tel: 0138 220 2382
GW EDINBURGH:
136 High Street. Tel: 0131 220 6540
GW FALKIRK:
12 Cow Wynd. Tel: 0132 462 4553
• GW GLASGOW:
81 Union Street. Tel: 0141 221 1673

GW Store UK Elite Store

FREE THIS MONTH! WARHAMMER BATTLE FOR SKULL PASS POSTER!

WHITE DWARF

LEGIONS OF MIDDLE-EARTH™

MUSTER AN ARMY • JOIN THE WAR

THE TWO TOWERS™

THE JOURNEY CONTINUES

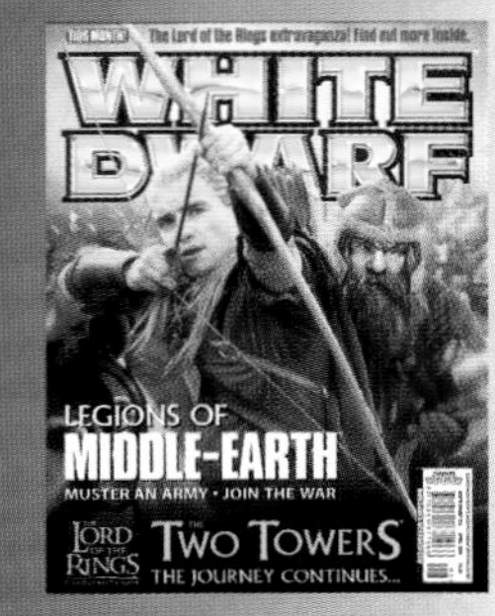

GAMES WORKSHOP DIRECT SALES

www.games-workshop.co.uk/storefront
Tel: 0115 91 40000 Fax: 0115 916 8002

GAMES WORKSHOP ONLINE

www.games-workshop.co.uk

FORGE WORLD

www.forgeworld.co.uk
Tel: 0115 916 8177
Fax: 0115 916 8044

THE BLACK LIBRARY

www.blacklibrary.com

SPECIALIST GAMES

www.specialist-games.com

Printed at Winkowski

Willow Road, Lenton, Nottingham, NG7 2WS

EDITORIAL

Beneath a thousand mail-shod feet, the ground trembles: the Legions of Middle-earth are here!

This month is an exciting time for players of The Lord of the Rings strategy battle game. First off, there's the release of the new Legions of Middle-earth expansion – a set of army lists and associated rules that lets you pick huge themed forces, and pit them against each other in titanic battles. Naturally, I turned straight to the Dwarf section, which looks very impressive, I can tell you! Not content with this release, we've also got The Two Towers, which lets you re-enact the tale of the book and film, with a whole host of new models to swell your forces. What this means is that you can build an impressive army and play competitve games like never before, but you can still use the new "Journey" supplement to settle down to some great scenarios and story-driven moments. With new models for just about every force in Middle-earth out in the next few months, it's never been a better time to play The Lord of the Rings!

Also this month, we have a battle report for the Fall of Medusa V campaign. Games guru Alessio Cavatore takes on our very own Old Grumbler, Matt Hutson, in what's set to be a real struggle for survival in the ruined city of Machavius.

Grombrindal, The White Dwarf

CORRESPONDENCE We welcome comments about White Dwarf, Games Workshop games and Citadel miniatures. All letters except subscriptions and Mail Order should be addressed to: White Dwarf, Games Workshop, Willow Road, Lenton, Nottingham NG7 2WS.

Please mark your envelope clearly with the name of the game you are writing to us about. If you want a reply you must enclose a self-addressed stamped envelope (overseas readers should include IRCs). We receive an enormous amount of mail. We do read every letter but it may take a little time for us to reply to you, so please be patient!

You can find Games Workshop on the World Wide Web at the following Internet address:

www.games-workshop.com

Product Code: 60249999320
ISSN: 0265-8712 19

ANGUS, Gardiners:
Tel: 01356 622 265
BANCHORY, Toy and Gift Shop:
Tel: 01330 825 586
CRIEFF, Pinetree Hobbycrafts:
Tel: 01764 653 706
DINGWALL, Sports and Model Shop:
Tel: 01349 862 346
DUNFERMLINE, Abbey Models:
Tel: 01383 731 116
EAST KILBRIDE, DTS Models:
Tel: 01355 238 988
EDINBURGH, Marionville Models:
Tel: 01313 177 010
ELGIN, Junner's Toymaster:
Tel: 0143 542 492
FRASERBURGH, Steven's Toymaster:
Tel: 01358 724059
FIFE (CUPAR), The Nappy Pin:
Tel: 01334 653 160
FORFAR, J. Yule and Sons:
Tel: 01241 872 195
FORT WILLIAM, The Granite House:
Tel: 01397 703 651
GALASHIELS, Books Plus:
Tel: 01896 752 843
GLASGOW, Static Games:
Tel: 01412 265 414
HADDINGTON, Cycle Services:
Tel: 01620 826 989
INVERNESS, Junners Toymaster:
Tel: 01463 233 234
ISLE OF LEWIS, A D MacDonald and Son:
Tel: 0851 705 650
KILMARNOCK, T4 Toys:
Tel: 01563 520 262
KINROSS, The Hope Chest:
Tel: 01577 862 516
KIRKCALDY, The Hope Chest:
Tel: 01592 260 116
NORTH BERWICK, Laws Cycles:
Tel: 01620 890 643
ORKNEY, Mclennan-Toymaster:
Tel: 01856 877 788
PAISLEY, Paisley Model Centre:
Tel: 01418 894 221
PERTH, T4 Toys:
Tel: 01738 639 450
PETERHEAD, George Donald Ltd:
Tel: 01779 474 737
SHETLAND, Harrys Dept Store:
Tel: 01595 693 097
STIRLING, Abacus:
21 Crawford Arcade, FK8 1AX,
Tel: 01786 478 784
STIRLING, Do It @ Your Leisure:
Tel: 01786 826 975
THURSO, Durrans:
Tel: 01847 893 169
TURRIFF, E Rae and Son:
Tel: 01888 562 610

NORTHERN IRELAND

GW BELFAST:
20A Castle Court (towards back of the Centre).
Tel: 0289 0233684
BALLYMENA, Camerons:
23 Broughshane St, Co Antrim,
Tel: 0482 564 8821
BANBRIDGE, David Rogers:
7 Bridge St, Co Down.
BANGOR, Replay Games:
High St, Co Down, Tel: 0489 145 2210
BANGOR, Stewart Miller & Sons:
40 Main St, Co Down, Tel: 0489 127 0108
COLERAINE, Moores:
7-11 Church St, Co Derry, Tel: 0126 544 44
CRUMLIN, Lilliput Construction Co:
92 Bramble Wood, Co Antrim.
ENNISKILLEN, Modellers Corner:
22 Darling St, Tel: 0486 632 2367
LISBURN, World of Wonder:
Riverside Centre, Tel: 0489 266 9996
OMAGH, Whites Toymaster:
3/7 Bridge St, Tel: 0662 242 427
PORTADOWN, D Jeffers:
8 Mandeville St, Tel: 0483 535 0889

EIRE

GW BLANCHARDSTOWN:
Unit 249a, Blanchardstown Shopping Centre, Dublin. Tel: 0035 318 223 868
GW DUBLIN:
Unit 3, Lower Liffey Street.
Tel: 0035 318 725 791
ATHLONE, Toy City:
N6 Centre, Co Westmeath, Tel: 090 647 9851
BALLINA, World of Wonder:
Dillon Terrace, Co Mayo, Tel: 096 76676
BLACKPOOL, World of Wonder:
23 Northpoint Bus Pk, Cork, Tel: 0214 210 445
BRAY, ER Harris & Sons:
Co Wicklow, Tel: 012 867 995
CARRICK ON SHANNON, Mulvey's:
Main Street, Leitrim, Tel: 071 962 2936
CASTLEBAR, McDermotts:
Co Mayo, Tel: 096 76676
CORK, Art and Hobby Shop:
Douglas Shopping Centre, Co Cork,
Tel: 021 436 3580
CORK, Art and Hobby Shop:
Wilton Shopping Centre, Co Cork,
Tel: 021 434 7207
CORK, Noddy's Toymaster:
13-14 Cornmarket St, Co Cork, Tel: 021 427 9508
CORK, Other Realms:
Paul Street Shopping Centre, Cork City,
Tel: 021 422 2224
CORK, World of Wonder:
Co Cork, Tel: 021 4210445
CLONAKILTY, Coughlan Educational Supplies:
11 Rossa St, Co Cork, Tel: 023 33068
CLONMEL, Hogan's Toymaster:
31 Parnell St, Co Tipperary, Tel: 052 23973
CLONTARF, Furlongs:
4 Vernon Avenue, Dublin, Tel: 01 853 0395
DUBLIN, Banba Toymaster:
48 Mary St, Tel: 01 872 7100
DUN LAOGHAIRE, Banba Toymaster:
Dun Laoghaire Shopping Centre, Co Dublin,
Tel: 012 804 011
DUNDALK, Pick n Save:
Long Walk S/Centre, Co Louth, Tel: 042 932 7356
DUNGARVEN, Murphy's Toy and Cycle Specialists:
9 Main St, Co Waterford, Tel: 058 41376
ENNIS, World of Wonder:
Woodqay Car Park, Co Clare, Tel: 065 684 8697
ENNIS, Banba Toymaster:
Clearwater S/Centre, Dublin, Tel: 01 864 3910
GALWAY, Games Realm:
8A The Corn Store, Co Galway, Tel: 091 563 006
GALWAY, It's Magic:
Eyre Square S/Centre, Co Galway,
Tel: 091 563 313
GALWAY, Model World:
14G Liosban Business Park, Taum Rd.,, Co Galway,
Tel: 091 765 655
GALWAY, Toy City:
Unit 3, Wellpark, Galway, Tel: 091 764 949
GOREY, John Webb:
Co Wexford, Tel: 055 21119
KILKENNY, Michael Crotty's:
77 High St, Co Kilkenny, Tel: 056 51038
KILLORGLIN, O'Sheas:
Lower Bridge St, Kerry, Tel: 066 976 1919
LIMERICK, Hollywood Empire:
30 Thomas St, Co Limerick, Tel: 061 313 477
LIMERICK, O'Callaghans:
Dock Rd, Co Limerick, Tel: 061 225 886
LIMERICK, The Gathering:
43 Lower Geraild Griffin St, Co Limerick
Tel: 061 315 133
LOUGHREA, Beatty:
Church St, Co Galway, Tel: 091 841 403
LOUGHREA, Mary's Toymaster:
2 Main St, Co Cork, Tel: 026 42491
LOUGHREA, Murphy's World of Wonder:
115, Main St, Co Cork, Tel: 022 21197
NENAGH, JKC:
25 Pearse St, Co Tipperary, Tel: 067 31391
NEWBRIDGE, World of Wonder:
Newbridge Retail Park, Kildare.
SLIGO, WA and AF Woods:
Co Sligo, Tel: 071 914 202 110 478
STILLORGAN, Nimble Fingers:
Co Dublin, Tel: 012 880 788
TRALEE, A Caball and sons:
9-12 Bridge Street, Co Kerry, Tel: 066 712 1847
TULLAMORE, Robbins:
William St, Co Offaly, Tel: 0506 21541
WATERFORD, The Hobby Shop:
38 The Quay, Co Waterford, Tel: 051 852 227
WESTPORT, World of Wonder:
Bridge St, Co Mayo, Tel: 098 25331
THURLES, Toymaster:
Friar St, Co Tipperary, Tel: 062 51326
TIPPERARY, Hogan's Toymaster:
31 Parnell St, Co Tipperary, Tel: 052 23973
TIPPERARY, Whelan's:
64-65 Main Street, Co Tipperary, Tel: 062 51326
WATERFORD, Fitzmaurice Toymaster:
Tel: 051 876 566
WEXFORD, Play & Learn:
8 Selskar St, Co Wexford, Tel: 053 23188
WICKLOW, Hopkins:
Main Street, Co Wicklow, Tel: 0404 67225

INTERNATIONAL ACCOUNTS

BELGIUM

BRUGGE, Fair Play
Spoorwegstraat 162, 8200,
Tel: 0032 (0)50 38 51 83
AARSCHOT, Conect'r
Gasthuisstraat 47, 3200, Tel: 0032 (0)16 56 88 30
HASSELT, D-Six
Kuringersteenweg 43-45, 3500,
Tel: 0032 (0)11 32 53 55
LEOPOLDSBURG, NV Moestermans
Maarschalk-Fochstraat 20, 3970,
Tel: 0032 (0)11 39 38 46
LEUVEN, The Dice Pool
Parijsstraat, 44, 3000, Tel: 0032 (0)16 29 49 94
MECHELEN, De Spelfanaat
Veemarkt 32, 2800, Tel: 0032 (0)15 34 59 07
OOSTENDE, King Arthur
Amsterdamstraat 63B, 8400,
Tel: 0032 (0)59 51 57 56
AALST, Hermelijn
Molenstraat 36, 9300, Tel: +32 (0) 53 41 48 66
AALST, Intertoys Aalst
Lange Zoutstraat 163, 9300,
Tel: +32 (53) 750143
ANTWERPEN, Celtic Cross
Zilversmidstraat 9, 2000,
Tel: 0032 (0)3 288 81 65
ANTWERPEN, Red Dragon Games
St Katelijnevest 55, 2000,
Tel: 0032 (0)3 231 71 61
BLANKENBERGE, De Speelhoek
Langestraat 41, 8370, Tel: 0032 (0)50 41 49 23
BRUGGE, Modelbouwcenter West-Vlaanderen
Langestraat 163, 2000, Tel: 0032 (0)50 34 20 71
BRUSSEL, Intertoys Laken
8-10 Avenue Busleyden, 1020,
Tel: 0032 (0)2 268 71 41
BRUSSEL, Intertoys Anderlecht
S Dupluislaan 315, 1070,
Tel: 0032 (0)2 523 84 73
DENDERMONDE, Tip Top
Moens, Sint-Gillistraat 75, 9200,
Tel: 0032 (0)52 21 17 98
DEURNE, The Gamestore
Bisschoppenhoflaan 7-9,2100
Tel, +32 3 325 55 35
GENT, Intertoys Gent
Volderstraat 17, 9000, Tel: 0032 (0)9 224 42 86
GENT, Miniatuurauto's Eeckhout
Burgstraat 87, 9000, Tel: 0032 (0)9 224 17 96
GENT, Lood &Spelen
Burgstraat 43, 9000, Tel: 0032 (0)9 224 47 34
GENT, Red Dragon Games Gent
Overpoortstraat 116, 9000
HALLE, Mishra's Playground
Ninoofsesteenweg 104, 1500,
Tel: 0032 (0)2 361 58 53
HALLE, Top 1 Toys Halle
Basiliekstraat 66, 1500, Tel: 0032 (0)2 356 04 03
HASSELT, Oberonn
Kempische Steenweg 27, 3500,
Tel: 0032 11 351 358
IXELLES, Intertoys Ixelles
104 Chaussee d'Ixelles, 1050,
Tel: 0032 (0)2 514 17 03
KORTRIJK, Albion
Doorniksestraat 52, 8500, Tel: +32 (56) 32 43 07
KORTRIJK, De Concorde
Brugsestraat 40, 8500, Tel: 0032 (0)56 37 05 65
LOKEREN, De Geest
Roomstraat 27, 9160, Tel: 0032 (0)9 348 49 50
MERKSEM, Game Garden, The
Bredabaan 376, 2170, Tel: 0032 (0)3 666 37 73
MOL, Intertoys Mol
Graaf de Broquevillestraat 9, 2400,
Tel: 0032 (0)14 32 08 24
NEERPELT, t' Spellenhuis
Fabriekstraat 10, 3910, Tel: 0032 (0)11 74 49 79
OOSTENDE, Timms
Vlaanderenstraat 48, 8400,
Tel: 0032 (0)59 80 49 63
OVERIJSE, Intertoys Overijse
Brusselsesteenweg 402A, 3090,
Tel: 0032 (0)2 687 42 53
ROESELARE, Black Border
Stationsdreef 68, 8800, Tel: 051/20 82 50
ROESELARE, Willi's Wereld
Henri Horriestraat 20, 8800,
Tel: 0032 (0)51 24 64 15
ST NIKLAAS, HQ
Ankerstraat 44, 9100, Tel: 0032 (0)3 776 35 45
TOURNAI, Intertoys Tournai
19 Rue Royale, 7500, Tel: 0032 (0)69 21 42 22

BULGARIA

SOFIA, Magic Worlds
1000, Slaveikov sqr.9
SOFIA, Moria
1303, Sredna Gora Str.133

CROATIA

CAKOVEC, Hama centar
Roban kuca "Medjimuka"
OSIJEK, Land of Magic
31000, Merkator Centar, Gacka 10
Tel: 00385 31275794
OSIJEK, Zelda,
Trg A. Starcevica
RIJEKA, Game Master
Krizaniceva 1c
SPLIT, Land of Magic
Kralja Zvonimira 15, 21000,
Tel: 00385 21482249
SLAVONSKI BROD, Lesic
Strossmayerova 7
VARAZDIN, Land of Magic:
Kaciceva 5, 42000, Tel: 00385 42200161
ZAGREB, Land of Magic
10000, Frankopanska 22, Tel: 00385 14870077
ZAGREB, Land of Magic
10000, Radiceva 13, 0038514923917

CZECH REPUBLIC

BRNO-ABOVRESKY, Cerny Rytir
Chladkova 3, Tel: 00420 605884082
CESKE BUDEJOVICE, Chaotit
Zacharyasova 5, Tel: 0042 602489158
HRADEC KRALOVE, Knihkupectvi Valhalla
Letcu 1651, Tel: 0042 495522009
LIBEREC, Ogri Doupe
Silkova 236/11, Tel: 00420603 893 336
PRAHA, Cerny Rytir
Za Poricskou branou 21, Tel: 00420 222312461
PRAHA, Ogri Doupe
Mikulandska 4/122, Tel: 00420 224 934 811
VSETIN, Atlantis
Prikra 42, Tel: 00 42 571411697

DENMARK

GW KØBENHAVN
Frederiksborggade 5KL, 1360, Tel: 33122217
AARHUS C, Dragons Lair
Sct. Knuds Torv 3, 8000, Tel: 8619 0063
ODENSE C, Dragons Lair
Kongensgade 71, st.th, 5000, Tel: 6591 9701
ROSKILDE, Fanatic Roskilde
Allehelgensgade 15, 4000, Tel: 4636 3548
SLAGELSE, Fanatic Slagelse
Skovsøgade 6A, 4200, Tel: 5854 4080
ESBJERG, Bunkeren
Kongensgade 19, 6700, Tel: 7518 1199
HELSINGØR, Hobby & Fritid
Rosenkildevej 2, 3000, Tel: 4921 4542
HILLERØD, Hobby & Fritid
Hostrupvej 4, 3400, Tel: 4825 2616
KØBENHAVN NV, Arena København
Rentemestervej 80, 2400, Tel: 3833 5700
KOLDING, B.O. Bøger Kolding
Kolding Storcenter 52, 6000, Tel: 7550 3834
NÆSTVED, Arena Næstved
Ramsherred 17, 4700, Tel: 5554 6700
RØDOVRE, Mr Games
Rødovre Stationscenter, 2610, Tel: 3672 0255
AALBORG, Aalborg Hobby Service
Nørregade 18, 9000, Tel: 9812 1315
AALBORG, Bog & idé Aalborg
Nytorv 5, 9000, Tel: 9811 6611
AALBORG SV, BO Bøger Aalborg
Ålborg St. Center 108, 9200, Tel: 9879 1545
AALBORG, EB Games
Bispensgade 10, 9000, Tel: 9811 5543
AALBORG, EB Games
Hobrovej 452, 9200, Tel: 9815 7520
AALBORG, Guns n' Games
Danmarksgade 45, 9000, Tel: 9813 4280
AARS, Ting og sager
Søndergade 6, 9600, Tel: 9862 4552
AABENRÅ, Legekæden Aabenrå
Storegade 17, 6200, Tel: 7462 2405
ALBERTSLUND, Bog & idé Albertslund
Stationstorvet 2, 2620, Tel: 4364 8877
ALLERØD, Bog & idé Allerød
M.D madsensvej 8, 3450, Tel: 4817 2770
AARHUS C, EB Games
M.P. Bruun's Gade 25, 8000, Tel: 8748 6060
AARHUS C, EB Games
Frederiksgade 26, 8000, Tel: 8741 6913
AARHUS C, Goblin Gate
Kystvejen 27, 8000, Tel: 8619 4311
AARHUS C, Hobby House
Nørregade 51, 8000, Tel: 8612 0062
AARHUS C, EB Games
Vestergade 58, 8000, Tel: 8613 1788
ASNÆS, Bog & Ide Asnæs
Asnæs Centret 2, 4550, Tel: 5965 0014
BALLERUP, EB Games
Ballerup Center 1, 2750, Tel: 4497 4422
BJERRINGBRO, Bog & idé Bjerringbro
Storegade 4, 8850, Tel: 8668 1077
BRØNSHØJ, Charlottes Legetøj
Frederikssundsvej 148, 2700, Tel: 3860 3626
CHARLOTTENLUND, Bog & idé Charlottenlund
Jægersborg Allé 5, 2920, Tel: 3964 3840
EBELTOFT, Ebeltoft boghandel
Adelgade 48, 8400, Tel: 8634 3844
ESBJERG, BO Bøger Esbjerg
Kongensgade 33, 6700, Tel: 7512 1177
ESPERGÆRDE, BO Bøger Espergærde
Espergærde Centret, Vester Torv 2, 3060, Tel: 4913 1946
FAKSE, Bog & idé Fakse
Torvegade 14, 4640, Tel: 5671 3013
FARUM, Bog & idé Farum
Farum Bytorv 64, 3520, Tel: 4495 1225
FREDERICIA, Bog & idé Fredericia
Gothersgade 37, 7000, Tel: 7624 5969
FREDERIKSBERG, EB Games
Falkoner Alle 46, 2000, Tel: 3536 8099
FREDERIKSBERG, Legekæden Frederiksberg
Godthåbsvej 36, 2000, Tel: 3819 7025
FREDERIKSHAVN, Bog & idé Frederikshavn
Søndergade 4, 9900, Tel: 9843 2584
FREDERIKSHAVN, Roses Boghandel
Søndergade 41, 9900, Tel: 9842 1454
FREDERIKSSUND, Legekæden Frederikssund
Jernbanegade 31, 3600, Tel: 4738 3959
FREDERIKSVÆRK, Hobby & Legetøj
Nørregade 38, 3300, Tel: 4772 1693
FREDDERKSSOND, Frederikssund Bøger & Papir
Østergade 1, 3600., Tel: 4731 0245
GILLELEJE, Lillys Legetøj
Vesterbrogade 9, 3250, Tel: 4830 3090
GRENÅ, Bog & idé Grenå
Torvet 8, 8500, Tel: 8632 1933
GREVE, BO Bøger Hundige
Hundige Storcenter, 2670, Tel: 4390 6008
HADERSLEV, Legekæden Haderslev
Nørregade 20, 6100, Tel: 7453 0385
HADSTEN, Mosquito Cykel Center
Kirkevej 1, 8370, Tel: 8698 0839
HADSUND, Lorentz Nielsen Bog & idé
Storegade 14, 9560, Tel: 9857 1833
HELSINGE, Schwartz Bog & idé
Østergade 17 - 19, 3200, Tel: 4879 4001
HELSINGE, Teaterbixen
Frederiksborgvej 10, 3200, Tel: 2092 2991
HELSINGØR, BO Bøger Helsingør
Sturups Plads 1, 3000, Tel: 4921 5600
HERLEV, Bog & idé Herlev
Herlev Bymidte, 2730, Tel: 4494 0477
HERNING, BO Bøger Herning
Bredgade 6, 7400, Tel: 9712 0747
HERNING, Buddy Legetøj
Herning Centret, Merkurvej 17, 7400,
Tel: 9722 0552
HERNING, EB Games
Dalgas Plads 7B, 7400, Tel: 9716 4600
HERNING, Færges Kælder
Smallegade 12, 7400, Tel: 3510 1897
HILLERØD, Legekæden Hillerød
Slotsgade 27, 3400, Tel: 4824 6161
HJØRRING, Bog & idé Hjørring
Strømgade 1, 9800, Tel: 9892 9998
HJØRRING, Rossels Boghandel
P. Nørkjærs plads 4, 9800, Tel: 9892 1744
HOLBÆK, Geppels legetøj
Smedelundsgade 22 E, 4300, Tel: 5944 1888
HOLBÆK, Storkfelt Bog & idé
Ahlgade 31, 4300, Tel: 5943 0074
HOLTE, Legetøjsbutikken
Holte midtpunkt 23, 1. 2840, Tel: 4546 1782
HORNSLET, ABC centret
Skolevangen 6, 8543, Tel: 8699 5033
HORSENS, Bog & idé Horsens
Søndergade 30, 8700, Tel: 7561 1711
HORSENS, Legekæden Horsens
Hospitalsgade 15, 8700, Tel: 7561 6011
HØRSHOLM, GAD Hørsholm
Hovedgaden 55 C, 2970, Tel: 4586 0408
HUMLEBÆK, Rodes
Torpenvej 4, 3050, Tel: 4919 1220
KALUNDBORG, Koch's Bøger & Papir
Kordilgade 9, 4400, Tel: 5951 0054
KJELLERUP, Ide & Hobby
Søndergade 12, 8620, Tel: 8688 1326
KØBENHAVN S, EB Games
Reberbanegade 3, 2300, Tel: 3296 7552
KØBENHAVN K, EB Games
Kalvebod Brygge 59, 1560, Tel: 3312 7172
KØBENHAVN K, EB Games
Nygade 3, 1164, Tel: 3332 0248
KØBENHAVN N, Steenbergs Bog & idé
Nørrebrogade 163, 2200, Tel: 3585 5277
KØBENHAVN K, Fantask
Skt. Pederstræde 35, 1453, Tel: 3393 8538
KØBENHAVN K, Bog & idé Fisketorvet
Fisketorvet 133, 1560, Tel: 3395 0700
KØBENHAVN S, Bog & idé Amager
Amager Centret 103, 2300, Tel: 3254 3666
KØGE, Køge Bog & Papirhandel
Nørregade 12, 4600, Tel: 5665 0082
KOLDING, EB Games
Skovvangen 42, 6000, Tel: 7550 1079
KOLDING, Good Games
Låsbygade 13, 6000, Tel: 7550 0304
LEMVIG, Legekæden Lemvig
Torvet 13, 7620, Tel: 9782 1511
LYNGBY, BO Bøger Lyngby
Lyngby Storcenter 54, 2800, Tel: 4587 0445
LYNGBY, EB Games
Lejemål 2750, 2800, Tel: 4587 0509
MARIBO, Legekæden Maribo
Østergade 3, 4930, Tel: 5478 2521
NÆSTVED, Georg Christensen Bog & idé
Axeltorv 10, 4700, Tel: 5572 2024
NÆSTVED, Holsted Bog & idé
Næstved Storcenter 16, 4700, Tel: 5573 4241
NÆSTVED, Langes Bog & idé
Torvestræde 3, 4700, Tel: 5572 0116
NAKSKOV, Tusind ting
Søndergade 12, 4900, Tel: 5492 2697
NYKØBING F, Bog & idé Nykøbing F.
Jernbanegade 8, 4800, Tel: 5485 2373
NYKØBING M, Morsø Boghandel
Algade 1, 7900, Tel: 9772 0700
NYKØBING Sj, Bog & idé Nykøbing Sj.
Algade 32, 4500, Tel: 5991 0006
NYKØBING F, Hundehuset
Jernbanegade 33, 4800, Tel: 5486 0846
ODDER, Legekæden Odder
Rosens Gade 32, 8300, Tel: 8654 4276
ODENSE C, EB Games
Kongensgade 43, 5000, Tel: 6612 9929
ODENSE C, BO Bøger Odense C
Vestergade 59-61, 5000, Tel: 6611 4033
ODENSE SØ, BO Bøger Rosengårdscentret
Rosengårdscentret 53 Gul Gågade, 5220,
Tel: 6615 9928
ODENSE SØ, EB Games
Ørbækvej 75, 5220, Tel: 6395 0070
RANDERS, Bog & idé Randers
Brødregade 6, 8900, Tel: 8643 0810
RANDERS, Byrge Sørensen Hobby
Rådhustorvet 4, 8900, Tel: 8642 5814
RANDERS, Randers Hobby Import
Adelgade 13, 8900, Tel: 8643 3923
RINGE, Fjords Bog & idé
Kirkepladsen 2, 5750, Tel: 6262 1125
RINGKØBING, Buddy Legetøj
Algade 4, 6950, Tel: 9732 0806
RINGSTED, Buddy Legetøj
Nørregade 15, 4100, Tel: 5767 1480
RISSKOV, Bog & idé Vejlby-Risskov
Veri Centret Frijsenborgvej 5, 8240,
Tel: 8621 5329
RØDOVRE, B.O. Bøger Rødovre
Rødovre Centrum 116, 2610, Tel: 3641 0485
RØDOVRE, EB Games
Rødovre Centrum 68, 2610, Tel: 3672 1227
RØNNE, Dorthe's Hobbystue
Lilletorv 14, 3700, Tel: 5695 9449
RØNNE, William Dam Bog & idé
Snellemark 36, 3700, Tel: 5695 0167
ROSKILDE, EB Games
Stationcenteret 2, 4000, Tel: 4637 1516
ROSKILDE, Flensborg Bog & idé
Stændertorvet 4, 4000, Tel: 4635 0008
ROSKILDE, Ønskeleg
Algade 28C, 4000, Tel: 4632 3463
SÆBY, Bøger & Papir Sæby
Grønnegade 22, 9300, 9846 1644
SKJERN, Bog & idé Skjern
Jernbanegade 14, 6900, Tel: 9735 1666
SILKEBORG, Bog & idé Silkeborg
Vestergade 31-33, 8600, Tel: 8682 0287
SILKEBORG, Byens Hobby & Fritid
Borgergade 49-51, 8600, Tel: 8681 5815
SILKEBORG, Gunzone
Frederiksberggade 1, 8600, Tel: 0045 8761 1112
SKAGEN, Legekæden Skagen
Sct. Laurentiivej 40, 9990, Tel: 9844 5465
SKANDERBORG, Schmidt Bog & idé
Adelgade 82, 8660, Tel: 8652 0027
SKIBBY, Bog & idé Skibby
Bymidten 2, 4050, Tel: 4751 2502
SKIVE, Jydsk Boghandel
Nørregade 19, 7800, Tel: 9751 2599
SLAGELSE, Bog & Idé Slagelse
City 3 Jernbanegade 7, 4200, Tel: 5852 0015
SLAGELSE, EB Games
Vestsjællandscentret 4, 4200, Tel: 5852 1120
SLAGELSE, Uldtotten
Nygade 2, 4200, Tel: 5853 5035
SORØ, Legekæden Sorø
Holberg arkaden 11, 4180, Tel: 5783 3705
SØNDERBORG, Bogcentret
Perlegade 77, 6400, Tel: 7442 2071
SØNDERBORG, Bog & idé Sønderborg
Perlegade 15, 6400, Tel: 7442 1820
ST HEDDINGE, Hobbystalden
Lejrstoftevej 19, Lejrtofte, 4660, Tel: 5650 8610
STENLØSE, EB Games
Stenlöse Center, 3660, Tel: 4717 2500
STENLØSE, Legekæden Stenløse
Stenløse centret 48, 3660, Tel: 4717 3220
STRUER, Hanne Madsen Bog & idé
Østergade 14, 7600, Tel: 9785 0408
SVENDBORG, B.O. Bøger Svendborg
Gerritsgade 28, 5700, Tel: 6217 2290
SVENDBORG, Farve & Hobby Hjørnet
Klosterplads 7, 5700, Tel: 6221 3131
TÅSTRUP, EB Games
City 2 Butik, 341 City 2 Butik, 341,
Tel: 4399 2245
TÅSTRUP, Genbrugsbøger
Køgevej 95, 2630, Tel: 4371 6115
THISTED, Bog & idé Thisted
Vestergade 14, 7700, Tel: 9792 0399
THISTED, Buddy Legetøj
Vestergade 4, 7700, Tel: 9792 1933
TØNDER, Jefsen Bog & idé
Storegade 5, 6270, 7472 2341
TORSHAVN, P/F Thomas Dam Wholesale
Boks 2148, Faro Islands, Tel: 298311400
VARDE, Bog & idé Varde
Vestergade 18, 6800, Tel: 7522 0040
VÆRLØSE, Bog & idé Værløse
Bymidten 45 - 47, 3500, Tel:+298 311400
VEDBÆK, Bog & idé Trørød
Trørød Torv, Trørødvej 70, 2950, Tel: 4589 1328
VEJLE, B.O. Bøger Vejle
Å-centret 10, Søndergade 24-26, 7100,
7582 0544
VIBORG, Battle Bunker
Jernbanegade 19, 8800, Tel: 8660 1740
VIBORG, L. K. Bog & idé
Sct. Mathias Marked 202, 8800, Tel: 8662 7762
VIBORG, Schous Bog & idé
Hjultorvet 5, 8800, Tel: 8725 7334
VIBY, Rybner Bog & idé
Viby Centret, 8260, Tel: 8611 9930
VORDINGBORG, Legekæden Vordingborg
Algade 63, 4760, Tel: 5534 0431

FALKLANDS

STANLEY, Falkland Collectables
The General Store, Tel: 00500 21174

FINLAND

GW HELSINKI
Simonkatu 9, 00100, Tel: 00358 975 154 525
HELSINKI, Fantasiapelit Helsinki
Vilhonkatu 4B, 00100, Tel: +358 9 650803
LAHTI, Puolenkuun Pelit
Rautatienkatu 16, 15110, Tel: +358 3 7515151
ESPOO, Pelimesta
Ulappakatu 1, 02320, Tel: +358 9 813328
JOENSUU, Fantasiapelit Joensuu
Kauppakatu 32, 80100, +358 13 2843144
JYVÄSKYLÄ, Fantasiapelit Jyväskylä
Kauppakatu 2, 40100, Tel:+358 14 216629
OULU, Fantasiapelit Oulu
Koulukatu 28, 90100, Tel: +358 8 374906
TAMPERE, Fantasiapelit Tampere
Rongankatu 5, 33100, Tel: +358 3 2225200
TURKU, Fantasiapelit Turku
Yliopistokatu 33A, 20100, Tel: +358 2 2328413
KUOPIO, Fantasiapelit Kuopio
Myllykatu 9, 70110, Tel: +358 17 361 1148
FORSSA, Fun Stuff & Cards
Hämeentie 7 Torikeskus, 30101, Tel: +358 34356585
HANKO, Hobby Jobi
Vuorikatu 10, 10900, Tel: +358 19 2485498
HEINOLA, Talousmuovi ja lelu
Kauppakatu 19, 18100, Tel: +358 3 7153905
HELSINKI, Fantasiapelit Varasto
PL 129, 00531 HKI, +358 9 7734756
HYVINKÄÄ, Royal Toys
Muottikatu 5, 05830, Tel: +358 19 439376
IISALMI, Taikatalo
Savonkatu 12, 74100, Tel: +358 17 826358
IMATRA, Kirja-Lahja Alex Ky
Mansikankuja 2, 55120, Tel:+358 5 4319555
JÄMINKIPOHJA, Vanha Kaarti
Kiimkallionntie 205A, 23210, Tel: +358 3 4762886
JÄMSÄ, Jaakko Saari
Välitie 1, 42100, Tel: +358 14 7497215
JÄRVENPÄÄ, Askertelutarvikeliike Taitaville
Helsingintie 13, 04400, Tel:+358 50 413 47 60
KAJAANI, Leppäkerttu
Kauppakatu 34, 87100, Tel: +358 8 6133 773
KERAVA, Antikvariaatti Kersa
PL 38, Torikatu 1, 04201, Tel: +358 9 2944210
KARHULA, Eagle Card
Eteläinen Karjalantie 7, 48600, Tel: +358 5 214238
KOUVOLA, Muoviepox
Valtakatu 3, 45100, Tel: +358 5 3117955
KUUSANKOSKI, Kirja Savinen
Kauppa-aukio 1, 45700, Tel: +358 5 3748271
LOHJA, Lohjan Kirjakauppa
Laurinkatu 48, 08100, +358 19 324150

NE Elite Store
NE Partner Store

MAARIEHAMN, Dillen
Torggatan 7, 22100, +358 18 15578
MIKKELI, Muppela
Porrassalmenkatu 21, 50100,
Tel: +358 15 361611
NUMMELA, Kimmon Peli &Lehti
Tuusantie 1, 3100, +358 9 2226041
PORI, Porin Pitkis
HerttuanTori 2.Krs, 28100, Tel: +358 2 633 2880
PORVOO, Askarteluaitta/Hobbyboden
Mannerheiminkatu 10, 06100,
Tel: +358 19 5243775
RAAHE, Raahen Astartelu ia Paperi
Lahdekorventie 32, 37130
RAUMA, Wanhan Rauman POP-peli
Nortamonkatu 14, 26100, Tel: +358 2 8234840
ROVANIEMI, Liigacenter Jässi
Rovakatu 28, 96200, Tel: +358 16 3560545
SALO, Salon Harraste
Vilhonkatu 21, 24240, Tel: +358 16 3560545
SAVONLINNA, Savonlinnan Antikvariaatti
Olavinkatu 51, 57100, Tel: +358 15 534412
SEINÄJOKI, Fantasialinna
Vapaudentie 51, 60100, Tel: +358 405616338
SEINÄJOKI, Pitkäkiekko
Verkatehtaan katu 4, 60100, Tel:+358 6 4177880
TAMPERE, Gamelife
Rautatienkatu, 33100, Tel: +358 3 2121244
TAMPERE, Info Koskikeskus
Koskikeskus, Iokero 28, 33100,
Tel: +358 3 2251850
VAASA, Nirunaru
Rauhankatu 19, 65100, Tel: +358 6 3127027
VALKEAKOSKI, Valkeakoskenkirja
Kauppakatu 3, 37600

GREECE

ATHENS, Fantasy Shop: Peristeri
Themistokleous 52 & Theokritou,
Tel: 0030 210 5774344
ATHENS, Action Hobbies
Cholargos, Tel: 0030 210 6564515
ATHENS, Fantasy Shop: Halandri
Kolokotroni & Gini 6, Tel: 0030 210 6897396
ATHENS, Fantasy Shop
3 Septemvriou 65, Tel: 0030 210 8231072
ATHENS, Fantasy shop: Ag. Paraskevi
Agiou Ioannou 24B, Tel: 0030 210 6005312
ATHENS, Fantasy Shop: Kifisia
Drosini & D. Kryiakou 16,
Tel: 0030 210 8016041
ATHENS, Fantasy Shop: Peiraias
Ypsilantou 116, Tel: 0030 210 4135757
ATHENS, Fantasy Shop: Exarcheia
Themistokleous 43-45, Tel: 0030 210 3828877
ATHENS, Kaissa Amarousiou
Kondili 7, Tel: 0030 210 6141675
ATHENS, Kaissa Chess & Games
Kallidromiou 8 & Ippohratous 114 72,
Tel: 0030 210 366488
ATHENS, Kaissa Glyfadas
Xorikon 4, Tel: 0030 210 8982 057
ATHENS, Kaissa Halandriou
Doukisis Plakentias, Tel: 0030 210 6898485
ATHENS, Kaissa Monokeros
Tritis Septemvriou, Tel: 0030 210 8813 990
ATHENS, Kaissa Pagratiou
116 34, Pl. Messologiou 2-4, Pagrati,
Tel: 00 30 210 7218 318
ATHENS, Kaissa Peiraia
Ipsilantou 174-176, Tel: 0030 210 4296 636
ATHENS, Kaissa Pigasos
Dilou 22, Tel: 0030 210 5786707
CHANIA, Kaissa Chanion
73 100, 109 Kydonias St, Tel: 0030 2821088996
CRETE, Fantasy Shop: Herakleion
Idomenes 2, Tel: 0030 2810 301312
CRETE, Kaissa Hania
Kydonias 107, Tel: 0030 28210 88996
HALKIDA, CD Corner
Miaouli 24, Tel: 0030 2221 087315
KALLITHEA, Fantasy Shop Kallithea
Irakleous 110a, Tel: 0030 29210 28782
LARISA, Kaissa Larisas
Koumoundourou 22, 0030 2410 537337
MAROUSI, Battle Bunker
Dionysou 9, Tel: 0030 2102528738
PATRA, Fantasy Shop:Patra
Pantanassis 75, Tel: 0030 2610 221014
PATRAS, Kaissa Patras
Gounari & Sisini 24, Tel: 0030 2610625632
PERISTERIOU, Kaissa Peristeriou
Dilou 22, Tel: 0030 2105786707
PIREUS, Dragons Eye Store
Fleming 42, Keratsini, Tel: 00302 106929169
THESSALONIKI, Fantasy Shop: Thessaloniki
Pl. Navarinou 2 & D. Gounari,
Tel: 0030 2310 240193
THESSALONIKI, Kaissa Thessalonikis
546 22, Skra 4, Tel: 00 30 2310 257 397
VOLOS, Fantasy Shop
Glavani 98-100 & Galias,Tel: 0030 24210 28782

HUNGARY

BUDAPEST, Silverland
1036, Lajos u. 40, Tel: 0036 125 04157
BUDAPEST, Trollbarlang
1061, Andrassy ut. 33, Tel: 0036 132 13279
GYOR, New Ork
9021, Arany J. u. 13 II em,
Tel: 0036 706 012 310
MISKOLC, Deron
3525, Deryne u. 7, Tel: 0036 464 11528
SZOMBATHELY, Sarkanytuz
9700, Kossuth L. u. 20, Tel: 0036 703 188 815
SZEKESFEHERVAR, Legendak Csarnoka
8000 Pityer u. 42, Tel: 0036 703 857 926
SZEGED, Csillagveg
6722, Gogol u. 15, Tel: 0036 203 371 501
VESZPREM, Sarkanytuz
8200, Kossuth ut. 10a, Tel: 0036 705 994 130

ICELAND

REYKJAVIK, Nexus
HVERFISGATA 1P03 125, Tel: +354 5529011

ISRAEL

HAIFA, Kitaro
Haifa grand mall, Tel: 00972 48503232
HERZLIA, Freak
Sokolov 29, Tel: 00972 99589077
RAMAT HASHARON, Tapuah
Osishkin 33, Tel: 00972 35404713
RAMAT HASHARON, Tapuah Fantasy
Sokolov 30
TEL-AVIV, Kitaro
Merkaz baalei Hamelacha 12a,
Tel: 00972 36299320
TEL AVIV, Freak
Even Gevirol 60, Tel: 00972 36961826

LITHUANIA

KAUNAS, JSC in Diza
Droiugystes str.15, 51226 Kaunas 31, Tel: 370 37763203

MALTA

MALTA, Forbidden Power
83 Triq Misrah Il-Barrieri, Msida,
Tel: 00356 21 227999
MALTA, K Hobbies Ltd
Mpesch Road, Fgura Pla 13,
Tel: 00356 21 686423

NETHERLANDS

GW AMSTERDAM
Rokin 36, 1012 KT, Tel: 020 622 3863
GW DEN HAAG
Schoolstraat 12B, 2511 AX, Tel: 070 392 7836
GW HAARLEM
Gierstraat 29, 2011 GA, Tel: 023 551 7677
GW ROTTERDAM
Van Oldenbarneveldplaats 452, 3012 AP,
Tel: 010 280 0268
ARNHEM, Spelkwartier Arnhem
Steenstraat 4, 6828 CJ, Tel: 026 370 2028
BREDA, Modelbouw Bliek
Boschstraat 23, 4811 GA, Tel: 076 521 8596
BREDA, Modelbouw Bliek
Boschstraat 23, 4811 GA, Tel: 076 521 8596
DEN BOSCH, De Dobbelsteen
Hinthamerstraat 90, 5211 MS, Tel: 073 614 5530
LEIDEN, Vliegershop
Turfmarkt 2, 2312 CD, Tel: 071 513 2783
MAASTRICHT, Vlieg-er-uit
Brusselsestraat 70, 6211 PG, Tel: 043 325 1653
ZWOLLE, Games-n-Stuff
Diezerpoortenplas 38, 8011 VX,
Tel: 038 421 6385
ALKMAAR, Bookers & Strippers
Boterstraat 19, 1811 HP, Tel: 072 512 1213
ALMERE HAVEN, Fantasia
Kerkgracht 41, 1354 AE, Tel: 036 531 6017
AMERSFOORT, Spellenwinckel
Scherbierstraat 4-6, 3811 EA, Tel: 033 470 0322
ASSEN, Plok
Stationstraat 1, 9401 KV, Tel: 059 231 3292
BERGEN OP ZOOM, Big Boys Toys
Lievevrouwestraat 23, 4611 JJ, Tel: 0164 25 0848
DEN HAAG, Spellenhuis
Zoutmanstraat 94, 2518 GT, Tel: 070 364 4782
ENSCHEDE, Pijplines
Pijpenstraat 34, 7511 GM, Tel: 053 430 5727
GRONINGEN, Krikke's Hobbyshop
Nieuwe Weg 28, 9711 TE, Tel: 050 312 9314
NIJMEGEN, Moenen & Mariken
Van Welderenstraat 70, 6511 MP,
Tel: 024 323 6119
TILBURG, Labyrinth Tilburg/Breda
Langestraat 176, 5038 SH, Tel: 013 544 3700
ALMELO, Somberg Modelbouw
Grotestraat 136, 7607 CW, Tel: 054 681 2981
ALPHEN AAN DEN RIJN, Top 1 Toys Arie vd Panne
Hooftstraat 66-68, 2406 GL, Tel: 0172 47 2254
AMSTELVEEN, Het Ganzenbord
Parlevinker 59, 1186 ZB, Tel: 020 641 2552
AMSTELVEEN, De Groot Toy Special Store
Rembrandthof 42, 1181 ZL, Tel: 020 347 3344
APELDOORN, Top 1 Toys - De Kinderdroom
Oranjerie 158, 7311WG, Tel: 055-5761098
BERGEYK, Wouters Technohobby
Pankenstraat 31, 5571 CP, Tel: 049 755 0248
BUSSUM, Bakx Modeltreinen
Laarderweg 3, 1402 BA, Tel: 035 691 8410
DELFT, Top 1 Toys Speldorado
Hippolytusbuurt 21-25, 2611 HM,
Tel: 015 213 4516
DEN BOSCH, Gameforce
Vughterstraat 60, D2, Tel: 73 7505883
DEN HAAG, Intertoys Theresiastraat
Theresiastraat 280-284, 2593 AX,
Tel: 070 347 3120
DEVENTER, Knibbel Comics
Nieuwstraat 38, 7411 LM, Tel: 057 061 6879
DORDRECHT, Hobby Modelbouw Dordrecht
Voorstraat 360, 3311 CX, Tel: 078 631 2711
EDE, Tinnen Soldaat
Weerdestein 24, 6714 CS, Tel: 0318 65 3296
EINDHOVEN, Gameforce Eindhoven
Visserstraat 18a, 5612 BT, Tel: 040 2447030
EMMEN, Spirithoes
Derksstraat 154, 7811 AJ, Tel: 0591 645787
GELEEN, Tactica
Anjelierstraat 3, 6163 CJ, Tel: 046 474 3016
GOES, Fantus Fantasy Store
Groene Weidje 16, 4461 JW, Tel: 011 325 8174
GORINCHEM, Netten Modelbouw
Kwekelstraat 30, 4201 JV, Tel: 018 363 6000
GOUDA, Intertoys v/d Wal
Nieuwe Markt 70, 2801 GP, Tel: 018 251 3525
GOUDA, The Movie Store
Lange Groenendaal 114, 2801 LV,
Tel: 018 252 2550
GRONINGEN, Wirwar
Oude Kijk in 't Jatstraat 40, 9712 EL, Tel: 050 314 8424
HENGELO, Top 1 Toys Mickey van Wezel
Burg. Jansenplein 14-17, 7551 EC,
Tel: 074 291 2200
HOORN, Het Gele Teken
Grote Oost 35, 1621 BR, Tel: 022 921 8623
LEEUWARDEN, Brattinga Speelgoed
St. Jacobsstraat 4, 8911 HT, Tel: 058 212 5682
LEIDEN, Tolkienwinkel
Hoge Rijndijk 195, 2314 AD, Tel: 071 541 2324
LELYSTAD, Treinenhoek
Botter 44-15, 8243 JE, Tel: 032 025 3160
MAASTRICHT, Hounjet
BurgemeesterCortenstr 18, 6226 GV,
Tel: 043 363 6778
MIDDELBURG, De Burcht
Londensekaai 19, 4331 JG, Tel: 06 2830 3895
NEUNEN, Schellens Speelgoed
Parkstraat 24, 5671 GG, Tel: 040 283 2984
OEGSTGEEST, De Tombe Toys for Boys... and Men
De Kempenaarstraat 77, 2341 GS,
Tel: 071 517 2977
OUD-BEIJERLAND, Mourits Model-Hobby
Croonenburgh 32, 3261 RG, Tel: 0186 62 1931
PANNINGEN, Top 1 Toys Marc Janssen
Markt 18, 4981 AN, Tel: 077-4634566
ROERMOND, Bloemboetiek Hermien
Nassaustraat 66, 6043 ED, Tel: 047 532 1710
ROOSENDAAL, Jadin
Oude Markt 58, 4701 PM, Tel: 0165 55 7964
SCHIEDAM, BTS
Groenelaan 49, 3114 CB, Tel: 010 473 8755
SCHIJNDEL, Top 1 Toys Anniek
Hoofdstraat 133, 5481 AD, Tel: 073-5477758
SLUIS, Top 1 Toys E. v/d Vijver
Oude Kerkstraat 7, 4524 CT, Tel: 011 746 1393
SOEST, Top 1 Toys Soest
V Weedestraat 16, 3761 CE, Tel: 035 629 0444
SPIJKENISSE, Lord of Magic
Spuistraat 7, 3201 AR, Tel: 0181 619061
TIEL, Goblincave
Zonnebloemstraat 12,4001, DZ,
Tel: 0344 654 689
UDEN, Goblin
Brabantplein 16a, 5401 GS, Tel: 041 327 0662
UTRECHT, Elf Fantasy Shop
Oude gracht 207, 3511 NH, Tel: 030 281 7157
UTRECHT, Whoops
Springweg 1, 3511, Tel: 030 230 4123
UTRECHT, Never Never Land (Wieder & Kugant)
Oude Gracht 202, 3511 NR, Tel: 030 233 2293
VELSERBROEK, Mol Plastic Modelbouw
Zadelmakerstraat 64, 1991 JE, Tel: 023 537 6016
VENLO, Modelbouw Luthart
Assendorperstraat 103, 8012 DH,
Tel: 077 354 2688
WASSENAAR, Top 1 Toys Kouwenhoven
Langstraat 79, 2242 KK, Tel: 070 511 0211
WORMERVEER, Mini-Wonders
Antillenstraat 1, 1521 AT, Tel: 075 640 1617
WINTERSWIJK, Top 1 Toys Winterswijk
Misterstraat 60, 7101 EX, Tel: 054 351 2827
ZOETERMEER, RC-Pitstop
"Dorpsstraat 179, 2712 AJ, Tel: 079 316 0560
ZUTPHEN, Vreemde Zaak
Groene markt 2, 7201 HX, Tel: 057 551 1566
ZWOLLE, Boekenhalte
Assendorperstraat 103, 8012 DH,
Tel: 038 422 1077
ZWOLLE, Top 1 Toys - De Wit
Diezerstraat 97/99, 8011 RD, Tel: 038-4217176

NORWAY

GW OSLO
Møllergata 7, 0179, Tel: 22332990
BERGEN, Here Be Games
Jonsvollsgata 7, 5011, Tel: +47 5532 87 90
KRISTIANSAND, Hobby Huset
Henrik Wergelandsgt. 26-36, N-4612,
Tel: 38020310
ÅLESUND, Kremmerhuset
Langelands v24,Spjelkavik, N-6022,
Tel: 70143770
ARENDAL, Hobby Huset Arendal
Torvgaten 1, N4836, 37404585
ARENDAL, Norli Arenasenter
Torvet 10, N-4800, 37025454
BÆRUM, Ringo Bærums Verk Leker
Vertshus veien 2, N-1317, Tel: 067133850
BERGEN, YES Vi Leker Oasen Leker
Oasen Storsenter, Tel: 055161280
BERGEN, Outland Bergen
Fortunen 4, 5013, Tel: 35061132
BERGEN, Ringo Lekeklossen
Østre Nesttunvei 16, N-5221, 55922650
BJØRKLANGEN, FX Hobby
FX Hobby A/S, Bjorkeveien 2,1940,
Tel: 63851195
BODØ, Underholdningsmagneten
Sandgt. 3, N-8006, Tel: 75525070
DOKKA, Yes vi leker Dokka
Bergfoss senteret N2870, Tel: 61112090
EGERSUND, Brio Glasmagasinet Øgrey
Storgt. 33-36, N-4370, Tel: 51461900
FAUSKE, Ringo Smart
Storgt. 72, N-8200, Tel: 75646022
FLISA, Ringo Bamsefar
Flisa Stormarked, N-2270, Tel: 62958290
FREDRIKSTAD, Leketorvet
Brock Gt 7-11, Tel: 69315630
FORDE, Ringo Leikehuset
Storehagen 9, N-6800, Tel: 57820102
GJØVIK, Ringo Leke-Olsen
Storgt. 10 , N-2815, Tel: 61108210
HAMAR, Lekehuset Maxi
Aslak Botts gt. 48, N-2316, Tel: 62533808
HARSTAD, Smått og Rått
Strand Gata, N9400, Tel: 77065774
HITRA, Ringo Hitra
Jorten Kjopsenter N7240, Tel: 72441245
HITRA, Yes Twins
Hitratorget 7240, Tel: 72441195
JESSHEIM, Brio Jessheim
Jessheim Storsenter, N-2050, Tel: 63973770
KONGSBERG, Ringo Rolf Liane AS
Kirkegaten 6, N-3616, Tel: 32731161
KONGSVINGER, Ringo Gågata Leker
Jernbanegt. 6, N-2211, Tel: 62817611
KRAGERØ, Brio Karis Hobby
Torvet 4, N3770, Tel: 35980484
KRISTIANSAND, Outland Kristiansand
Markensgt. 24, N-4611, Tel: 38099420
KROKSTADELVA, Helmax Leker,
Buskerud Storsenter Sandstranda 24, N-3054,
Tel: 32879910
LANGESUND, Ringo Tarangers Eftf. Per
Torvet 4, N-3970, Tel: 35973662
LARVIK, Ringo Sokrates
Tjölling Veien 38, 3262, Tel: 33185437
MO I RANA, Ringo Lekehjornet Mo
Nordahl Griegs Gt. 8, N-8622, Tel: 75151717
MOLDE, Yes vi leker Leke Jørnet
Torget 1 N6413, Tel: 71219363
MOSJØEN, Hobbysentret
C.M. Håvigsgt. 18, N-8651, Tel: 75170170
MOSS, Brio Frisenfeldt
Dronningensgt. 10, N-1530, Tel: 69251290
MYSEN, Brio Saker og Ting
Jernbane gaten 13, N-1850, Tel: 69890194
NARVIK, Brio Lek Center Narvik
Bolagsgata 1 Amfisentret, N-8514, Tel: 76963472
NARVIK, Ringo Barnas Verden
Kongensgt. 66-70, N-8514, Tel: 76946505
NESBRU, Ringo Eventyrland
Vogelund Veien 6 N1394, Tel: 66779410
OSLO, Yes Nesodden Bokhandel
Tangen Centrum, Nesodden, Tel: 66911855
OSLO, Brio Notabene Lambertseter
Langbølgen 5, N-1150, Tel: 22280551
OSLO, Outland Jernbanen
Jernbanetorget 1, N-0154, Tel: 22177010
OSLO, Outland Paleet
Karl johans Gate 37-43, Tel: 22330410
OSLO, Brio CC Vest
Lille Akerveien 16, N-0383, Tel: 22731777
RANDABERG, Ringo Sito
Randberg veien 372 N4070, Tel: 53429100
SANDNES, O Saeland
Langgaten 44, N-4031, Tel: 51661509
SANDVIKA, Hobby Larsen
Sandvika Storsenter, N-1300, Tel: 67540107
SKI, Brio Titt-Inn
Jernbanesvingen 6, N-1401, Tel: 64857777
SKIEN, Ringo Bjørns Leker
Liertorvet N3717, Tel: 35525209
SKIEN, Sokratis Hobby Gården
Skistredet 7, N-3707, 35528764
SOLA, Ringo Sola Gaver og Leker
Solakrossen, N-4050, Tel: 51651763
SONGDAL, Ringo Sogndal Glasmagasin
Sogningen Storsenter, N-6851, Tel: 57671880
SORTLAND, Ringo Bamse Leker
Skibsgården, N-8400, Tel: 76113374
STAVANGER, Veslefrikk
Skagen 12, N-4006, Tel: 51895232
STAVANGER, Outland Stavanger
Kirke gt 2, N-4006, 51938080
STOKMARKNES, Stokmarknes Aktietrykkeri
Markedsgt. 12, N-8455, Tel: 76117750
SYKKLYVEN, Ringo Blindheim
Kyrkeveien, 6239, Sykklyven, Tel: 70251029
TØNSBERG, Gledeshuset
Ø. Langgate 47, N-3110, Tel: 92251707
TROMSØ, Tromsø Bruktbokhandel
Kirkegt. 6, N-9008, Tel: 77686974
TRONDHEIM, Gotham,
Kongens gate 21, 7011, Trondheim,
Tel: 73512888
TRONDHEIM, Outland Trondhein
Munkegaten 58, 7011, Trondhein, Tel: 73520545
TRONDHEIM, Tronderfrim
St Olavs Gt 11 , N-7012, Tel: 73520840
TYNSET, Ringo Tynset Bokhandel
Brugt. 2A, N-2500, Tel: 62480038
VADSØ, Brio Vadsø
W. Andersensgt. 4, N-9811, 78942229

POLAND

BIALYSTOK, Departament Gier
ul. Legionowa 9/1, lok.153, 15-281
Tel: 0048 857 993 360
BIELSKO BIALA, Gnom
43-300, Szkolna 15, Tel: 0048 338 124 686
GDANSK, Spider Games
ul. Dywizjonu 303 nr.2, 80-462,
Tel: 0048 58 551 93 33
GDANSKI, Fenris
ul. Orkana 1, 83 000 Pruszcz
Tel: 0048 600 980 005
GDYNIA, Futurex
81-572, Waleriana Szefki, 2D/B8,
Tel: 0048 587 811 180
GDANSK, Iskra
80-239, Miszewskiego 16, Tel: 0048 585 201 952
GLIWICE, Game Station
ul. Boh. Getta Warszawskiego 12, 44-100,
Tel: 0048 504 255 194
JELENIA GORA, Avalon Galeria Karkonoska
Ul. 1 Maja 27, 58500,
KATOWICE, Bard Centrum Gier
40-049, Kosciuszki 8, Tel: 0048 322 571 817
KIELCE, Sklep RPG Gracz
25-300, Mala 12 (w bramie),
Tel: 0048 507 013 387
KRAKOW, Bard Centrum Gier
31-135, Batorego 20/17, Tel: 0048 126 320 735
LODZ, 'Ajk' Firma Ksiegarska
90-103, Piotrkowska 90, Tel: 0048 426 398 301
LODZ, Gamelord
90 425, Piotrkowska 101, Tel: 0048 631 1161
LUBIN, Balrog
59-300, Grottgera 9, 0048 602 714 813
LUBLIN, Krzys
20-009, Kapucynska 6, Tel: 0048 815 322 986
NOWY SACZ, Hobbit
33-100, Jagiellonska 50a, Tel: 0048 604 133 612
OPOLE, HMS II Computers
45-018, Krakowska 41a, Tel: 0048 774 547 413
POZNAN, Bard Centrum Gier
61-806, Sw. Marcina 41, Tel: 0048 618 538 277
POZNAN, Sklep Wilczek
ul. Zielona 1, Tel: 0048 615 036 52888
SWIEBODZIN, Czempioni
Os. Poludniowe 39, 66-200,
Tel: 0048 606229457
TORUN, Sklep Papierniczy
87-100, Szeroka 46, Tel: 0048 566 522 593
WARSZAWA, Arkana Ksiazki
Pl. Wilsona 4, Tel: 0048 228 399 417
WARSZAWA, Cytadela
02-777, Aleja Komisji Edukacji Narodowej 98,
Tel: 0048 601 323 209
WARSZAWA, Ksiegarnia Bellona
00-068, Krakowskie Przedmiescie 11,
Tel: 0048 228 261 707
WARSZAWA, Faber Faber SJ
02-515, Pulawska 11, Tel: 0048 228 491 265
WARSZAWA, Ksiegarnia Saska CENTAUR
03-966 Brazylijska 9, Tel: 0048 226 175 746
WARSZAWA, Sklep Morion SC
01-499, Powstancow Slaskich 124 Paw.155,
Tel: 0048 22 4239120
WARSZAWA, Warsaw Model Centre
ul. Powsinska 42/44. 02-903,
Tel: 0048 22 602 305 070
WARSZAWA, Warsaw Model Centre
ul. Bitwy Warszawskiej 1920 r. nr 4,
Tel: 0048 228 224 646
WARSZAWA, Warsaw Model Centre
ul. Ostrobramska 75 c, Tel: 0048 226 113 796
WROCLAW, Skavenblade Centrum Gier
ul. Ladna 15a, 50-353, Tel: 0048 600 426 371
WROCLAW, Skelp Pracownia Fantastyczna
ul. Sokolnicza 7/17, Tel: +48 71 354 43 44
WROCLAW, Bard Centrum Gier
50-079, Ruska 46C (Pasaz),
Tel: 0048 713 417 472
WROCLAW, Ogryn
50-052, Szewska 6/7, Tel: 0048 717 851 957
ZIELONA GORA, Avalon
DT Centrum, ul. Bomaterow Westerplatte 21A,
65-001

ROMANIA

CLUJ-NAPOCA, Otala
Regele Ferdinand 7, 400429, Tel: 00 4072
720696

RUSSIA

KRASNODAR, Alegris-Jug (South)
Krasnaya st, b43, Tel: 008612 730331
MINSK, Valahanovich ent
Jahn Kolas st, Exhibition center OLYMP,
Tel: 008029 6358212
MINSK, Valahanovich ent
Masherova av b4, Palace of Sports, second floor
Tel: 008029 6548426
MOSCOW, Alegris
Metro station Alieksiejewskaya Prospekt Mira 103,
Tel: 70952168126
MOSCOW, Alegris
Metro station Dubianka, Miasnickaya St. 20/1,
Tel: 70959283337
MOSCOW, Urfin Juice
Metro "Ulitsa 1905 goda" Zvenigorodskojo shosse
4, Tel: +79057846355
NORLISK, Na Styke Mirov
Komsomolskaya st, second floor, Dom Byta, 127
474,Tel: 008029 6548426
NOVOSIBIRSK, Icehummer
Krasnuy av, b50, Dom Byta
SARATOV, Detskiy Mir
Kirov av, b43, Detskiy Mir, second floor, gallery,
Tel: 64 5840
ST PETERBURGH, Art-Miniatures
Sedova st, b11, third floor, trade center Evrika,
Tel: 00812 3321828
TAMBOV, Hobby and Igrushki
Internatsionalnaya st, b54-b, Torgoviy Mir,
Tel: 0075 2728811

SERBIA-MONTENEGRO

BELGRADE, Exit Hobby Store
Cika Ljubina 1, Tel: 00381 11 62 78 27
BELGRADE, ANET Hobbystore
Visegradska 6, 11000, Tel: 00 381 11 3612 525
BELGRADE, ANET Hobbystore
11000, Zvecanska 1a, Tel: 00381 112652236
BELGRADE, White Dragon
11000, Vojvode Milenka 44,
Tel: 00 381 63827222
NOVI SAD, Valhala
21000,Masarikova 18, Tel: 00 381 21315538
NOVI SAD, Dragon
21000, Kralja Aleksandra 4,
Tel: 00 381 636 24038
PODGORICA, Neutron Podgorica
Trg Republike, Tel: 00 381 69 060 669
ZRENJANIN, Takeda
23000, Sarajlijina 5, Tel: 00 381 2364572

SLOVENIA

LJUBLJANA, Crna Luknja
1000, Poljanska 19, Tel: 00386 012802220
LJUBLJANA, Pri Goblinu
1000, Dolenjska Cesta 11, Tel: 00386 40833230

SOUTH AFRICA

BLOEMFONTEIN, The Dungeon
13 Short Street, 9301, Tel: 0027 51 447 2034
CAPETOWN, The Boys and Mens Hobby Shop
Shop 123, Tiger Valley Shopping Centre,
Tel: 0027 21 914 8688
CAPETOWN, Wizards
Shop G19, Stadium on the Main Road,
Tel: 0027 216830360
DORINGKLOOF, Battle Planet
No. 4WBH Centre, 177 Cecile Street,
Tel: 0027 8245 93933
DURBAN, The Hobby Specialists
Shop F174, Gateway Shopping Centre, no.1 Palm Boulevard, Uhlanga Ridge, New Town Centre, Umlanga,
Tel: 0027 031 564 9706
DURBAN, Wizards Warehouse
Shop L18, Windermere Centre, 163/177 Windermere Road, Morningside, 4001. Tel: 0027 31 312 8271
GAUTENG, Wizards Warehouse
Shop G4, Colony Shopping Centre, 3345 Jan Smuts Avenue, Craigihall Park, 2196. Tel: 0027 11 880 9252
JOHANNESBURG, Esswex Retail
Shop 20a Northcliff Corner Shopping Centre,
Tel: 0027 11 8883619
JOHANNESBURG, Wizards Warehouse
Lower level, Eden Vale, Tel: 0027 21 683 0360
LINMEYER, Dragons Den
203 Peter Avenue, Tel: 0027 082 824 4124
PRETORIA, The Smelly Troll
297 Lynnwood Road, Tel: 0027 0833 079107
RANDBURG, Otherland
Shop G10 B, Brightwater, Rebpublic Rd,
Tel: 0027 117944571
RUSTBERG, Quantum Books & Games
Boschdalstand 309/10, HelenJoseph Drive, 0300,
Tel: 0027 83 292 9373
SOUTH-AFRICA, Battle Planet
No 4 WBH Centre, 177 Cecile Street, Tel: 00 27
824593933

SWEDEN

GW GÖTEBORG
Kungsgatan 28, 411 19, Tel: 0046 311 33 958
GW STOCKHOLM
Regeringsgatan 30, 111 53, Tel: 0046 8 213 840
GÄVLE, Hobbyshopen
Drottninggatan 25, 80311, Tel: 026186299
UMEÅ, Fantasia
Storgatan 44, 903 26, Tel: 090770360
ESKILSTUNA, Lasses Leksaker
Kungsgatan 21, 632 20, Tel: 016130335
KARLSTAD, Spel och Fantasi
Kungastan 6, 65224, Tel: 054 15 10 70
MALMÖ, Utopia, Malmö
Regementsgatan 8, 211 42, Tel: 040 127250
NORRKÖPING, Hobbyhörnan
Drottningg 18, 602 24, Tel: 011162120
NORRKÖPING, Lekhuset
Järngatan 21, 602 23, Tel: 011287070
NORRTÄLJE, Fantasybutiken
Bältartorpsvägen 8, 761 32, Tel: 0176 57400
STOCKHOLM, Science Fiction Bokhandeln
Västerlång Gatan 48, 111 27, Tel: 08215052
SUNDSVALL, Orionspel och böcker
Köpmangatan 23, 852 32, Tel: 060155947
UPPSALA, Prisfyndet
Kungsgatan 39, 753 21, Tel: 018106607
VÄSTERÅS, Zetterlunds
Storagatan 33, 722 12, Tel: 021 10 44 91
VÄXJÖ, Helges Håla
Klosterg. 4, 352 30, Tel: 08715 25 01
ÄNGELHOLM, Leksaksmagasinet
Framtidsgatan 1,262 84, Tel: 0431 80527
ARVIKA, Perry Data
Köpmangatan 4, 67131, Tel: 057010669
ASARUM, Lek & Fritid
Granvägen 2, 374 52, Tel: 0454329906
AVESTA, Vega Video
Kungsgatan 16, 774 30, Tel: 022680078
BORÅS, Hobbex
Skaraborgsv 62-64, 506 30, Tel: 033418380
DEGERFORS, Buskul
Agensgatan 2, 693 30, Tel: 00 46 586 92 034
ESKILSTUNA, Barnens Hus
Folkestaleden 40, 635 10, Tel: 016481138
FALKÖPING, MysPys
Storgatan 22-26, 521 42, Tel: 051581150
FALKENBERG, Brio Falkenberg
Storgatan 35, 311 31, Tel: +46 (0) 346 807 60
FALUN, Tv-spelsbörsen
Falugatan 2, 791 71, Tel: 02327775
FINSPÅNG, Alltilek
Bergslagstorget, Kalkugnsgatan 1, 612 30,
Tel: 012214120
FÄRJESTADEN, Leksaksmagasinet
Ölands Köpstad, 386 31, Tel: 048534570
GISLAVED, Albe Leksaker
Södra Storgatan 10, 332 33, Tel: 037110733
GÄLLIVARE, Lekia
Metall Vägen 14, 982 38, Tel: 097066502
GUSTAVSBERG, Lilla Guls Barnsligheter
Gustavsberg Centrun, 134 40, Tel: 0857036800
HALMSTAD, Brio-Halmstad
Stormgatan 6, 302 60, Tel: 035159175
HUDIKSVALL, Albins Leksaker
Storgatan 24, 824 30, Tel: 0650595082
JÄRFÄLLA, Hobbex

GW Store

UK Elite Store

Flygavfarten, 17538, Tel: 0858018091**JÖNKÖPING, Play Planet**
St Göransvägen, 55454, Tel: 036122834
KALMAR, Ojtoy
Skeppsbrog. 12, 392 31, Tel: 048022002
KALMAR, Kalmar Lek & Hobby
Södra Långgatan 32, 392 32, Tel: 48024717
KARLSHAMN, Leksakshuset
Ronnbyg 37, 374 35, Tel: 045410381
KARLSKOGA, Leklådan
Bergsmansg 17, 691 31, Tel: 058633333
KARLSKRONA, Fact & Fiction
Norra Kungsgatan 7, 37133, Tel: 045516710
KARLSKRONA, Leksakshuset
Lallerstedtsgt.5, 37 154, Tel: 045524082
KATRINEHOLM, Leksaksboden
Köpmangatan 19, 64130, Tel: 0150 79720
KIRUNA, Lekhuset
Box 2081, 921 02, Tel: 098082550
KÖPING, MD Hobby
Schellegatan 7, 73732, Tel: 0736426178
KRISTIANSTAD, Spel På Vallgatan
Östra Vallgatan 2, 291 31, Tel: 044101091
KUNGÄLV, Lek & Hobby
Västra Gatan 62, 442 31, Tel: 30313940
KUNGSBACKA, Lek & Hobby
S.Torggatan 6, 434 30, Tel: 030014136
LAHOLM, Leksaksaffären
Trädgårdsgatan 14, 31222, Tel: 043010069
LANDSKRONA, Leksakshuset
Timmermansg. 45, 261 38, Tel: 041810790
LIDINGÖ, Karena
Stockholmsv 55c, 181 34, Tel: 087656680
LIDKÖPING, Brio Lidköping
Framnäs City 531 54, Tel: 00 46 510 289 00
LIDKÖPING, Game Maniacs
Änghagsgatan 11, 531 00, Tel: 0705 190274
LINKÖPING, Sagoland
Svedengatan 18, 58273, Tel: 013122290
LINKÖPING, Skogstrollet
Barnhemsg 5a, 582 20, Tel: 013124006
LJUNGBY, Brio-Ljungby
Eskilsgatan 1, 341 30, Tel: 037213481
LULEÅ, Barnens Hus
Barnv 25, 973 40, Tel: 0920220095
LUND, Spel på Clemenstorget
Clemenstorget 6, 22221, 046127810
LYCKEBY, Serieslussen
Riksv 34, 371 62, 045529959
MALMÖ, Lek & Spel pa Djäknegatan
Djäknegatan 2a, 211 35, Tel:040 120410
MORA, Lek & Hobby
Skalmyrsv. 33 Noret Köpcentrum, 792 30, Tel: 025071628
NACKA, Amusar
Siroccogatan 10, Terminalgatan 3, 131 34, Tel: 086440540
NYKÖPING, Laka TV Spel
Galleria Axet, Västra Storgatan 13, 61131, Tel: 0155281000
ÖREBRO, Lekcenter
Nygatan 32, 70211, Tel: 0196114983
ÖREBRO, Modellex AB
Engelbrektsgatan 30, 702 12, Tel: 0196111534
ÖRNSKÖLDSVIK, Sound & Vision
Skolgatan 11, 891 33, Tel: 066019924
ORMINGE, Happies
Orminge Centrum, 132 00
OSKARSHAMN, Brio-Oskarshamn
Lilla torget 572 30, Tel: 0491 170 66
ÖSTERSUND, Hobbyboden
Köpmangatan 31, 831 30, Tel: 063513310
PITEÅ, Barnens Hus
Backev 55, 941 47, Tel: 091119910
RIMBO, Fantasybutiken
Köpmannagatan 7, 76231, Tel: 017572777
SALA, Elons Leksaker
Rådhusgatan 10, 733 30, Tel: 022410314
SKELLEFTEÅ, Barnens Hus
Uppfinnarv 5, 931 42, Tel: 091013990
SKELLEFTEÅ, Lek & Hobby
Nygatan 49, 931 31, Tel: 091012980
SOLENTUNA, Barnens Hus
Bollstanäsv. 1, 192 78, Tel: 086269940
STENUNGSUND, Barnhuset
Stenungstorg, 444 30, Tel: 030380384
STOCKHOLM, Dragons Lair
Kungsholmstorg 8, 112 21, Tel: 08 654 60 50
STRÖMSTAD, Kjells Lek & Hobby
Södra Hamngatan 8, 452 30, Tel: 052615989
SVEDALA, Elbe Lekis
Storg 40, 233 31, Tel: 040400318
SÄFFLE, Bergers Lek & Bosättning
V:A Storgatan 1, 661 30, Tel: 053310345
SÖDERHAMN, Barnens Hus
E-Center, 826 40, Tel: 027014220
TOMELILLA, Alfs Leksaker
Norregatan 6, 273 30, Tel: 041710008
TROLLHÄTTAN, Partaj
Ladugårdsvågen 12, 461 70, Tel: 052079499
TUMBA, Leksakskungen
Tumba Torg 7, 147 30, Tel: 0853038000
TUMBA, Kom & Lek
Bryggarv. 5-7, 147 30, Tel: 0853060011
TÄBY, Hobby & Prylar
Vallatorp 1F, 18752, Tel: 0851050426
UMEÅ, Barnens Hus
Björnv 11, 906 40, Tel: 090777702
UPLANDS VÄSBY, Lekia
Dragonv. 86, 194 00, Tel: 859030933
UPPSALA, Barnens Hus
Bolandsgatan 15a, 753 23, Tel: 018602970
VARBERG, Spelbutiken
Norrgatan 10, 432 41, Tel: 0340678610
VETLANDA, Leksakslagret
Lasarettsgatan 21, 574 40, Tel: 038319990
VIMMERBY, Brio Vimmerby
Södra Industrigatan 15, 598 40, Tel: 049231188
VISBY, Lekstugan
Hästgaten 18, 621 57, Tel: 0498215050
VÄSTERVIK, Lekstugan
Hamn Gatan 38, 593 30, Tel: 049036171
VÄSTRA FRÖLUNDA, Toys
Markonigatan, 421 21, Tel: 031459401
VÄXJÖ, Helge Håla
Klosterg. 4,352 30, Tel: 08715 25 01
YSTAD, Tv Spelshörnan
Tobaksgatan 16, 271 41, Tel: 041166680

TURKEY

ISTANBUL, Sihir
Besiktas, Sinanpasa 235. Tel: 0090 212 227 9955
ISTANBUL, Gerekli Seyler
Tesvikiye, Kalici Sk. 111. Tel: 0090 212 291 0689
ISTANBUL, Ureten
Bakirkoy, Bahcesaray Sk. 6/A. Tel: 0090 212 660 8964
IZMIR, Excalibur
Alsancak, 1447 Sk. 4. Tel: 0090 232 464 7669

UKRAINE

KIEV, Charge
Lagerna str 40 (Metro Beresteska), Apt 29, Tel: 0038 0444567671

UK club directory

More information on page 116

GCN Gaming Club Network

1st Company Veterans (Warhammer World)
Contact: Chris and Scott
E-mail: info@1stcompanyveterans.net

Aftermath (East Anglia)
Contact: Lee Lowe
Phone: 07921 859 581
E-mail: leelowe@btopenworld.com

Armageddon Inc. (Bucks)
Contact: James Schofield
Phone: 01494 865 905

Battlenet (Norwich)
Contact: Richard Miller
Phone: 07710 702297
E-mail: Richard@battlenet.co.uk

Battlescar (Poole)
Contact: Paul Cleveland
Phone: 01202 385 632
E-mail: paul@battlescar.co.uk

Blackfish (North Walsham)
Contact: Guy Blashill
E-mail: guyblashill@yahoo.co.uk

Bracknell Forest Gamers
Contact: Daniel Currey
Phone: 07951 816 613
E-mail: d.currey@talk21.com

BRBBA (Bognor Regis)
Contact: Frank Hill
Phone: 07896 319683
E-mail: mrfrankhill@yahoo.com

Bridgend YMCA Games Club
Contact: Matt Churchill
Phone: 01656 668298
E-mail: velvetfiend@yahoo.co.uk

Brighton Warlords
Contact: Peter Cooke
Phone: 0797 409 4240
E-mail: Peter.cooke423@ntlworld.com

Buckenham Bone Crushers
Contact: Paul Girling
Email:www.banhamandthebucks.co.uk/wargames

Chelmsford Bunker
Contact: David Chilvers
E-mail: bunkersecretary@yahoo.co.uk

Clapham Wargames Guild (London)
Contact: Thomas Petit
Phone: 07966 969 309
E-mail: info@claphamwargamers.org.uk

Clayton Warlords(Hampshire)
Contact: Roger Smith
Phone: 07711 556 296
E-mail: Roger_gs_smith@hotmail.com

Coppull & Chorley Knights
Contact: Jonathan Taylor-Yorke
Website: http://cack-wargamesclub.net

Colchester Games Club
Contact: David Freeman
E-mail: info@colchestergamesclub.org.uk
Phone: 07859 775 572

Cross Swords Gaming Club
Contact: Anthony Cross
E-mail:antandshell@cross247.wanadoo.co.uk
Phone: 01752 837 133

Dice and Dagger (Bude)
Contact: Kurt Baker
E-mail: celtofkernow@aol.com

Dudley Darklords
Contact: Paul Sheldon
Phone: 01384 288 360

Dursley Games Club
Contact: Dan Bishop
Phone: 01453 549 377

Dysartes
Contact: Nick Johnson
Phone: 01924 374097

Edinburgh Pub Bowl League
Contact: Dave Avery
Phone: 07837 380713
E-mail: daveryedin@hotmail.com

Gambit Games UK
Contact: Gareth Wynn
E-mail: Gareth.wynn808@ntlworld.com

Gatekeepers Wargames Club (Shrewsbury)
Contact: James Sherry
Phone: 01743 369605 or 07792 469648
E-mail: n.sherry@btopenworld.com

Gobstyks (Lincoln)
Contact: Will Platten
Phone: 01522 803310
E-mail: info@gobstyks.co.uk

Hammer N Ales
Contact: Daniel Few
Phone: 07816 889028
E-mail: sonofsmy@hotmail.com

Hyde Clarendon Strategy Games Club
Contact: Paul Mather
E-mail: paul.mather@tameside.ac.uk

Jersey Privateers Gaming Club
Contact: Paul Noel
Phone: 01534 738192
E-mail: noelwarlock@aol.com

K.I.A (Midlands)
Contact: Che Webster
E-mail:Blackfalcon@bruxx.net

Kirriemuir Wargames Club
Contact: Michael Anderson
Phone: 01382 454068
E-mail:www.kirriemuirwargamesclub.co.uk

Last Stand (East Anglia)
Contact: John White
Phone: 07861 136140
E-mail: whitewater0034@hotmail.com

Leeds Night Owls
Contact: Steve Nolan
Phone: 0113 225 0461

Maccwargames (Macclesfield)
Contact: Duncan Harradine
Phone: 01625 612 579
E-mail: Harradine2002@yahoo.co.uk

Madgamers (Maidenhead)
Contact: Denis Jackman
Phone: 01628 540934
E-mail: DENIS_JACKMAN@hotmail.com

Middlesborough Gamers Club
Contact: Shaun Atherton
Phone: 01642 272 021

Mitcham Marauders (Mitcham)
Contact: Jason Fowler
Phone: 07766 3403472
E-mail: Mitcham-marauders@yahoo.co.uk

Newmarket Dwarf Wargames Society
Contact: Chris Peachey
Phone: 07967951289
E-mail: nktdwarf@hotmail.com

North West Warriors (Kendal)
Contact: Adam Turner
Phone: 07905 410 067
E-mail: Orc69@hotmail.com

Northumbrian Adventurer's Guild
Contact: Mark Anderson Coulter
Phone: 07906 193711
E-mail: nagonline@hotmail.co.uk

Nuneaton Model and Gaming Club
Contact: Brian McCormack
Phone: 07976 884 558

Oxford Gaming Club
Contact: Mike Sharp
Phone: 07802 764143
E-mail: Mike.sharp4@btopenworld.com

Phoenix Gaming Club (Rushden)
Contact: Darrell Lee
Phone: 07951 728142

Plymouth Association of Wargamers
Contact: Orlando Murrish
Phone: 0175 251 1402

Portbury Knights
Contact: Alan Vowles
Phone: 07771 985488
E-mail: alanvowles@msn.com

Rainhill Wargames Club
Contact: Paul Tennant
E-mail: paultennant@hotmail.com

Royal Guild of Minted Boards (Cheshire)
Contact: Christopher Fry
Phone: 07976 878732
E-mail: Chris_Fry@FryupFilms.com

Redcar Ironbeards
Contact: Ian Widdowson
Phone: 01642 503207

Sad Muppets Society (Basingstoke)
Contact: David Offen-James
E-mail: david@sadmuppets.org

The Spiky Club (Reading)
Contact: David Cole
E-mail: spikyclub@hotmail.com

South Oxfordshire Wargamers
Contact: Darren Basset
Phone: 0199 370 0226

St Aidans Warriors Club
Contact: Paul Fletcher
Phone: 01415 770196
E-mail: paulmcgregorfletcher@hotmail.com

Stirling Wargamers
Contact: Paul Brooks
Phone: 07879 612 033
E-mail: paul@treeandleaf.plus.com

Stortford Stormers
Contact: Richard Bower
Phone: 01279 465 574
E-mail: rb@abbyy.co.uk

Suffolk and Essex Gamers
Contact: Mark Aldhouse
Phone: 01440 785589*-

Swarmm Wargames Club
Contact: Matt Holden
Phone: 01473 827 208
E-mail: matt@holdenhouse.freeserve.co.uk

Swindon and District Wargamers
Contact: Paul Nettle
Phone: 01793 700609
E-mail: nettle.tribe@ntlworld.com

Tanelorn Wargames Club
Contact: Martin Turner
E-mail: Martin.Turner@Hess.com

TGC (Tamworth)
Contact: Phil Hannigan
Phone: 01827 287446
E-mail: philhannigan2002@yahoo.co.uk

That Dam Gaming Club (Newmillerdam)
Contact: Kyle Simms
E-mail: koolaworld90@hotmail.com

Tolworth 1st Founding
Contact: Peter Corps
Phone: 07788 790136

Tunbridge Wells Wargame Society
Contact: Colin Stone
Phone: 0175 340 0211
E-mail: colin@castone.freeserve.co.uk

Walburton Wargamers
Contact: Mike Roddham
Phone: 01245 554185
E-mail: walbertonwargamers@yahoo.co.uk

Watford Wargames Federation
Contact: Robert Phipps
Phone: 01494 465244
E-mail: rp@a-b-a.co.uk

Warlords of Walsall
Contact: John Davis
Phone: 01922 724278
E-mail: warlords_of_walsall@hotmail.com

Woking 1st Founding
Contact: Peter Corps
Phone: 07788 790136

Yeovil Games
Contact: Chris Lowe
Phone: 07811 843747

York Garrison (York)
Contact: Robey Jenkins
Phone: 07967 277994
E-mail: garrison_wargaming@yahoo.com

NE Elite Store NE Partner Store

ORDERING DIRECT

Fast, secure and straight to your door!

Games Workshop Direct is a fast, accurate and convenient service that lets you order your miniatures and other hobby products from the comfort of your home.

- We aim to despatch all orders in three days, straight to your door.
- You can order ANY Games Workshop product.
- Our Advance Order service lets you order models and products before they are released, guaranteeing you'll get them on the day of release.
- Available now are a range of models available only through Direct. Check out what's on offer this month!

HOW YOU CAN ORDER!

- **On the internet:** Visit our secure Online Store at: www.games-workshop.co.uk/store
- **In-Store:** Order from any Games Workshop Hobby Centre at the in-store order point.
- **By Phone:** Call the Hobby Specialists on: *0115 91 40000 (UK),* opening hours, Monday-Saturday: 10am-6pm, Sunday: 11am-5pm. *0115 918 4040 (Northern Europe)*
- **By FAX:** Fax your order on: *0115 916 8002 (UK) or 0044 115 916 8162 (Northern Europe)*
- **By Post:** Or the traditional way: Games Workshop Direct Sales, Willow Road, Lenton, Nottingham, NG7 2WS

+++DIRECT EXCLUSIVE+++
GWAIHIR
99111499048 £12

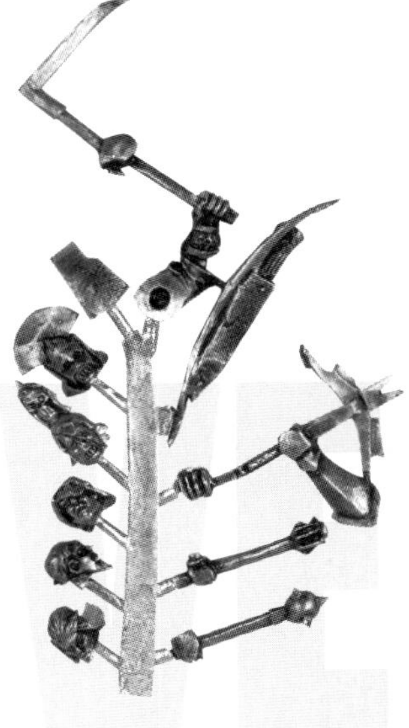

+++DIRECT EXCLUSIVE+++
CONVERSION SPRUE
9947149905501 £2
(Uruk-hai, Orc and Elf heads, two Human heads, Elf bow, Orc and Human weapons, Uruk-hai crossbow)

CALL THE HOBBY SPECIALISTS: 0115 91 40000

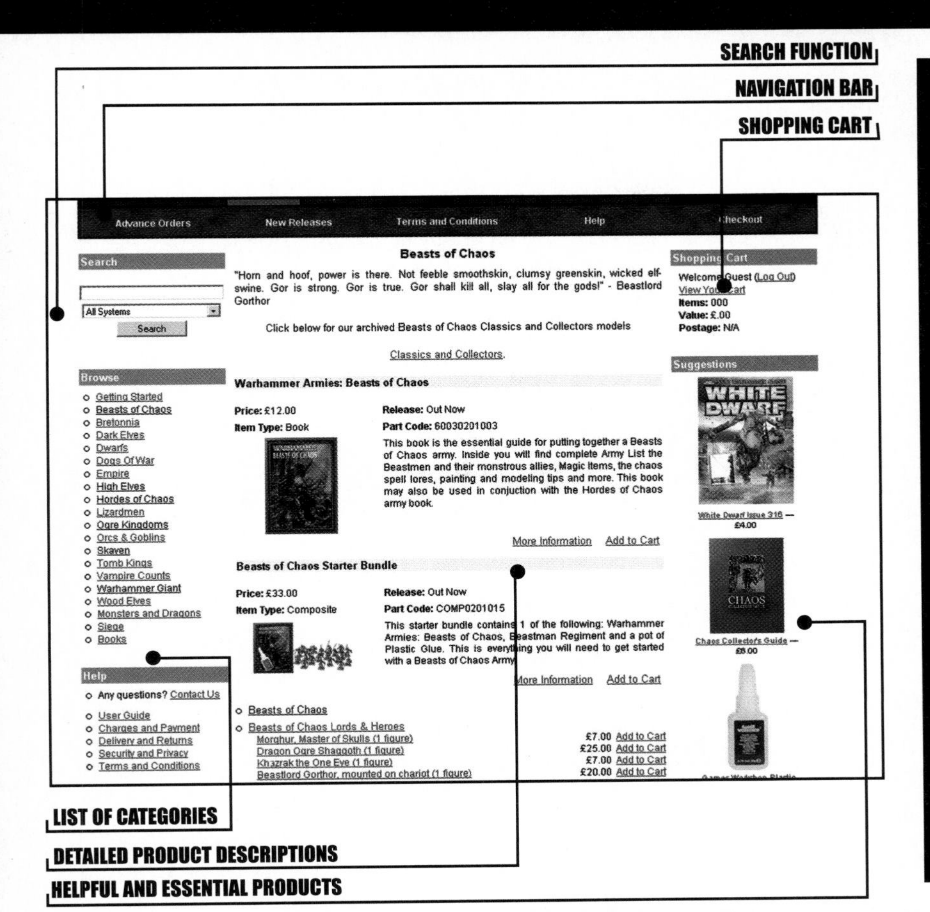

SHOPPING Online

The Games Workshop Online Store is open 24 hours a day, seven days a week.

Get exactly what you want, when you want it.

- **Huge range**
- **Secure**
- **Easy to use**
- **Open 24 hours**

This month's Online Store features:

- Legions of Middle-earth (pages 28-48): *www.games-workshop.co.uk/store/legionsofmiddleearth*
- The Two Towers (pages 50-59): *www.games-workshop.co.uk/store/thetwotowers*
- Medusa V (pages 71-78): *www.games-workshop.co.uk/store/CoD*
- Lizardmen (pages 66-69): *www.games-workshop.co.uk/store/lizardmen*
- High Elves (pages 82-85): *www.games-workshop.co.uk/store/highelves*

DEATH FROM ABOVE ARMY DEAL

As featured on page 104, Nicola Taylor's Tyranid army has been recreated as a bundle on the Online Store. Now you too can own this fast attacking 'Nid force.

INCLUDES:

- 1 Hive Tyrant
- 1 Death Leaper Lictor
- 5 Warrior boxes
- 1 Genestealer Brood box
- 2 Gaunt boxes
- 5 Gargoyle blisters
- 1 Biovore
- 1 Carnifex

\+

The following extra parts to make conversions:

- 1 Plastic Dragon Wings
- 6 Termagant sprues, 6 biomorph sprues
- 9 Dark Pegasus Right and Left wings.

NEW! THE LORD OF THE RINGS!

Uruk-hai

VRASKU BODY
9947146203701 **£5**

VRASKU CROSSBOW
9947146203702 **£0.60**

Rohan Outriders

ROHAN OUTRIDER ON FOOT 1
9947146410601 **£4**

ROHAN OUTRIDER ON FOOT 2
9947146410602 **£4**

Dunlendings

DUNLENDING CHIEFTAIN
9947146410701 **£4**

DUNLENDING STANDARD BODY
9947146410702 **£3**

DUNLENDING STANDARD
9947146410703 **£0.60**

DUNLENDING WITH SHIELD 1
9947146410803 **£2.50**

DUNLENDING WITH TWO-HANDED WEAPON 1
9947146410801 **£2.50**

DUNLENDING WITH BOW 1
9947146410805 **£2.50**

DUNLENDING WITH SHIELD 2
9947146410804 **£2.50**

DUNLENDING WITH TWO-HANDED WEAPON 2
9947146410802 **£2.50**

DUNLENDING WITH BOW 2
9947146410806 **£2.50**

You can find all these products online by logging on to: www.games-workshop.co.uk/store

Rohan Heroes

ERKENBRAND ON FOOT
9947146410501 **£5**

THEÓDRED ON FOOT
9947146410401 **£5**

ROHAN CAPTAIN 2
9947149906801 **£4**

AVAILABLE TO ORDER NEXT MONTH

Rohan

ROHAN CAPTAIN 1
9947146411201 **£4**

ROHAN STANDARD
9947146411301 **£3**

Haldir's Elves

LÓRIEN ELF CAPTAIN 1
9947146303001 **£4**

LÓRIEN ELF CAPTAIN 2
9947146303002 **£4**

continued on next page...

COLLECTORS' GUIDES

In-depth catalogues showing all the miniatures for each range.

- Full range
- Components
- Direct exclusives
- Golden Demon winners
- Army showcases
- Conversion showcases

Available now from Games Workshop Hobby Centres:

The Lord of The Rings Collectors' Guide

Warhammer 40,000 Collectors' Guides
- NEW! Forces of the Imperial Inquisition
- Imperial Guard
- Eldar & Dark Eldar
- Orks
- Tau & Necrons
- Tyranids

Warhammer Collectors' Guides
- Bretonnians
- Chaos
- Dwarfs
- Elven
- Lizardmen
- Monsters & Mercenaries
- Orcs & Goblins
- Skaven
- Undead

NEW! see page 22

 continued from previous page...

Osgiliath Veterans

OSGILIATH VETERAN WITH BOW
9947146411001 **£2.50**

OSGILIATH VETERAN WITH SPEAR
9947146411002 **£2.50**

OSGILIATH VETERAN WITH SWORD
9947146411003 **£2.50**

Defenders of Rohan

ARAGORN (HORNBURG)
9947146410901 **£5**

LEGOLAS (HORNBURG)
9947146303101 **£5**

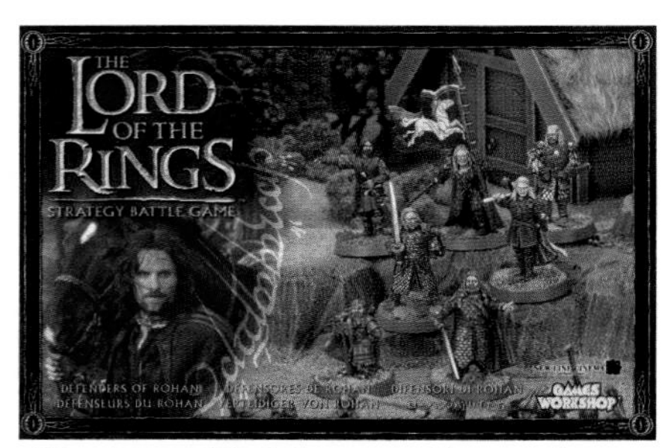

Also available as a boxed set

DEFENDERS OF ROHAN
99111464109 **£25**

GIMLI (HORNBURG)
9947146501501 **£5**

THÉODEN (HORNBURG)
9947146410902 **£5**

ÉOMER (HORNBURG)
9947146410904 **£5**

HÁMA (HORNBURG)
9947146410905 **£5**

GAMLING WITH STANDARD
9947146410903 **£5**

You can find all these products online by logging on to: www.games-workshop.co.uk/store

ADVANCE ORDER!

WARHAMMER®

Rulebook £30

see page 64.

Battle for Skull Pass £40

see page 65.

£60 Special Gamers Edition'

see page 81.

COLLECTORS EDITION

Collectors Edition Rulebook' £60

see page 80.

Can't wait to get your hands on the latest releases?

- Get the latest products and models for your armies on the day of release, delivered to your door, with our Advance Order service, via the Online Store, by calling Direct or by post.
- Choose from loads of models and products not yet released in our Hobby Centres.
- Postage for Advance Orders is only £2*, so you can afford to get more models for your money.

Advance order now:

15th July (released 26th August)

- Ent £20
- Haldir's Elves Command..................£6
- Isengard Troll £15
- Morgul Stalkers £6
- Dead Marsh Spectres £6
- Osgiliath Veterans...........................£6
- Defenders of Rohan £25
- Rohan Captain, foot and mounted £10
- Rohan Standard Bearer, foot and mounted £9

Advance order now:

22nd July (released 2nd September)

- Space Marine Megaforce..............£100
- Dawn of War: Tempest................£6.99
- The Corrupted £6.99
- 2007 Calendar £12

Advance order now:

29th July (released 9th September)

- Battle for Skull Pass £40
- Warhammer Rulebook £30
- Warhammer Collectors' Edition Rulebook............................£60
- Warhammer Special Gamers' Edition £60
- Battle for Skull Pass paint set..........£12
- Warhammer Dice (tin).......................£6
- Warhammer Fanatics Special Edition model £7

Advance order now:

12th August (released 23rd September)

- Orcs & Goblins Army Set £145
- Tau Empire Megaforce..................£100

£2 postage only applies to Advance Order products being delivered to addresses in the UK or Ireland. Orders including Advance Order products will be held until the last available product is released.

Subscriptions guarantee you will not miss an issue, and offer savings over buying individual copies. There are a number of ways to subscribe.

- **Call Games Workshop direct on 0115 91 40000**
- **Log on to *www.games-workshop.co.uk/store/wd1yearsub/***
- **Visit your nearest Games Workshop store**
- **Complete the form below and return to:**

GW DIRECT SALES, WILLOW ROAD, LENTON, NOTTINGHAM, NG7 2WS

SUBSCRIPTION OFFER 1

Take out a year's subscription for just £36 and saving you a great *£12* off the cost of the cover price – effectively giving you three issues free!

SUBSCRIPTION OFFER 2

Take out a two year subscription for just £60 – saving you a massive *£36* off the cost of the cover price, effectively giving you nine issues free!

I would like to subscribe to White Dwarf starting with issue number: WD☐☐☐ (if no issue number is stated or if the issue number selected is no longer available we shall start your subscription with the next available issue)

I would like to subscribe for:

1 YEAR 12 issues (WDSUB1) **£36.00** ☐ **2 YEARS** 24 issues (WDSUB2) **£60.00** ☐

I am an existing subscriber ☐ I am a new subscriber ☐ (please tick a box)

MY DETAILS

Mr/Mrs/Ms/other:............................ ...Forename: .... Surname: ....

Address: .... Postcode:................................

.... Country:................................

Tel (inc STD code):..

The subscription is a gift for the person detailed below ☐ (tick box if appropriate)

Mr/Mrs/Ms/other:............................ ...Forename: .... Surname: ....

Address: .... Postcode:................................

.... Country:................................

Tel (inc STD code): ....

METHOD OF PAYMENT

Postal Order (UK only)/Cheque ☐ (made payable to Games Workshop Ltd)

VISA ☐ MasterCard ☐ SWITCH ☐ No: ☐☐☐☐ ☐☐☐☐ ☐☐☐☐ ☐☐☐☐☐☐☐

Valid from: ☐☐☐☐ Expiry date: ☐☐☐☐ Issue No: ☐☐

Cardholder's Name: ....

Signature:.. Date: ....

(signature of parent or guardian required if recipient is under 16 years of age.)

Reply by the 25/08/2006 to take advantage of this offer.